BE THE DRIVING FORCE

Leading Your School on the Road to EQUITY

DON PARKER

Foreword by William D. Parker

Solution Tree | Press

a division of
Solution Tree

555 North Morton Street
Bloomington, IN 47404
800.733.6786 (toll free) / 812.336.7700
FAX: 812.336.7790

email: info@SolutionTree.com
SolutionTree.com

Visit **go.SolutionTree.com/leadership** to download the free reproducibles in this book.

Printed in the United States of America

Library of Congress Cataloging-in-Publication Data

Names: Parker, Don, 1975- author.

Title: Be the driving force : leading your school on the road to equity / Don Parker.

Description: Bloomington, IN : Solution Tree Press, 2023. | Includes bibliographical references and index.

Identifiers: LCCN 2023011382 (print) | LCCN 2023011383 (ebook) | ISBN 9781954631496 (paperback) | ISBN 9781954631502 (ebook)

Subjects: LCSH: School principals--United States. | Educational leadership--United States. | Teacher-principal relationships--United States. | School environment--United States. | Educational equalization--United States. | Children with social disabilities--Education--United States.

Classification: LCC LB2831.92 .P37 2023 (print) | LCC LB2831.92 (ebook) | DDC 371.2/0120973--dc23/eng/20230517

LC record available at https://lccn.loc.gov/2023011382

LC ebook record available at https://lccn.loc.gov/2023011383

Solution Tree
Jeffrey C. Jones, CEO
Edmund M. Ackerman, President

Solution Tree Press
President and Publisher: Douglas M. Rife
Associate Publishers: Todd Brakke and Kendra Slayton
Editorial Director: Laurel Hecker
Art Director: Rian Anderson
Copy Chief: Jessi Finn
Senior Production Editor: Christine Hood
Text and Cover Designer: Kelsey Hoover
Acquisitions Editor: Hilary Goff
Assistant Acquisitions Editor: Elijah Oates
Content Development Specialist: Amy Rubenstein
Associate Editor: Sarah Ludwig
Editorial Assistant: Anne Marie Watkins

Acknowledgments

Solution Tree Press would like to thank the following reviewers:

Doug Crowley
Assistant Principal
DeForest Area High School
DeForest, Wisconsin

Louis Lim
Principal
Bur Oak Secondary School
Markham, Ontario, Canada

Lance McClard
Assistant Superintendent
Ste. Genevieve R-II School District
Ste. Genevieve, Missouri

Bo Ryan
Principal
Greater Hartford Academy of the Arts
   Middle School
Hartford, Connecticut

Ringnolda Jofee' Tremain
K–8 Principal
Trinity Leadership Arlington
Arlington, Texas

Dawn Vang
Administrative Assistant
Pembroke Elementary School
Virginia Beach, Virginia

Table of Contents

Reproducibles are in italics.

About the Author

Don Parker, PhD, is a transformational keynote speaker and professional development provider. He specializes in social-emotional learning (SEL), supporting teachers to build trusting relationships with students, restorative practices, trauma-informed practices, and improving the culture and climate of schools to enhance students' and teachers' feelings of belonging.

Dr. Parker is a former principal who served at Posen School in Posen, Illinois, where he improved the school climate, staff collaboration, parent engagement, and student achievement. Previously, he was the principal of Lincoln Avenue School, a K–8 school in Dolton, Illinois, where he improved the culture, implemented a resilience program, managed the implementation of restorative justice, and increased attendance and student achievement.

Dr. Parker has been an educator since 1997 with a background as a teacher, dean of students, assistant principal for student life, assistant principal for curriculum and instruction, and assistant principal for activities and athletics. His teaching experiences include working in inner-city Chicago public schools. Dr. Parker was also an adjunct professor who taught graduate courses for students seeking their master's degree in curriculum and instruction at National-Louis University in Bolingbrook, Illinois. His diverse background in education provided him with the knowledge of how to best apply evidence-based methods and student interventions to improve student behavior and increase student achievement.

Dr. Parker has a strong belief in creating a school climate in which the entire staff strive for excellence to meet the academic and social-emotional needs of each student. He has presented throughout the United States at distinguished educational conferences, including the Association for Supervision and Curriculum Development (ASCD), Every Student Succeeds Act, National Principals, Illinois Principals, Oklahoma Secondary and Elementary, Raising Student Achievement, and Innovative Schools Summit, to name a few. He is also an expert workshop facilitator and offers the following professional development sessions: "Building Trusting Relationships With Challenging Students," "Building Resilience in Students," "Culturally Responsive Schools," "Taking Students From Trauma to Triumph: Supporting ACE Students," "Burning Up Instead of Burning Out! Teacher Mental Health Awareness," "Culture Strong: Strengthening School Culture," "Restorative Practices," and "Be the Driving Force: Leading Your School on the Road to Equity." Dr. Parker is also the author of the book *Building Bridges: Engaging Students Through the Power of Relationships*.

Dr. Parker received a bachelor's degree in physical education and health from Wartburg College, a master's degree in educational administration from Governors State University, a doctorate in educational leadership from Argosy University, and his Illinois superintendent certification from St. Francis University.

Dr. Parker resides in Chicago with his wife and two daughters, the younger of whom has FoxP1 syndrome and autism. He and his family regularly promote autism and FoxP1 gene mutation awareness and support the FoxP1 and autism communities.

To learn more about Dr. Parker's work, go to www.DrDonParker.com or follow him @DrDonParker1 on X (formerly Twitter), Instagram @DrDonParker5, Facebook at Dr. Don Parker and Don Parker, or LinkedIn at Dr. Don Parker.

To book Don Parker for professional development, contact pd@SolutionTree.com.

Foreword

By William D. Parker

Whenever Dr. Don Parker (no relation) and I talk by phone or through a video feed, he almost always says, "William D. Parker—my brother from another mother!" His humor and laughter are infectious. His attention to detail—remembering stories about my family and work, for instance—makes me feel like Don knows me and considers me a friend. Before long, he is sharing something he has gleaned through research and practice that I can apply in my work as an educator. None of these small moments with Don go unnoticed. Educators know that strong pedagogy includes building rapport with students just as much as it does conveying important content through engaging lessons.

Don's book, *Be the Driving Force: Leading Your School on the Road to Equity*, is a book I wish he had written during my formative years in school administration. It is a powerful resource because it is personal, reliable, and practical. You will notice every chapter is designed with a story that captures the imagination and propels readers into lessons that are well researched and easy to apply in any school setting. Don wisely carries along the analogy of driving a car to help leaders understand the importance of principles, vision, climate, equity, policies, procedures, communication, responsive learning, and so much more.

When I began my work in school administration in 2004 as a high school assistant principal, I was optimistic that I could be a positive influence in my school community. However, I was only a few days on the job when I was already overwhelmed. My efforts to be helpful so often seemed sidetracked by unforeseen conflicts among students, teachers, and community members. By the end of my second year in administration, I was almost at a breaking point. One night, my wife kindly but firmly communicated that she and our children had accepted that I was a husband and father on the weekends only—the rest of the time, the school owned me, she said. Thankfully, it was during this time that I made an important life-changing decision: I wrote a letter of resignation. I placed it in a folder and put it on the corner of my desk. I told myself that either I would begin to maintain a better work-life balance or I would hand in my letter at the end of the school year.

Fast-forward a few years later to when I was recognized as the 2012 Oklahoma Assistant Principal of the Year by the Oklahoma Association of Secondary School Principals and the National Association of Secondary School Principals. On the night I received my award, my wife and children attended. I remember thinking how grateful I was to have rediscovered important lessons for serving my family and my school with better focus, meaning, and outcomes. I was an educator who had survived, found solutions, and continued serving schools.

Many educators, however, are leaving their positions at alarming rates. This is especially true of school leaders. An August 16, 2022, a survey of 1,000 principals and students by the National Association of Secondary School Principals (NASSP) reported that "one out of two school leaders claim their stress level is so high they are considering a career change or retirement" (NASSP, 2022).

This book is an illustration of strong pedagogy for educational leaders. Just as Don communicates so effectively with students, teachers, and others in his work as a career educator, his book carries the same sentiment that he delivers in person. The engaging stories set the stage. The careful research provides context. The practical solutions he provides will equip you with tools for moving forward. The reflection questions and self-inventory practices will challenge you to take decisive action. I dare say, *Be the Driving Force* may be the antidote to the resignation letters many educational leaders have considered writing in their own careers. Read ahead to rediscover the meaning in your mission as a school leader. As you do, may you be inspired to be the driving force of change for your school community.

William D. Parker is the Founder of Principal Matters, LLC, an educator, author, and speaker. He is the host of Principal Matters: The School Leader's Podcast. *He also proudly serves as the executive director for the Oklahoma Association of Secondary School Principals (OASSP) and the Oklahoma Middle Level Education Association (OMLEA).*

INTRODUCTION

*P*RINCIPALS SIGNIFICANTLY INFLUENCE the culture, climate, priorities, and personnel practices within their buildings, placing them in the preeminent position to close the insidious achievement gap that continues to plague schools. Leadership actions and behaviors either drive education equity or tap the brakes on it. Which kind of leader are you?

If ensuring that every student receives what's needed to develop to their full academic and social potential regardless of race, ethnicity, gender, income level, identity, or any other societal factor is the desired destination, then what is the road map to get you there? Unfortunately, all too often, the education system veers in directions that reinforce the very inequalities it was designed to overcome. This book aims to provide support to principals and other school leaders who seek to be education equity's driving force, leaders who consistently identify and remove the barriers blocking student success.

As you strive to be the driving force for your school, I'll guide you with an analogous approach. Just as each component of a vehicle is crucial to its overall performance, each facet of your leadership is critical to promoting equity in your school.

When it comes to being the driving force to enhance equity in education, school leaders (principals especially) must provide all students with the opportunity to learn in an equitable environment. This means that school leaders must work to create environments where each student has access to the same quality of education, regardless of race, socioeconomic status, background, or identity. Equity must exist for *all* students to learn and thrive within the buildings you lead. It's hard to accept that a lot of the work we, as educators, have been doing for a long time has helped only some students but not all.

Students of color and low income, and other marginalized students, have not always benefited from the way U.S. schools are structured due to factors such as insufficient funding, lack of access to advanced courses, and limited support for non-native English speakers. According to The Education Trust (2018) report *Funding Gaps 2018: An Analysis of School Funding Equity Across the U.S. and Within Each State*, these students are less likely to attend high-performing schools and likely to have less access to experienced teachers and resources, which contribute to achievement gaps and limit their educational opportunities. For these reasons, there is a need for policy changes and targeted interventions to address these disparities (Morgan & Amerikaner, 2018). The challenge is that sometimes we aren't sure how to stop counting what we are doing and make what we are doing count. The strategies in this book will help you get started and can help K–12 teachers and leaders at any school.

> **The challenge is that sometimes we aren't sure how to stop counting what we are doing and make what we are doing count.**

As principals and leaders, we start by taking a whole-child approach. Students' social-emotional needs, such as a sense of belonging, emotional support, positive relationships, autonomy and independence, and a sense of competence, must be met (Hamre & Pianta, 2001). We, as educators, should work toward meeting them as rigorously as we work to help students learn academic content. It is crucial that we understand students and where they are coming from—both where they live and their perspective (Joseph, 2021). This equity work requires and demands that we move out of our comfort zones and into a place of discomfort to accept students however they show up to the doors of our schools and classrooms. Responding to the cry for equity in our schools and communities is more important than ever.

When educators are more knowledgeable about issues students are dealing with, including poverty, racial discrimination, gender identity, pressure to join gangs, drugs, homelessness, abuse, neglect, emotional instability, trauma, and fear, schools can put programs and practices in place to better support them. Western Governors University (2021) writes:

> By becoming more aware of matters that affect categories such as poverty, ethnicity, gender, and more, educators can create actionable

plans that can circumvent the effects these situations have on a student's education. We may not be able to single-handedly solve all of these issues, but by understanding more about them we discover how they affect a student's learning capabilities, and can correct for them effectively.

Principals who understand how educational structures and procedures work and how they can impact students are better equipped to provide needed support for those students. Sometimes district leadership and school principals are a part of the systemic issues, whether unwittingly or otherwise. Teachers can alert principals to these complications and help get everyone on the same page about how to address them. To encourage such communication, principals must give teachers an active voice and encourage equity among staff and other stakeholders. If teachers felt comfortable bringing awareness and identifying inequities without fear of consequence, schools would be better off. Educators who understand how to work with administrators are crucial in helping advance equity in their classrooms, schools, and communities.

The reason equity is a burning topic in education right now is because some educational institutions, particularly in high-poverty, low-income, and middle-class communities, do not provide an environment conducive to learning for all. Data from the National Center for Education Statistics (2021b) reveal significant learning gaps in mathematics and reading scores between students in high-poverty schools and those in low-poverty schools. This phenomenon appears across major student reporting groups by race, ethnicity, and socioeconomic status. According to Grady Wilburn, Brian Cramer, and Ebony Walton (2021):

> Black students, Hispanic students, and White students, as well as students eligible for the National School Lunch Program (NSLP) all show a growing divergence in achievement between the group's lowest- and highest-achieving students. A period of gains at the 10th percentile over the 2003 to 2009 period (except for Black and Hispanic students in eighth-grade reading) is followed by losses or stagnation between 2009 and 2019.

Achievement gaps exist not only between White students and students of color, but also between students from affluent communities and students from communities with lower socioeconomic statuses. This is a long-standing problem that calls for strong leaders with innovative ideas.

Actively promoting equity in schools removes barriers so each student can succeed. When all students have the resources they need, more students and schools will achieve at greater levels. The quality of education that students receive directly correlates to their future quality of life (Organisation for Economic Co-operation and Development, 2007). Education equity has the power to shape every student's future. The more resources and equitable opportunities available to them, the better. For this reason, it is vital for school leaders and teachers to address any barriers students face to succeeding in school and in life. As a result of reading this book, you will be energized to be the driving force to enhance equity at your school!

The Driving Force

I chose the title *Be the Driving Force* because it correlates the critical components of a car with the critical components of school leadership. Just as a car cannot operate without its engine, a school cannot function without a strong, committed principal. And just as each key component of a car contributes to a smooth- or rough-running whole, each key component of a principal's leadership style contributes to—or detracts from—an enhanced-equity outcome. Writing this book afforded me the opportunity to combine my love of cars with my devotion to school leadership and promoting equity. And I aim to make it both an enjoyable and informative ride.

People use cars for many purposes, but the most important purpose is to get us from where we are to where we need to be. I look at education as a vehicle that can transport students from where they are now to where they want to be in the future.

From as far back as I can remember, my parents and teachers told me that education was among the few playing-field levelers for students from low-income or middle-class backgrounds such as myself. My parents and teachers drilled this thought into me: If I received a good education and took school seriously, I could go anywhere and achieve anything I desired. This convinced me to take school seriously. I completed high school and went on to earn my teaching degree. I became a physical education teacher and basketball coach. I found so much fulfillment in this role and loved doing it so much that, for a time, I was determined to retire in this position. After several years, the department chair of the PE department left the school to become the head coach and department chair in a different district. My principal approached me and told me that he would like for me to be the department chair and take on managerial duties. I appreciated the opportunity, but I was pretty comfortable in my role and unsure if I was well suited for the added responsibility.

My principal insisted that I could do it. Actually, he kind of made it clear that I didn't have a choice. I remember him saying that yes, it was more responsibility, but nothing compared to what he faced in his role. He told me how difficult it was to be a school leader, and I didn't really understand how a school functioned or have any appreciation for all the effort he put into making it run smoothly.

His words struck a chord with me. At this particular time in my career, I loved what I was doing. However, this discussion with my principal sparked an interest in learning more—in this case, learning more about the way schools worked and how to be an effective school leader. As I reflect on being a school principal for the past six years and the rich experiences I've been blessed to enjoy, I am reminded of this paradigm-shifting conversation.

School leaders have students' futures in their hands. We can be the mechanics of solidly performing schools delivering quality, equity-based educations. When we are performing at our best, we open the road for students to pursue their dreams, with education as their vehicle to get them where they want to be.

In This Book

In the chapters that follow, you will find a useful road map for developing the characteristics necessary to ignite passion for schoolwide equity among all stakeholders. More than that, you also will find practical action plans for ensuring the necessary follow-through. It is one thing to hold an ideal in high esteem; it is entirely another to see it realized. As with any successful journey, this one begins from within.

The first chapter, "Building Self-Confidence as the Key," examines the role of self-confidence for effective leaders. Every human being faces times of self-doubt. Even the most tenured practitioners may occasionally question their own approach, their overall value to the enterprise, or how others perceive their contributions. But when something as crucial as educational equity hangs in the balance, overcoming these self-doubts is paramount. It is also achievable. This chapter offers important insights, anecdotal narratives, and scholarly research detailing how to access your inner strength and exude a quality outer character that catches on with your colleagues.

Chapter 2, "Embracing the Principal as the Engine," examines best practices for ensuring school leaders are primed and ready for the sometimes daunting, but always worthwhile, tasks at hand. All engines require the occasional tune-up, and if school leaders wish to provide peak performance, they must adjust their approach as needed. This chapter discusses school leadership's role as the heart of the educational body.

Much like an engine does for a car, a school principal sends the signals that turn the institution's gears.

Given that ensuring school equity is a leader's destination of choice, they need to develop the road map that is right for their school. Direct paths are always the most efficient, but obstacles occasionally force a circuitous route. Chapter 3, "Maximizing Equity Through Leadership Styles," explores various leadership styles and how to select the right one for you and your school. From servant to authoritative to transformational, leaders should understand their preferred leadership style and also learn what works best with their school and staff. Ultimately, knowing the tools and strategies you can draw on from various styles makes you the most effective leader in meeting all types of scenarios and situations. It's an important topic and an even more important undertaking. For society's sake, we can no longer afford leadership styles that continue to kick the school equity can down the road. Eventually, the can strikes a wall or falls over a cliff. What then?

Chapter 4, "Creating the Vision to Desired Destinations," takes an in-depth look at composing vision and mission plans that work, along with strategies for achieving the necessary buy-in. That buy-in is far more readily achieved in a climate where stakeholders feel valued and heard, fostering the sort of cooperative atmosphere with which high-achieving districts seem to be so blessed. It's likely, however, that a spirit of cooperation did not simply materialize in those progressive, high-achieving schools we'd like to emulate. Such a spirit is purposefully—and occasionally painstakingly—built through creating a positive, equitable school climate, which is the topic of chapter 5, "Adjusting the School Climate."

Next, chapter 6, "Growing Equity From Integrity," acknowledges the role of leadership integrity in closing the educational equity gap. A corroded chassis won't stand up well to bumps in the road, nor will school leaders whose integrity is assailable. This chapter explores character and backbone. On the road to educational equity, one can no longer "go along to get along."

With that in mind, a careful and thorough review of school policies and procedures is often in order before equity can be anything other than a lofty but unrealized concept. Chapter 7, "Revising School Policies and Procedures," discusses the sort of policy pitfalls that have led to the marginalization of many groups of students, from those whose access to advanced courses are limited based on race to others whose gender identity leaves them with inadequate support systems, and still others whose experiences with harsh discipline lead them to drop out. It is in this arena, perhaps more than all others, that meaningful, long-lasting, equitable changes can arise.

All the positive change in the world, however, means little if people aren't aware of what's happening at your school. Chapter 8, "Managing Effective Communication," offers strategies and tips for clearly communicating with school stakeholders, including students, staff, and the community. Not all people communicate in the same way, and your challenge is to meet the needs of all stakeholders to keep them engaged and informed.

Speaking of communication, it is the more compelling teachers who frame classwork in terms their students can readily identify. Surely, you've seen students tune out when they feel that coursework lacks relevance in their lives. Chapter 9, "Implementing Culturally Responsive Practices," takes an informative look at reaching students where they live. In other words, teachers who take the time and make the effort to understand the cultures and backgrounds of their students, adjusting their approach accordingly, will have greater success. As an equity-enhancing leader in your school, it's up to you to foster this culturally responsive mindset. Since most teachers receive a tremendous motivational boost when they perceive that students are becoming more actively engaged, this is a leadership investment that can pay relatively quick dividends.

Finally, another investment that can pay both short- and long-term dividends is addressing the level of burnout school leaders and staff may experience. Few would argue that a school leadership position is challenging. We all can attest that our jobs as educators are, at times, downright exhausting. We may experience crises that are confounding and discouraging. And we do ourselves and our entire school communities a tremendous disservice if we do not weave time into our schedules for self-care. Chapter 10, "Charging Your Battery Through Self-Care," addresses these important issues.

Conclusion

By the time you've completed *Be the Driving Force*, you'll have journeyed through areas of the educational leadership landscape that have been the subject of much research and debate. Perhaps you'll sketch out a road map of your own along the way, jotting down key concepts and detailing specific avenues you'd like to pursue.

The career you've chosen offers tremendous potential for good. By developing your self-confidence, heart, vision, warmth, and integrity, you'll position yourself to lead effectively. When you tackle policies and procedures that stand in the way of equity and ensure that your school communities are aware of both your challenges and your progress, you'll act as a shining example to others.

If you cultivate culturally responsive teaching in your classrooms while also making time for meditation or physical fitness, you'll spread an enthusiasm for both learning and wellness. And when you exemplify a leadership style that has equity at its center, you lay the foundation of a better world. Not tomorrow, but now.

CHAPTER 1

BUILDING SELF-CONFIDENCE AS THE KEY

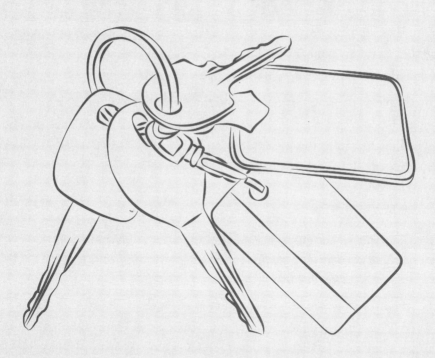

Effective leaders believe in themselves and their abilities. Self-confidence primes the pump for others to trust that leaders are steering them toward achieving their personal and professional goals. It takes a key to start a car—and it takes belief and confidence in yourself to make you the right key to ignite your school's success.

*M*Y MOM HAS always had a difficult time with keys. On one particular day, she'd lost her car keys and asked my dad to copy his set for her. She climbed into her car's driver's seat and tried to insert the key in the ignition. She could not get it in and mumbled repeatedly that my dad must have given her the wrong key. Finally, my dad came out to the garage and leaned in through the driver's side window to look at the key. He assured my mom that he had given her the correct one. Reassured that she had the correct key, she was more confident that she could get it to work. She began twisting and turning it and tried harder and harder to get the key to work. Eventually, after a forceful push, mom slid the key into the ignition. My dad and I shared a look, rolled our eyes, and shook our heads, smiling.

Now ask yourself, why did my mom have such a hard time getting the key to work? It's certainly possible the key did not go in easily because it was new and needed to be broken in, or perhaps she was not holding the key at the right angle. But the real reason she could not get the key to work was because *she did not believe she had the right key*. Once my father assured her that indeed she did, she believed that it would work and refused to give up until she achieved her goal.

As simple as this everyday action might seem, like my mom, many educators struggle because they are filled with self-doubt. They lack confidence in their skills and abilities to be effective leaders who enhance equity. They feel like they don't have the right key.

> **Many educators struggle because they are filled with self-doubt. They lack confidence in their skills and abilities to be effective leaders who enhance equity.**

When I started my career as a teacher, I did not envision myself becoming a principal. One of the reasons I had resolved to spend my entire career as a physical education teacher is because I did not believe becoming a principal was possible for me. I'm grateful that this perception changed with time, as I learned more about educational administration and leadership and how to grow confidence. After several years of experience as a principal, I was still figuring out how to be effective in this role and still had a lot to learn. But as I continued, I noticed I was becoming more effective. My confidence had increased. Instead of doubting myself and my decisions, I began to believe in myself.

The Merriam-Webster online dictionary (n.d.a) gives several definitions of the word *confidence,* including:

1. "A feeling or consciousness of one's powers or of reliance on one's circumstances"

2. "Faith or belief that one will act in a right, proper, or effective way"

3. "A relation of trust or intimacy"

All these definitions in some form or fashion involve the concept of trust. Rahul Eragula (2015), award-winning author and education researcher, states:

> This trust that contributes so much to confidence is defined as the reliance on the integrity, strength, ability and surety of a person or thing. Confidence is one of the most important ingredients in determining success, and a healthy self-esteem keeps leaders from falling into insecurities and increases their confidence levels. (pp. 1070–1071)

As principals and other educational leaders, the hill we must climb to achieve equity can seem daunting. The inevitable struggles can shake the confidence of any educator at times. The sheer number of decisions educators must make, and the knowledge of their far-ranging consequences, can breed insecurity. Many things can shake a leader's confidence, as noted in an article by Presence Learning (2020):

> There's no doubt that principals have a profoundly stressful career as the leader of a school, responsible for typically dozens of teachers and hundreds of students. Much of the focus has been put on teacher burnout, but the pressure of long hours and competing priorities typically travels up the ladder and rests on the shoulders of principals as well.

Principals also have a duty and professional and moral obligation to advance equity at their school. Along with this comes the pressure of removing barriers and making the environment more welcoming for all students, especially low-income students and students of color, where the achievement gap is most prevalent. The level of excitement that exists with so many great ideas and aspirations to lead when one accepts a leadership role is matched with enormous job responsibilities and a high level of anxiety and stress, which can lead to uncertainty.

Principals also have a duty and professional and moral obligation to advance equity at their school.

Self-doubt to lead effectively and advance equity can be crippling. But it may be encouraging to know that those who came before you, even those who have achieved well-documented levels of success, once entertained self-doubts of their own. Back when I taught physical education, I did not think I possessed the potential to become a successful principal, let alone an author and a motivational speaker. It took getting a solid push (a push I'm grateful for to this day), accepting the challenge, and gaining the confidence that comes with putting training into practice. My steadfast aim now is to help others do the same, all the while building a greater framework of educational equity.

This chapter discusses how school leaders must have confidence in themselves and their ability to lead their school in promoting equity. When leaders are confident in themselves, they can effectively communicate their vision and goals to their team and community. They are also more likely to take bold and necessary steps to address systemic inequities that may exist in their school. To grow their confidence, school leaders can seek out professional development opportunities, collaborate with other leaders, and reflect on their successes and challenges. They can also build relationships with staff and students, which can help create a sense of trust and support within the school community. Ultimately, when school leaders have confidence in themselves, they can create a positive school culture that fosters equity, inclusion, and academic success for all.

What the Research Says

There is consensus among the research that self-confidence is one of the most important characteristics of effective leadership. Joanne Kelleher (2016), school administrator and adjunct professor at St. John's University, states that managers with low self-efficacy perform poorly under pressure. Matthew Lynch (2020), professor, author, and expert on education equity, reform, and innovation, builds on this idea: "Education leaders must possess the self-confidence to be successful, which has to do with your capacity to fulfill multiple roles, and is built through your experiences and dealings during your life." Self-confidence is so paramount that it is the fundamental basis from which leadership grows (Dao, 2008).

When we think about the difference between average leaders and great leaders, the dividing line also involves which leaders have the self-confidence to believe the work they do will have a positive impact. To be self-confident is a vital component of having *self-efficacy*, the belief in your capacity to drive action toward the achievement of specific goals.

Connecting Confidence and Efficacy

Principal self-efficacy is connected with effective leadership, high-performing schools, positive school turnaround processes, and high-level teaching and learning. Educational researcher John Hattie (2012) defines principal efficacy as "the degree to which principals believe they can influence student achievement and school success" (p. 154). He argues that principal efficacy is a key factor in effective school leadership, as principals who have high levels of efficacy are more likely to take risks, make difficult decisions, and lead their schools in ways that promote positive outcomes for students. Hattie (2012) also notes that principal efficacy can be developed through experience, reflection, and ongoing professional learning. He suggests that principals should seek out opportunities to learn from other leaders, engage in ongoing self-reflection, and continually evaluate their own practices and their impact on student learning to help develop confidence.

Kelleher (2016) points out, "Principals' thoughts and actions influence the school culture, and research indicates that a principal can have a negative effect during a period of change. For these reasons, principals must have a strong sense of self-efficacy" (p. 70). Principals need strong self-efficacy and confidence because their confidence level affects their performance level, which, in turn, affects the entire school's performance.

It's not that self-confident leaders don't have to grapple with failure and change their approach. Principals and other educational leaders often feel overwhelmed, causing them to question their confidence. However, self-confident leaders achieve success in part because failing merely intensifies their desire for future accomplishments (Reddy, 2021).

To eliminate self-doubt, leaders should understand the relationship between self-confidence and efficacy, and how they affect leadership. Self-confidence is so similar to self-efficacy that they are often used as interchangeable terms, but there is a key difference: where self-confidence is focused on one's own abilities, leadership self-efficacy refers specifically to one's confidence in being able to successfully lead a group (Oyer, 2015). Michael McCormick (2001), professor and author of publications regarding self-efficacy, leadership education, and development, states, "Self-confidence and self-efficacy are not identical concepts but are closely associated in that self-confidence is a trait that impacts leadership performance through the mediating mechanism of leadership self-efficacy" (p. 24).

> *To eliminate self-doubt, leaders should understand the relationship between self-confidence and efficacy, and how they affect leadership.*

So, what a person believes about their efficacy influences their prospects of success, and these beliefs influence the initiation of a person's coping behavior, the level of effort they exert on a task, and how long their commitment will be sustained when faced with adversity. Additionally, those who consider themselves efficacious are more likely to put in sufficient effort to produce successful outcomes, whereas those with low self-efficacy are more likely to end their efforts too soon and fail (Oyer, 2015). In other words, people who believe in themselves and know that they are capable keep going and continue to forge ahead amid challenges.

The catch for those who lack self-confidence is that developing self-confidence is not just a matter of waking up one day and saying, "I'm going to be self-confident now." Leadership expert Peter Stark (2014) expresses how leadership skills like problem solving, decision making, communication, and other skills can be taught, but it's more difficult to teach a person confidence. If leaders don't believe in themselves, they are leaders in title only until they gain true confidence. Donald H. McGannon states, "Leadership is action, not position" (cited in Singer, 2023, p. 1).

Ultimately, to be a principal is to be a decision maker. The number of difficult decisions educational leaders routinely face, the number of people those decisions affect, and the high stakes of those decisions can breed self-doubt. A lack of confidence hinders leaders from acting, not necessarily because they are unsure of what to do but because they question their capacity for doing it.

They may question whether any decision they make or action they take is the right thing to do, which could lead them to taking no action at all. They might be indecisive or delay decisions for fear of doing the wrong thing. This could be especially challenging during a crisis and can hinder important decision making (Strammer, 2021). Strammer (2021) states that "confidence helps leaders to leave their comfort zone and pursue ambitious courses of action. Rarely do individuals or teams achieve remarkable things by staying in familiar spaces."

I will present more specific strategies for building self-confidence later in this chapter (see Building Self-Efficacy, page 17), but for now, it is important to acknowledge that self-confidence does not always lead to the right decision. However, the decision-making process remains the key that ignites action and provides the assurance to take responsibility. School leaders demonstrating confidence in their decisions portray that confidence even when they are not 100 percent sure about their decisions. When good intention is behind a decision, the decision maker's conscience is clear and confidence unruffled. When the decision turns out to go the wrong way, self-confident leaders know they can use the information and experience gained from that failure to plan out a new road map to success.

> **A lack of confidence hinders leaders from acting, not necessarily because they are unsure of what to do but because they question their capacity for doing it.**

Over time, as leaders gain more experience and become more competent in knowing what to do and how to be more effective, their confidence grows too. But during this process of growth, in many cases, leaders, and especially school principals, internalize how they think staff members perceive their actions. They are expected to exude confidence even when they may be experiencing fear, nervousness, or anxiety. Constantly worrying about how others perceive you can lead to feelings of uncertainty and self-doubt, the roots of impostor syndrome. These are exactly the emotions I experienced during my first couple of years as a new principal.

Avoiding Impostor Syndrome

As a kid growing up in a lower-middle-class community, I was familiar with the phrase, "Fake it until you make it!" I found myself doing just that and learned I was experiencing impostor syndrome. The term *impostor syndrome* was coined by psychologists Pauline Rose Clance and Suzanne Imes (The Decision Lab, 2023). They spent many years in the 1970s counseling highly accomplished professors, administrators, and students who were enormously concerned with being revealed as frauds. "The leaders they coached regularly credited their success to extreme overwork or relationships that protected or elevated them. People with impostor syndrome struggle to internalize accomplishments" (Dynamic Transitions, 2021).

According to Crystal Raypole (2021), impostor syndrome is also called *perceived fraudulence*. It involves feelings of self-doubt and personal incompetence that persist despite your education, experience, and accomplishments. Impostor syndrome represents a conflict between your own self-perception and the way others perceive you. Andrea Thompson and Jessica Gomez (2021) write:

> If you lack self-confidence and are riddled with doubt about your ability to carry out a task, the focus is on what you can or cannot do—a surface-level concern. But when you experience an impostor moment, it isn't whether or not you feel capable of executing a task, it is your perception of who you think you are versus the person you present yourself to be.

Impostor syndrome is a surprisingly common condition: "70% of people in the U.S. report that they have experienced it at least once" (Dynamic Transitions, 2021). Impostor syndrome affects all kinds of people from all walks of life: women, men, medical students, marketing managers, actors, and executives (Abrams, 2018). When I disclosed to other principals and educational leaders about the times in my career when the feeling was the strongest, many of them told me that they had experienced similar feelings.

So how do we get over this feeling of impostor syndrome and start building our confidence as leaders? According to Valerie Young (2021), co-founder of the Impostor Syndrome Institute and widely recognized as the leading expert on impostor syndrome:

> The only way to stop feeling like an impostor is to stop thinking like an impostor. People who don't feel like impostors are no more intelligent or capable than the rest of us. The only difference between them and us is that during that same situation that triggers an impostor feeling in us, they think different thoughts. Which is really good news, because it means all we have to do is learn to think like a non-impostor.

This advice is as practical as it gets. Changing the way one thinks and transforming one's mind is one of the most powerful things a person can do. So, what other steps can principals and other educational leaders take to reduce feelings of impostor syndrome and increase their self-efficacy and confidence?

> *Changing the way one thinks and transforming one's mind is one of the most powerful things a person can do.*

In *Conquering Imposter Syndrome*, authors Andrea Thompson and Jessica Gomez (2021) suggest that principals suffering from impostor syndrome can benefit from support that builds self-awareness and strategies to counter it. Their advice: *Take control of your inner voice and confront negative thoughts.* Tell yourself who you really are to silence judgment that may be coming from within or from others. Thompson and Gomez (2021) suggest that internally repeating the following positive statements helps leaders recognize their intrinsic value: "Start with 'I deserve to be here.' Follow up with 'I am good at what I do, and I'm willing to build upon my successes' and 'I am open to compliments and constructive feedback as I continue my growth.'"

Thompson and Gomez (2021) further encourage leaders to grow in their space, practice skills, and avoid comparing themselves to others. They further suggest that comparing oneself to others is less productive than comparing yourself to yourself, noting how far you've grown, for example. Stick to terms that outline how well you are doing today compared to how well you did yesterday. Their conclusion: *Leaders should appreciate and acknowledge their journeys while realizing that they belong.*

Building Self-Efficacy

One of the best sources for strategies to build self-confidence and self-efficacy remains the eminent psychologist Albert Bandura, whose research spawned the psychological theory of self-efficacy. Courtney Ackerman (2018) writes, "[Bandura] noticed that there was a mechanism that played a huge role in people's lives that, up to that point, hadn't really been defined or systematically observed. This mechanism was the belief that people have in their ability to influence the events of their own lives."

In his book *Self-Efficacy in Changing Societies*, Bandura (1995) shares four main influences that are likely to develop people's efficacy: (1) mastery experiences, (2) vicarious experiences, (3) verbal persuasion, and (4) physiological and affective states. Of these four, Bandura finds that mastery experiences are the strongest influencers of self-efficacy. This happens when people successfully complete a task and then develop an expectation that they will succeed when faced with a similar task in the future. This yields a mindset that success leads to more success, and is is especially true when triumph results from determination in the presence of difficulties, obstacles, or resistance. Leaders that reflect on successful experiences in their life, both personally and professionally, can create a positive trajectory for professional growth (Walker & Carr-Stewart, 2006).

According to Bandura (1995), vicarious experiences entail looking at the achievements of peers or coworkers who are similar to yourself and imagining you can accomplish the same things they are. This is another strategy for building self-efficacy. Observing others in genuine leadership settings empowers new principals to use the skills and knowledge they learned vicariously. Bandura (1995) also discusses verbal persuasion and mentoring from role models and leaders who are respected in the field. He states that receiving encouragement from someone we respect and trust strengthens our belief in our own ability. He refers to this as *persuasory feedback*, which encourages one to persist in the face of adversity. When mentors encourage and affirm, principals' efficacy and confidence can skyrocket.

Principals' self-efficacy and self-confidence also grow when principals remain in a healthy physiological and emotional state. According to Bandura (1995), stress and anxiety can negatively affect self-efficacy by taking a toll on leaders' emotional and physical health. Leaders and principals must regulate their emotions and maintain a good level of physical health to reach optimal levels of efficacy and self-confidence.

Kelleher (2016) summarizes Bandura's four main forms of influence on self-efficacy and self-confidence:

> If a principal experiences a string of successes, identifies appropriate role models, receives encouragement, and remains relatively stress-free, [they] will most certainly develop high self-efficacy, which will benefit the principal and the school community that [they] serve]. (p. 71)

These four factors can build confidence in leaders since positive experiences and words of encouragement from colleagues and mentors fuel and maintain efficacy.

> *Principals' self-efficacy and self-confidence also grow when principals remain in a healthy physiological and emotional state.*

In her article "You're OK, I'm OK," Kelleher (2016) provides three methods of her own for boosting leaders' self-efficacy: (1) professional development, (2) reflection, and (3) self-knowledge. She contends these have all been shown to improve self-efficacy. In particular, she emphasizes how professional development increases efficacy when it includes authentic problem solving involving the ordinary activities of school administrators. Such activities lead to developing the useful, robust, situated knowledge that expert leaders possess. Kelleher (2016) writes, "Prior experiences of success and the quality of the mentorship experience influenced new principals' judgment about their self-efficacy. Reflecting on successful experiences has the potential to increase self-efficacy" (p. 73).

What It Looks Like in the Real World

Before becoming a school principal, I was an assistant principal, and my role required a myriad of responsibilities. I made many mistakes early in my tenure as a school administrator. Then it dawned on me that the very things that I worried about were manifesting. My fears were coming true. After noticing this, I committed to being intentional about personal growth and development, and learning that confidence must be accompanied by ability, as well as controlling my thoughts, including, as much as possible, my subconscious mind. I read many books, but the ones that resonated with me the most were *The Power of Your Subconscious Mind* by Joseph Murphy (2009), *Think and Grow Rich* by Napoleon Hill (2005), and *The Secret* by Rhonda Byrne (2010).

Byrne's (2010) book focuses on the law of attraction, which suggests that positive thoughts and emotions can attract positive outcomes and experiences in life. It provides a step-by-step guide on how to harness the power of positive thinking to achieve success, happiness, and fulfillment in life. By encouraging readers to focus on what they want rather than what they don't want, the book helped me develop a positive mindset and increased my confidence levels. Additionally, Byrne (2010) suggests various techniques, such as visualization and affirmations, and the importance of maintaining mindfulness for success, to reinforce positive thoughts, which helps me stay motivated on my journey toward achieving my goals.

Maintaining Mindfulness for Success

By focusing more on the success I aimed to achieve in running my school, I worried less about the things that could go wrong on any given day. Gaining these new mindfulness skills truly helped me accomplish my school leadership goals. Rather than wasting time and energy on fears of my own making, I found a new way of thinking. Not only did I find that my self-confidence improved, but I also noticed positive outcomes, supporting my growing belief that I was on the right path.

Psychologists have studied the power of the subconscious mind and how it controls people's beliefs and actions. They have noted that people's fears often tend to come true, especially when they are highly emotional about them. So, the first step in harnessing the power of the subconscious mind is to eliminate the thoughts loaded with negative emotions. Eliminating negative thoughts by countering them as soon as possible with positive thoughts and positive self-affirmation statements is an important step toward success (Mayer, 2018).

I began studying the power of the subconscious mind and harnessing the power of positivity during my tenure as an assistant principal. Strengthening my subconscious mind with positivity and the newly discovered feelings of self-confidence that derived from doing so became even more critical when I got my first job as a principal. My self-confidence came through during the interview process, as different stakeholders on the committee asked me questions, which led directly to me being offered and accepting the job.

The superintendent met with me afterward to enlighten me about the status of the school. She warned that the school climate was in shambles, and the previous principal had been released in February of the prior school year. A huge divide had developed, she said, between the elementary-level and the junior high–level teachers. In addition, teachers schoolwide were not exhibiting faith in their students' abilities, and student achievement was correspondingly low. Furthermore, a lack of accountability had hindered any potential for progress.

After sharing this information with me, she told me that she wanted my focus to be on improving the school's culture and climate. Once that was accomplished, then student achievement would follow. The task before me was formidable, but I believed I was up for the challenge because my self-confidence had grown coupled with experience in my assistant principal role and by constantly studying, researching best practices and leadership, and seeking advice from mentors. My previous work experiences and the challenges that I had overcome at this point in my career only boosted my belief.

The truth, however, was that I was entering personally uncharted waters. I had been successful at running several departments, but not an entire school. As with anyone, I brought strengths and weaknesses. But it was my abiding belief in myself that helped me find ways to get the job done, even when encountering problems and tasks I had not previously faced. The one thing I was absolutely sure of—because of the work that I'd put in to improve my confidence and self-efficacy—was that I would be successful if I continue to believe in myself and that I was the right person for this job, and that I was going to succeed if I worked hard.

New school leaders can take several steps to improve their skills and boost their confidence. Some of the things I did was seek mentorship and coaching to benefit from the guidance and expertise of experienced leaders. New leaders can also seek mentorship from their colleagues or join coaching programs to get feedback and advice on their leadership style. I attended professional development workshops and conferences on school leadership to learn and stay up to date with the latest practices and trends in education. This can also help leaders develop new skills and gain fresh insights into effective leadership.

Connecting with other school leaders and educators can be a valuable source of support and encouragement. I joined my state's principal association, which is something that all, and especially new leaders, can do to build relationships and learn from others. I also reflected on my practice. New school leaders can do this as well to improve their skills by evaluating their performance regularly. This can involve seeking feedback from colleagues or using self-assessment tools to identify areas for improvement. Lastly, I learned how to take calculated risks. School leaders can boost their confidence by taking calculated risks and trying new approaches to leadership. I suggest starting small, such as introducing a new initiative in your school, and gradually building up to bigger challenges.

In light of these ongoing efforts, a quote by U.S. Supreme Court Justice Sonia Sotomayor comes to mind: "A surplus of effort can overcome a deficit of confidence" (The Quotable Coach, n.d.). Like most leaders, I grew my confidence by working hard and gaining more experience. New leaders must understand that as they work toward becoming strong leaders and increasing equity in their schools, persistence and hard work can compensate for a lack of confidence or natural ability in achieving one's goals.

Enhancing Self-Belief

A major characteristic of any successful school leader is self-belief. Many challenges to enhancing equity in your school will seem unsurmountable. Various problems will arise that are difficult to solve, and numerous equity goals may feel frustratingly just out of reach. Those who successfully fight through these challenges rely not only on their past experiences and training but also on their belief and trust that they are the perfect fit for their leadership role. Even if they must do some finessing—or outright wrangling—to resolve a challenge, they must have confidence that they have built a solid foundation for decision making and are the key to their school's success.

A major characteristic of any successful school leader is self-belief.

Matthew Lynch (2020) writes:

> Remember, as a leader, you call the shots, and as a result, your employees will follow your lead. If you don't feel confident in your abilities, how can you empower them to be confident in theirs? An organization led by someone who lacks self-confidence will not be very successful, and at its best, it will be lackluster. (p. 1)

This insightful quote aptly captures the indispensable role of self-confidence in the realm of educational leadership. It illuminates the profound importance of a leader's unwavering confidence in their own capabilities to inspire and enable their team. By embodying a resolute self-belief, leaders not only cultivate an atmosphere of trust and optimism throughout their school community, but also establish a fertile ground for transformative progress and the attainment of equitable outcomes. As we delve further into the exploration of effective leadership principles in advancing equity, bear in mind the formidable influence of self-belief as a catalyst for unlocking the full potential of educational institutions and the students in our care.

Taking Action to Build Confidence and Self-Belief

There are a lot of things you can do to build your confidence and self-belief. Some of them are small changes to mindset; others you may have to work on for a bit longer to make them habitual. Consider taking some of the following actions to increase your confidence and self-belief.

ACTION 1:　**Think of things you're good at.** Everyone has strengths and talents. What are yours? Make a list of all your personal and professional strengths. Recognizing what you're good at, and building on it, will help you grow confidence in your own abilities.

ACTION 2:　**Seek out a mentor.** Mentoring has been shown to have positive effects on building the confidence of new school leaders by providing them with guidance, support, and a sounding board for their ideas and concerns. A study by Lisa Bertrand, David Stader, and Sherry Copeland (2018) found that new school leaders who participated in a mentoring program reported increased confidence in their leadership abilities, greater job satisfaction, and improved performance. Additionally, the study found that mentors played a key role in providing emotional support, helping mentees navigate challenging situations, and providing constructive feedback.

Find a mentor who has advanced equity at their school. Don't be shy about asking an effective school leader to serve as your mentor. Mentors can provide guidance, support, and advice as school leaders work to promote equity in their own schools. Stay in touch with mentors who have helped you get where you are now and leverage the relationship to help you get where you want to be.

ACTION 3: **Talk positively to yourself.** You're not going to feel confident about yourself if you have negative commentary running through your mind telling you that you're not ready or you're not good enough. Examine your self-talk and how that might be affecting your self-confidence. Decorate your office with positive inspirational quotes and work on controlling your subconscious mind.

ACTION 4: **Learn more about equity work.** Attend training and professional development focused on equity and diversity. These opportunities can provide knowledge, tools, and strategies to promote equity in your school.

ACTION 5: **Read literature on equity.** Reading books, research articles, and other literature on equity can help you deepen your understanding of the issues and challenges facing diverse student populations. This knowledge can help you develop more effective policies and practices to support all students. As a leader, you must ensure that school systems are built on fairness and inclusion, with protections, such as interventions and resources, built in to make sure each student has the opportunity to achieve their academic goals.

ACTION 6: **Make a choice to believe in yourself.** Believing in yourself is a choice. It's your responsibility to take charge of your own self-concept and what you believe to be true about yourself. You must choose to believe that you can do anything you set your mind to—because the reality is, you can. Write three things you can do to start developing a positive mindset.

ACTION 7: **Celebrate your wins.** Focusing on the positive accomplishments in your life will help you maintain confidence. You might reward yourself for starting a new hobby or reaching personal or professional goals.

Recognizing your successes will help you feel more confident about your skills and abilities, and inspire you to pursue future achievements (Tendig, 2021). Write three accomplishments, big or small, and how you will celebrate yourself.

ACTION 8:   **Keep a positivity journal.** Start your day by writing or making a voice note to yourself about your positive attributes or compliments. Focus these compliments on both professional and personal traits and skills.

Conclusion

The best leaders in any field innovate to improve the experience of their consumers or constituents. They employ confidence to develop and implement new and better means of achieving desired outcomes. In the automotive technology field, for example, fewer and fewer cars today require the sort of traditional ignition key that once so vexed my mother. Push-button starts are increasingly common. The question for you is, how can you best build the confidence necessary to be the driving force for education equity at your school? What new shifts are needed in your mental gears? What "push to start" do you need to help you begin to really lead?

Questions for Reflection

Working individually or with a collaborative group, ask yourself the following reflective questions.

1. What messages do you tell yourself that may affect your confidence as a leader?

2. What opinions do others have about you that negatively affect your confidence as a leader?

3. Who are you as a leader, and what equity goals do you want to accomplish?

4. What do you need to continue doing as a leader to advance equity, and what do you need to stop doing that is not equitable?

5. What do you need to adjust to enhance equity and provide the optimal experience for every student at your school?

Leadership Confidence Survey

For each item, circle the response that best describes your self-confidence as a leader.

1. I sometimes internalize how I think I am being perceived by my staff.

1	2	3	4	5
Strongly disagree	Disagree	Neutral	Agree	Strongly agree

2. I attribute my success to extreme overwork or relationships that protect or elevate me.

1	2	3	4	5
Strongly disagree	Disagree	Neutral	Agree	Strongly agree

3. Sometimes I question my leadership ability and my effectiveness as a leader.

1	2	3	4	5
Strongly disagree	Disagree	Neutral	Agree	Strongly agree

4. I enjoy reading articles, books, and journals about school leadership and equity and putting what I read into action.

1	2	3	4	5
Strongly disagree	Disagree	Neutral	Agree	Strongly agree

5. I often leave my comfort zone and pursue ambitious courses of action to enhance equity.

1	2	3	4	5
Strongly disagree	Disagree	Neutral	Agree	Strongly agree

6. I am confident about many of the decisions I make to help move my school forward.

1	2	3	4	5
Strongly disagree	Disagree	Neutral	Agree	Strongly agree

7. I do not compare myself to others; instead, I focus on my own personal and professional growth.

1	2	3	4	5
Strongly disagree	Disagree	Neutral	Agree	Strongly agree

8. I am committed to learning more about equity to raise my self-confidence about doing equity work at my school.

1	2	3	4	5
Strongly disagree	Disagree	Neutral	Agree	Strongly agree

9. I reflect on previous successful experiences to boost my self-confidence for future success.

1	2	3	4	5
Strongly disagree	Disagree	Neutral	Agree	Strongly agree

10. I focus on positive ideas to promote equity rather than think about potential resistance.

1	2	3	4	5
Strongly disagree	Disagree	Neutral	Agree	Strongly agree

11. I feel like I am making a positive impact on enhancing equity at
my school.

1	2	3	4	5
Strongly disagree	Disagree	Neutral	Agree	Strongly agree

12. I am confident that I am the key to success in enhancing equity at
my school.

1	2	3	4	5
Strongly disagree	Disagree	Neutral	Agree	Strongly agree

Survey Results:

12–18	Your confidence in your leadership is low.
19–24	Your confidence in your leadership is moderately low.
25–36	Your confidence in your leadership is average.
37–46	Your confidence in your leadership is moderately high.
47–60	Your confidence in your leadership is high.

CHAPTER 2

EMBRACING THE PRINCIPAL AS THE ENGINE

A school leader is to a school what the engine is to a car. The heart of every vehicle, the engine powers the wheels. Without an engine, vehicles are nothing more than stationary metal carriages. An engine employs gasoline and a spark to cause a controlled explosion inside of a cylinder, producing power. This chapter shares innovative ways in which school leaders can be that spark, producing the power that schools need to enhance equity.

*A*FTER COLLEGE GRADUATION, I could finally afford to buy a car of my own! I had been wanting one since high school, but I could not afford it at the time. I still could not afford a brand-new car, so I combed the used car ads until I found ones that were in my price range. I found one that really interested me—it was the make and model that I liked, and the color that I preferred. My father picked me up to meet the seller so he could help with my decision. He wanted to inspect the car to make sure it was reliable, safe, and in good condition.

The first thing my father asked the seller to do was start the engine and open the hood. My father listened to the engine sounds, inspected how it looked, and checked the oil to see if it was clean. He told me to sit in the driver's seat and lightly press down on the gas pedal. Then he told me to apply more pressure as he listened to the engine rev. My dad looked at me, then looked at the seller and said, "We'll take it!" I asked my dad if he wanted to finish inspecting the rest of the car before he made his final decision. He told me that the engine was strong and in excellent condition. He went on to explain that the engine was his major point of concern; he wanted to ensure it was in great shape before we purchased the vehicle. My dad emphasized that the engine is the heart of a car. It's a complex machine that converts heat from burning gas into the force that sets the wheels in motion.

The same has been said about leadership in schools and businesses alike—the leader of a school or business is its heart. School leaders are considered the engine and heart of the school because of their critical role in shaping the school's vision, culture, and operations. They are responsible for developing policies and practices that support student learning, create a positive school climate, and foster strong relationships with staff, students, and families.

This chapter highlights the importance of school leaders in promoting student learning and achievement, improving school climate and culture, and building strong partnerships with families and communities. It also discusses the challenges and opportunities facing school leaders in the educational landscape regarding equity and offers suggestions for equitable practices.

What the Research Says

Business leaders are responsible for making sure every aspect of business operations runs smoothly. They also are charged with ensuring that the business's public image is positive. School leaders similarly work with every aspect of the school. The functions of a principal at an elementary, middle, or high school are similar, whether the setting is public or private. A principal provides strategic direction. According to Mary Dowd (2018), "Principals develop standardized curricula, assess teaching methods, monitor student achievement, encourage parent involvement, revise policies and procedures, administer the budget, hire and evaluate staff and oversee facilities." These responsibilities are important, but what may rank as a priority above all is enhancing equity at the school for the benefit of each student.

Principals enhance equity by immersing themselves in all aspects of the school system. Leadership expert Brené Brown (2018) states:

> From corporations, nonprofits, and public sector organizations to governments, activist groups, schools, and faith communities, we desperately need more leaders who are committed to courageous, wholehearted leadership and who are self-aware enough to lead from their hearts, rather than unevolved leaders who lead from hurt and fear. (p. 5)

When the leader of a business or a school is performing well, that typically correlates with the business or school also performing well. This statement can apply to a principal who is working diligently to enhance equity as well. If the principal is making strides to increase equity at their school, then the school should be making strides and progress in this area. School leaders who are working to advance equity at their school may face a range of obstacles that can hinder progress. These obstacles may include resistance to change, a lack of resources, inadequate data, and limited buy-in from members of the school community.

To overcome these challenges, school leaders can take several steps. For example, building coalitions with stakeholders, such as staff, students, and families, can help create a coalition of support for equity initiatives. School leaders can also leverage existing resources, such as staff or time, to address equity issues. Collecting and analyzing data on equity gaps can help identify areas for improvement and track progress over time.

Additionally, fostering a culture of equity through modeling inclusive practices, promoting awareness and understanding of equity issues, and engaging in ongoing professional development can help create a shared understanding and commitment to equity among all members of the school community. Finally, developing a comprehensive equity plan with clear goals, strategies, and metrics for success, and communicating it to members of the school community can help ensure continued progress toward equity. There are many things a principal can do to ensure the school is moving in the right direction, starting with monitoring and supporting staff.

Monitoring and Supporting Staff

As the heart of the school or business, leaders must influence every facet of the organization. They must be the engine that inspires equity-minded actions by others, as well as inspiring teachers to be tremendous classroom educators. Even considering the plethora of tasks and responsibilities of leaders, one of the main things we must do is monitor how well others in the organization are doing their jobs. John E. Jones, president of Dickinson College, states, "What gets measured gets done, what gets measured and fed back gets done well, what gets rewarded gets repeated" (as cited in Williamson, 2020). As a school administrator, I faced many tasks, but my supervisor reminded me always to monitor the work of my staff. In her words, "What gets monitored gets done."

> *As the heart of the school or business, leaders must influence every facet of the organization.*

She placed a tremendous emphasis on my bureaucratic tasks, but monitoring staff progress was just as important, and most times, more important. Kottler (2018) emphasizes, "Leaders help to organize groups in such a way that they accomplish desired tasks, and presumably do so more efficiently than if the employees were left to their own devices" (p. 8). In his book *Pause. Breathe. Flourish.*, Will Parker (2020) writes, "Leadership is influence. It means helping others to achieve more. It is taking someone from one location to another or motivating someone to do what they otherwise would not accomplish on their own" (p. 83).

These principles made me realize that if I considered myself a leader, and if my job is to monitor staff, build them into strong leaders, and hold them accountable for what they are supposed to be doing to promote equity, then I had better make sure I was a role model for others and also hold myself accountable. Leaders cannot be the sole driving force to enhance equity. They should constantly set equity expectations for others and concentrate on growing future leaders who carry on equity work.

There are several ways of doing this.

1. **Communicate that equity is a top priority through various channels such as schoolwide meetings and staff evaluations:** Model equitable practices by consistently making decisions that prioritize fairness and inclusivity and seeking out and addressing instances of bias or discrimination (Fergus & Noguera, 2021).

2. **Provide ongoing training and support to staff to develop their capacity for equity work:** This can involve offering professional development opportunities that focus on culturally responsive teaching, restorative justice practices, and other strategies for promoting equity in the classroom. It can also involve creating opportunities for staff to engage in ongoing dialogue about equity issues and share best practices and resources (Thomas & Lindgren-Streicher, 2021).

3. **Identify and support emerging leaders who have a demonstrated a commitment to equity and social justice:** This can involve providing mentoring, coaching, and professional development opportunities that help emerging leaders develop their skills and expertise in equity work. It can also involve providing opportunities for emerging leaders to take on leadership roles within the school and collaborate with other staff members to promote equity and inclusion (Turner & Sanders, 2021).

Overall, setting equity expectations for staff and growing future leaders who carry on equity work requires a sustained and intentional effort by school leaders. By prioritizing equity, providing ongoing support and training, and cultivating emerging leaders, school leaders can create a culture of equity and inclusion that benefits all members of the school community (Pacheco & Zeichner, 2021).

> *Setting equity expectations for staff and growing future leaders who carry on equity work requires a sustained and intentional effort by school leaders.*

Promoting Teacher-Leader Collaboration to Improve Student Learning

Leadership starts at the top. School leaders should never underestimate how much their actions, words, and behaviors impact others, determining school outcomes. As leadership receives more attention as an essential ingredient in improving schools and student learning, Jason A. Grissom, Anna J. Egalite, and Constance A. Lindsay (2021) offer this perspective:

> The impact of an effective principal has likely been understated, with impacts being both greater and broader than previously believed: greater in the impact on student achievement and broader in affecting other important outcomes, including teacher satisfaction and retention (especially among high-performing teachers), student attendance, and reductions in exclusionary discipline. (p. 4)

School leaders are a high-leverage point for improving student achievement because they play an important role in developing great teachers and creating working conditions that keep great teachers in the field. As principal effectiveness relates to student achievement, research shows that the impact of replacing a below-average elementary school principal with an above-average principal leads to greater academic gains, specifically an additional 2.9 months of mathematics learning and 2.7 months of reading learning each year for students in the school. The significance of the change in leadership had more influence in growth scores than two-thirds of mathematics educational interventions and one-half of reading interventions (Grissom et al., 2021). Grissom and colleagues (2021) further specify the significance of an effective principal:

> To further put the magnitude of these impacts in context, compare them with estimates of teacher impacts from research studies. The comparison shows that the impact of having an effective principal on student achievement is nearly as large as the effect of having an effective teacher. (p. 17)

The reason a principal's impact is so great, even more so than a highly effective teacher, is that principals affect all students in the building, while teachers affect primarily the students they have in class, which is a much smaller portion of the school population.

In no way do I mean to downplay the positive influence that effective teachers have on student achievement. I know how valuable and enormously important they are. I spent years in the classroom working to have a positive impact before becoming a school administrator. Both roles are vital. The real magic happens when principals and teachers consistently collaborate, supporting one another to enhance equity by giving students what they need to grow academically and socially. It is key to understanding how a good principal supports high levels of teaching and learning but "it is neither teachers alone nor principals alone who improve schools, but teachers and principals working together" (Schmidt-Davis & Bottoms, 2011, p. 2). Principals are expected to lead their schools within a framework of collaboration and shared decision making with teachers and other staff members. Doing this effectively requires knowing how to motivate staff behavior and foster positive relationships with them to ensure they feel empowered to do their best work on behalf of their students.

> **The real magic happens when principals and teachers consistently collaborate, supporting one other to enhance equity by giving students what they need to grow academically and socially.**

Motivating and Collaborating With Staff

Principals can motivate and collaborate with their staff in a variety of ways, including the following.

- Recognize and appreciate them for their hard work and dedication, and celebrate their accomplishments. You can do this through public praise, awards, and certificates.

- Communicate regularly and clearly with staff, keeping them informed of changes, goals, and expectations.

- Create an open-door policy, so staff members can come and talk to you about their concerns, ideas, and feedback.

- Foster a positive work environment by promoting teamwork, collaboration, and a sense of community.

- Organize social events, team-building activities, and professional learning communities (PLCs) in which staff can share ideas and learn from one another.

- Lead by example and model the behaviors you expect from staff.
  This can include being accountable, transparent, and fair, as well as
  demonstrating a commitment to ongoing learning and growth. Your
  actions span beyond instructional leadership and can be connected
  with these noticeable behaviors.

Effective principals regularly engage in these kinds of actions, which should be done simultaneously so they all work together to motivate staff to achieve the vision and goals of the school. Research shows that when considered separately, most school variables have considerably insignificant effects on learning. The real payoff comes, however, when individual variables combine to reach critical mass, and that's when significant change can take place. A study by Jaime E. Welborne (2019) found that "critical mass" in equity-focused school improvement occurs when schools develop and implement several interconnected equity-oriented practices simultaneously. These practices include setting explicit equity goals, providing professional development in equity-focused teaching practices, creating opportunities for teacher collaboration, and engaging families and communities in the school's equity work.

The principal is the one who can bring these variables together, creating the conditions for positive change (Wallace Foundation, 2011). The principal must establish the vision for equity and empower others in the school to utilize their talents and efforts to reach it.

Charging teachers and staff to do their job effectively and work hard to overcome educational inequities, along with other barriers to student learning, demands that school leaders influence and motivate teachers to persist. Provide opportunities for staff to collaborate and share best practices, as well as offer coaching and feedback to help staff members refine their equity practices. Foster a sense of community by creating opportunities for staff members to build relationships and work together toward a common goal through organizing team-building activities, encouraging staff members to participate in schoolwide events, and providing opportunities for staff to engage in shared decision making and problem solving (Peters & Boser, 2021).

Effective principals model persistence. They demonstrate what it looks like to be "all in" so teachers can follow suit. Gina Ikemoto, Lori Taliaferro, Benjamin Fenton, and Jacquelyn Davis (2014) write, "Too often, principals are effective in spite of— rather than because of—district conditions. They are superheroes who work around the clock and circumvent barriers to create an oasis of high performance in the midst of unsupportive systems" (p. 1). Even the best principals may struggle to remove some of the obstacles that exist in respective school settings. Still, they find creative ways to support teachers in achieving desired equity and student-growth outcomes. Without this ability to help level the playing field for teachers and staff, the faculty will be unable to level the playing field for their students.

Kenneth Leithwood, Christopher Day, Pam Sammons, Alma Harris, and David Hopkins (2006) state:

> Leadership has very significant effects on the quality of the school organization and on pupil learning. There is not a single documented case of a school successfully turning around its pupil achievement trajectory in the absence of talented leadership. One explanation for this is that leadership serves as a catalyst for unleashing the potential capacities that already exist in the organization. Those in leadership roles have a tremendous responsibility to get it right. (pp. 14–15)

Without this ability to help level the playing field for teachers and staff, the faculty will be unable to level the playing field for their students.

Fostering Positive Relationships With Staff

Getting it right entails being that leader who establishes positive relationships with staff. These are leaders who demonstrate that they understand this axiom: *People will support a cause but will support people faster.* True leaders do not just develop processes, procedures, and systems; they also develop people and relationships. When people encounter mutual respect, and the value that each person brings to the team is championed, they are far more likely to buy into the established processes, procedures, and systems.

People will support a cause but will support people faster. True leaders do not just develop processes, procedures, and systems; they also develop people and relationships.

Karen Seashore Louis, Kenneth Leithwood, Kyla Wahlstrom, and Stephen Anderson (2010) offer a definition of *leadership* that states, "Leadership is all about organizational improvement; more specifically, it is about establishing agreed-upon and worthwhile directions for the organization in question and doing whatever it takes to prod and support people to move in those directions" (pp. 9–10). When a leader is the heart of the organization, exhibiting empathy and investing routinely in the staff, people feel compelled to work toward the collective vision of equity. Prodding is rarely necessary in a collaborative culture where everyone shares responsibility.

Great teachers want to work with great principals. They prefer principals who collaborate over those who dictate. It's been said that "people don't quit their job, they quit their boss." In the education world, this saying would go, "Teachers don't quit their school, they quit their principal." As someone who has studied teacher burnout and teacher attrition, I know the factors affecting teachers' decisions to switch schools—or leave the profession altogether. Studies identify several reasons why teachers switch schools or leave the profession, including poor working conditions, low salaries, lack of administrative support, and feeling undervalued and disrespected by society (Marshal, Pressley, Nuegebauer, & Shannon, 2022). A study by the Learning Policy Institute found that teacher turnover is higher in schools serving low-income students, and turnover rates are particularly high among novice teachers and teachers of color (Darling-Hammond, Hyler, & Gardner, 2017).

Another study by the National Center for Education Statistics (2021a) found that the most common reason for leaving the profession among public school teachers was job dissatisfaction, with 43 percent of teachers citing this as the reason for leaving. Teacher attrition grows worse by the year. If part of being the engine of a school is positioning students to achieve at the highest level, then ensuring that they have the strongest possible teachers in front of them is key.

Understand that being a strong principal entails being able to keep strong teachers at your school. According to Stephanie Levin (2021), effective principals ensure students have access to educational opportunities. They create welcoming and inclusive learning environments and include staff on decisions. "They also attract and retain highly effective teachers, organize schools to support the whole child, and lead and support deeper learning instruction" (Levin, 2021, p. 2). Powerful outcomes occur when principals establish strong relationships and clearly foster shared beliefs among staff and the school community.

These benefits can be traced back to principal effectiveness. Effective schools are run by effective principals who are proficient in leading programs and people. It is hard to find a high-performing school without a high-performing principal (Xu, 2018). Sometimes, principals might find it difficult to motivate staff and build positive relationships in schools that struggle with standardized high-stakes test scores or have low rankings from their state or province. However, remember that these rankings don't necessarily mean such schools have ineffective principals or teachers. Schools have placed such a laser focus on standardized test scores and high-stakes testing that people are sometimes misled into equating poor test scores with incompetence in the principals.

Rather than being discouraged, principals leading schools where test scores are not at the desired level need to put their shoulders back and continue leading to ensure that staff maintain the necessary morale to accelerate learning.

> **Rather than being discouraged, principals leading schools where test scores are not at the desired level need to put their shoulders back and continue leading.**

Staff must believe in themselves and continue building relationships with students, teachers, and other school staff. They must continue influencing in this way until their positive impact is demonstrated by not only test scores but also other indicators of success such as increased attendance, decreased discipline referrals, decreased number or percentage of students failing courses, and positive survey results from students, staff, and parents.

School leaders improve teaching and learning in the schools they lead by influencing beliefs, attitudes, the school climate, and teacher efficacy. Moreover, they create a shared vision and mission for the school, which can foster a sense of collective responsibility for student success and create a culture of continuous improvement (Hallinger & Heck, 2011). They are the driving force to school success, the engine propelling schools toward enhanced equity.

What It Looks Like in the Real World

After building my self-esteem and receiving the "push to start" that I needed, I developed the right mindset to complete the necessary tasks required of school leaders to promote equity. I wholeheartedly wanted my students to succeed, and I measured my success based on theirs. It reminded me of my high school coaching years and even the coaching philosophy lessons I learned as an undergrad student.

Out of all the great coaching philosophies and theories I learned in college, the one I will never forget is that coaches should give their players the praise in victory and take the blame in defeat. My duty as a coach was also to put my players in a position to win—on and off the court. To me, that meant preparing them for competition as well as life beyond high school. It meant trying my best to afford them every opportunity to get where they desired to be after high school, whether that was playing at the next level, attending college as a non-athlete, or seeking a career.

> *Coaches should give their players the praise in victory and take the blame in defeat.*

I cared deeply for my players and always vowed to take responsibility for them and for the team. Before, during, and after the season, I met one on one with my players to discuss their personal goals, how the season was going for them, and what they needed for their continued development. The players were immersed in the process and took on a large level of responsibility, but also felt supported in meeting team and individual goals.

You can take a similar approach to your staff, meeting with them one on one, discussing their personal and professional goals, and immersing them in the process of leading the school toward equity. The next section discusses how you can approach ongoing meetings with teachers and staff.

Ongoing Meetings With Teachers and Staff

Great principals take a similar approach with teachers and staff. They play a major part in the way teachers and students perform. Teachers and students receive the glory when goals are met, and principals takes responsibility when they aren't. In my own school, realizing how effective my one-on-one meetings had been with my players, I conducted this same practice with each teacher on my staff. These meetings were beneficial not only for goal setting, but also for relationship building, the importance of which cannot be overstated.

During these meetings, we talked about which goals would best serve students. We went over student academic progress and addressed behavior. We discussed what was going well and where improvements were needed. These one on ones are not to be confused with typical evaluation processes. They were over and above the traditional preconference, observation, midyear check-in, and postconference. Instead of being used for evaluation, these meetings provided support and let teachers know they're respected professionals who have great responsibility and a voice in the key decisions affecting their daily work in the classroom. After all, they are the ones doing the day-to-day work of teaching and building relationships with students. This practice keeps teachers engaged; it helps them feel supported and valued as team members who are so vital to a school's overall achievements.

During these meetings, we also reviewed student data together. The first school where I served as a principal used the STAR assessment to measure student growth, which students took in the fall, winter, and spring. The objective of these assessments is to evaluate students' performance in the Common Core standards and establish learning goals for the next benchmark.

Our district's data-analyst specialist impressed upon district principals that, at minimum, each student enrolled in school should grow by one year. During the one-on-one meetings with teachers in the fall, we reviewed and explained these data. Then teachers set a goal of how much growth their students would make by the time the assessment was administered again in December. We met again in December after the data were in to see how students were progressing toward the goal. The teachers and I collaborated and set ambitious goals, aiming for students to achieve more than just one year's growth over the course of the school year. Teachers gained confidence as they understood that I believed in their ability to meet these goals.

During these meetings, I shared how I was working to improve the school's culture and climate. I monitored student behavior and worked with safety facilitators to ensure the school's student behavior policy was followed and implemented the district's new restorative justice initiative. *Restorative justice* is an approach that focuses on repairing the harm caused by misbehavior or conflict and restoring positive relationships among students and between students and adults. This approach encourages dialogue and collaboration to address harm, instead of punishment or exclusion. It aims to create a safe and supportive school environment where all students feel valued and respected (McCluskey, Lloyd, Kane, & Riddell, 2021). Implementing restorative justice practices was another example of equity actions we took to positively influence student outcomes.

Demonstrating Professionalism

An essential part of carrying yourself as a professional is being aware of how staff, students, parents, and supervisors view you. You want to be seen as a competent, capable, and strong leader, so it's important to carry yourself in that manner. Just as important, you must believe this image is truly who you are, which means overcoming any form of impostor syndrome, as outlined in chapter 1 (page 15).

My desire for staff to believe in me just as much as I believed in myself dictated the way I dressed, spoke, prepared, and interacted with my staff daily. I employed the same lessons I'd learned as a high school dean of students working to help shape the identities of challenged students. I told students that their self-identity dictated their activity; if they considered themselves to be good people, then they would consistently do good things. Similarly, if I considered myself to be a strong leader, then my actions would follow. Reinforcing this idea reminded me that I could continue to make good decisions. An indicator of future performance is past performance.

> **I told students that their self-identity dictated their activity; if they considered themselves to be good people, then they would consistently do good things. Similarly, if I considered myself to be a strong leader, then my actions would follow.**

Part of my own leadership growth process was acknowledging that I didn't know everything and that I still had much to learn, but it also meant knowing that I possessed the ability to learn it. In the very beginning and over the course of the year, I consistently delivered the message that I would support my staff, and that I was committed to helping the school—and all within it—succeed.

As the principal, I was also the "face" of the school, and I realized that carrying myself in a positive manner would go a long way toward the public perceiving the school in a positive manner. Teachers, too, are ambassadors for their schools. I asked my staff to follow my example, always exuding a high level of public-facing professionalism. We discussed what professionalism meant to them and what it meant to me, arriving at a mutual understanding that we could refer to throughout the year.

Symbolism can play an important role in establishing the kinds of positive administrator-teacher relationships that lead to improved school cultures and advances toward education equity. Although I did not realize its power at the time, I later learned how a gesture I made during a staff meeting left a lasting impression. "As your principal," I said to the group, "I will always support you and our students. I will have your backs." Then I turned my back to them and said, should adversaries arise, they would "have to go through me to get to them." Later that same month at a family reading night, several of my teachers told me the effect this had on them. They told me that they were going to work to not only achieve school goals and educational equity benchmarks, but also support me as the principal and leader. They went on to share how many of the staff members were relieved and pleased to feel supported. They were on board with our mutually agreed-on professionalism standards and enthusiastic about the positive effects this would have on students. This was an important milestone, deepening my understanding of how profoundly a principal's actions and leadership style affect their ability to be a school's driving force.

Taking Action to Become the Engine at Your School

Consider taking some of the following actions to become the heart, or engine, of your school.

ACTION 1: **Seek out mentorship or coaching from experienced principals who can provide guidance and support.** Engaging in one-on-one mentorship or a small-group coaching relationship has the capacity to fortify a principal's self-assurance and catalyze their professional growth. Through the guidance and support of an experienced mentor or coach, principals can tap into reservoirs of wisdom, bolstering their decision-making process and augmenting their strategic leadership acumen. This transformative process fosters a fertile ground for self-reflection, introspection, and deliberate practice, enabling principals to develop a deep sense of self-efficacy and poise in tackling equity-related challenges. As they witness their mentor's exemplary leadership and receive constructive feedback, a principal's confidence can increase, equipping them with the resilience and conviction needed to navigate uncharted territories and spearhead sustainable change.

ACTION 2: **Attend professional development workshops or courses to improve skills and gain new insights to boost confidence.** Principals committed to enhancing equity within their school communities gain substantial benefits from participating in professional development workshops or courses tailored to fostering their skills and illuminating new insights. These intentional learning experiences equip principals with a repertoire of effective tools, strategies, and techniques, and fortify their professional knowledge base.

        Attending these workshops and courses not only broadens a principal's intellectual horizons but can also ignite a sense of efficacy and assurance. Through exposure to cutting-edge research, emerging trends, and collaborative discussions, principals develop a heightened self-awareness and self-confidence in their ability to champion equity. Moreover, the networking opportunities afforded by these professional development settings enable principals to connect with like-minded peers, fostering a supportive community of practice that sustains their ongoing growth.

ACTION 3: **Build relationships with staff and other stakeholders to gain a deeper understanding of the school's needs and strengths to help you feel more confident in your decision making.** Your proactive cultivation of relationships with staff and stakeholders is crucial to foster a knowledge base regarding your school's unique needs and strengths. By forging meaningful connections with team members and other stakeholders, you can glean invaluable insights, harness collective wisdom, and build a cohesive sense of purpose within the school community. You have the opportunity to leverage diverse perspectives, promote collaborative problem solving, and create a culture of trust and shared ownership. As you develop an intimate understanding of the intricate fabric of your school, you can make informed, contextually sensitive decisions that align with the collective aspirations and values of your stakeholders.

ACTION 4: **Reflect on successes and challenges.** Your confidence as a school principal can experience significant growth through intentional reflection on both successes and challenges encountered in your school. Engaging in a rigorous process of critical self-reflection allows you to discern patterns, identify areas for growth, and leverage your achievements as building blocks for future success. Moreover, by examining challenges with a growth mindset, you can extract valuable lessons, adapt your strategies, and embrace a resilient approach, ultimately bolstering your confidence in navigating complexities and driving positive change within your school community.

Conclusion

Promoting equity in schools requires school leaders to actively monitor and support their staff. Leaders should regularly observe classroom instruction to identify areas where teacher training and support may be needed to improve student outcomes. By providing ongoing professional development opportunities and resources, leaders can help to promote teacher growth and ensure that all students have access to high-quality instruction. Additionally, leaders should foster positive relationships with their staff and create a culture of collaboration and trust. Regular meetings with teachers and staff can help to build these relationships and ensure that everyone is working toward the same goals.

Teacher-leader collaboration is also essential for promoting equity in schools. By working together, teachers and leaders can develop strategies to improve student learning and address issues of equity within the school system. Leaders can motivate and collaborate with their staff by providing opportunities for shared decision making and encouraging teachers to take leadership roles in areas where they have expertise. Additionally, leaders should demonstrate professionalism by modeling positive behaviors and holding themselves and others accountable for meeting high standards. By taking action to become the equity leader at their school, school leaders can promote a culture of equity that supports the success of all students.

Questions for Reflection

Working individually or with a collaborative group, ask yourself the following reflective questions.

1. How can you show a commitment to doing the necessary work to constantly improve the school and enhance equity for students?

2. As the heart or "engine" of the school, how can you influence every facet of the organization and inspire action among staff to be more equity-minded?

3. How might you monitor staff to ensure they are supporting and implementing equitable practices?

4. How do your actions, words, and behaviors impact others and determine school outcomes?

5. How can you motivate teachers to persist and remove barriers to equity that exist in your school?

Leading Equitable Practices Survey

For each item, circle the response that best describes your role as the "engine" for equity at your school.

1. I regularly engage in ongoing self-reflection and professional development to better understand issues of equity and bias.

1	2	3	4	5
Strongly disagree	Disagree	Neutral	Agree	Strongly agree

2. I provide professional development opportunities to staff on topics related to equity and diversity.

1	2	3	4	5
Strongly disagree	Disagree	Neutral	Agree	Strongly agree

3. I work collaboratively with teachers to develop strategies for addressing issues of equity within the school.

1	2	3	4	5
Strongly disagree	Disagree	Neutral	Agree	Strongly agree

4. I engage in ongoing conversations with families and community members to better understand the unique needs of their children.

1	2	3	4	5
Strongly disagree	Disagree	Neutral	Agree	Strongly agree

5. I ensure that all students have access to high-quality, diverse resources and instruction.

1	2	3	4	5
Strongly disagree	Disagree	Neutral	Agree	Strongly agree

page 1 of 3

6. I require teachers to incorporate culturally responsive teaching practices into the school curriculum and monitor their progress.

1	2	3	4	5
Strongly disagree	Disagree	Neutral	Agree	Strongly agree

7. I ensure students in my school from historically marginalized communities feel valued and have a sense of belonging.

1	2	3	4	5
Strongly disagree	Disagree	Neutral	Agree	Strongly agree

8. I allocate resources in an equitable manner and address inequitable funding within the school system.

1	2	3	4	5
Strongly disagree	Disagree	Neutral	Agree	Strongly agree

9. I work to address the achievement gap between students from various racial, ethnic, cultural, and socioeconomic backgrounds.

1	2	3	4	5
Strongly disagree	Disagree	Neutral	Agree	Strongly agree

10. I incorporate student voice and input in decision-making processes related to equity and diversity.

1	2	3	4	5
Strongly disagree	Disagree	Neutral	Agree	Strongly agree

page 2 of 3

11. I ensure that all students have access to technology and other necessary resources to support their learning.

1	2	3	4	5
Strongly disagree	Disagree	Neutral	Agree	Strongly agree

12. I measure and track progress toward achieving equity goals within the school system.

1	2	3	4	5
Strongly disagree	Disagree	Neutral	Agree	Strongly agree

Survey Results:

12–18	Leadership actions toward promoting equity are low.
19–24	Leadership actions toward promoting equity are moderately low.
25–36	Leadership actions toward promoting equity are average.
37–46	Leadership actions toward promoting equity are moderately high.
47–60	Leadership actions toward promoting equity are high.

MAXIMIZING EQUITY THROUGH LEADERSHIP STYLES

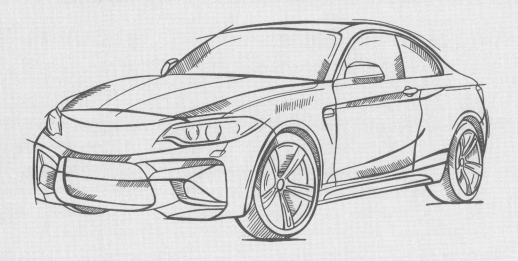

Just as buyers seek a car that complements their personal style, school leaders must choose a leadership style that aligns with their unique personality and approach to effectively advance equity in their schools. A sleek sports car effortlessly maneuvers through winding roads like an authoritative leader who values structure and clear direction. Alternatively, a transformative leader is like a hybrid vehicle, seamlessly blending innovation and collaboration to propel the school community forward. By understanding their own style and selecting the leadership vehicle that best represents them, educators become the driving force to navigate the road to equity, ensuring they reach their destination with purpose and impact.

WHEN PEOPLE BUY a car, three major factors typically weigh into their decision: (1) price—the buyer must be able to afford the car; (2) practicality—the car must meet the buyer's needs; and (3) style—the style of the car must fit the buyer's personality and preferences. Usually, the buyer must compromise.

After working as a teacher for two years, I was ready to buy the kind of vehicle that I really wanted. I always loved Jeep Cherokees because they looked really cool to me. There it was, that cool-looking vehicle, easily maneuvering over rough terrain and handling harsh road conditions. To me, this was practical, and I needed a vehicle that could handle the rough terrain that comes with Chicago winters, potholes, and railroad tracks, which all take a toll on a car. At that time, it fit my style perfectly.

I told my dad and younger brother that I was thinking about buying a Jeep Cherokee, but they both advised against it. My dad said that I should buy a Buick. My brother said that I should get a BMW because it was a smooth and attractive car. I listened to both their perspectives and weighed the information they gave me. Then I told them the reason my dad loved his Buick was because it's a classy car, and he is a classy older gentleman. I told my brother that he loved BMWs because, like him, they're smooth and attractive. I reminded them that they purchased the kinds of cars that fit their style, and I had to do the same thing, so I would be comfortable with my decision. Similarly, when it comes to leading a school and enhancing equity, principals have to lead in a way that is effective for their particular school. Their leadership style must be a match to drive the necessary change. Although some compromises must be made, the goal to enhance equity cannot be among them.

Just like with purchasing a new car, as principals work in their school to enhance equity, they have to work within the school's budget to get what they can afford. They also must do what is practical and makes sense for their school, students, and staff. Most importantly, principals must figure out their leadership style and use it to serve the dual purpose of bringing out the best in their staff and enhancing equity at their school.

> *Principals must figure out their leadership style and use it to serve the dual purpose of bringing out the best in their staff and enhancing equity at their school.*

This chapter discusses the crucial topic of school leadership styles and their role in advancing equity within educational settings. Effective leadership is a key driver in creating inclusive and equitable schools, and understanding the different leadership styles is vital for leaders who aspire to foster a culture of fairness, diversity, and excellence. While many leaders have a preferred and comfortable leadership style, they must be adaptable and flexible to meet the diverse needs of any school community. Each leadership style has unique characteristics and approaches that can be harnessed to influence and motivate staff toward achieving equity goals. By understanding and utilizing these different styles, leaders can create an environment that encourages collaboration, respects diversity, and empowers all stakeholders.

This chapter explores several leadership styles that can be effective in promoting equity within schools, including servant leadership, authoritative leadership, transformational leadership, ethical leadership, democratic leadership, affiliative leadership, and coaching leadership. I will highlight the unique strengths of each style and discuss how each one can be utilized to advance equity in the educational context.

Principals must carefully consider their own strengths, values, and leadership philosophy to determine which style aligns best with their personal disposition and the needs of their school community. By understanding and selecting or blending any of the appropriate leadership styles, principals can effectively champion equity, cultivate a positive school climate, and empower their staff to drive transformative change.

What the Research Says

Principals need a framework that defines their approach so they can lead teachers and staff effectively. The Indeed Editorial Team (2023) advises that "adopting a leadership style assists you in determining how to make decisions, which goals to prioritize, and most importantly, how to interact with others." When you choose the right leadership style for enhancing equity at your school, you will be more equipped to solve complicated problems, mediate conflicts, and reorient the direction of the school or orchestrate transformational change in educational organizations (Indeed Editorial Team, 2023).

Closing the achievement gap takes leadership. Remember all that striking data about closing the achievement gap in the introduction? That doesn't happen without making it a leadership priority. The great news is that in high-achieving schools, strong educational leaders make a major difference in their students' lives. Educational leaders have certain qualities and leadership styles that empower them to make an impact. American University (2020a) offers the following common traits among effective school leaders. They have the ability to:

- Establish a sense of purpose
- Work relentlessly for students
- Set a clear vision
- Build community relationships
- Lead people and build collaboration
- Balance strategic and operational goals
- Adjust to change

The key questions are, *Which leadership style best enables you to be most effective in reaching your school's goals?* and *Which leadership style best fits your personality?*

> **Which leadership style best enables you to be most effective in reaching your school's goals?**

School leadership is ever-evolving. Leadership styles in schools and districts utilized successfully by principals and administrators influence the culture of a school. Each style has its pros and cons. This is the reason to pinpoint your leadership style and understand how effectively it influences your school (Shkurina, 2018). Timothy M. Lupinacci (2019) writes:

> Too many people fail to see their unique leadership role and miss opportunities to influence others. Leaders must continue to grow. Although it is difficult to devote regular time to leadership growth and learning, it is a discipline that is crucial for long-term success and achievement. Leadership traits can be learned and nurtured, allowing each of us the opportunity to become a better leader.

To grow as an equity school leader, principals need to know the different aspects of various leadership styles and decide if they will be consistent with one or be fluid and adapt their leadership style based on whatever situation or school environment they lead. There are many styles of educational leadership, including *ethical, democratic, affiliative, coaching, servant, authoritative,* and *transformational.* These leadership styles, when applied thoughtfully and with a deep commitment to equity, have the potential to drive positive change, create a more inclusive and just educational environment, and support the success of all students.

Following is a brief overview of each leadership style, and then a more in-depth look at servant leadership, authoritative leadership, and transformational leadership, which are the three styles most commonly used in schools. Note that many of them have overlapping characteristics and values.

Ethical Leadership

Ethical leadership refers to the practice of leading with integrity, fairness, and moral values (Arar & Saiti, 2022). It involves making decisions and taking actions that align with ethical principles and promote the greater good. By modeling ethical behavior and demonstrating a commitment to equity, the principal sets the tone for the entire school community.

An ethical leader promotes transparency and open communication, ensuring that staff members understand the school's values and goals regarding equity. They actively engage in discussions about equity-related issues and encourage staff to share their perspectives and concerns. By creating a safe and inclusive space for dialogue, the principal empowers staff members to actively participate in shaping equitable practices within the school.

An ethical leader also promotes accountability by establishing clear guidelines and policies that promote fairness and equal opportunities for all students. They ensure that decision-making processes are inclusive, involving staff members in shaping equitable policies and practices. Additionally, an ethical leader holds themselves and others accountable for upholding these standards and addressing any biases or inequalities that may arise.

Democratic Leadership

Democratic leadership is a style of leadership that emphasizes collaboration, participation, and shared decision making. It involves actively involving team members or stakeholders in the decision-making process, seeking their input, and valuing their perspectives (Ligette, 2022). A democratic leadership style, when employed by principals in leading their staff, can be a powerful tool in promoting equity in schools. Principals can utilize this leadership approach to create a collaborative and inclusive environment where staff members have a voice and are actively involved in decision-making processes related to equity.

A democratic leader encourages open communication, actively seeks input from staff members, and values staff perspectives and ideas. They create opportunities for staff to participate in discussions, committees, and decision-making forums. By involving staff members in shaping equity initiatives, policies, and practices, the principal ensures that multiple viewpoints are considered and that decisions are more likely to reflect the needs and aspirations of the school community.

In a democratic leadership approach, principals facilitate a sense of shared ownership among staff members by encouraging teamwork and collaboration. They foster a culture of trust, respect, and inclusivity, where everyone feels valued and empowered to contribute to the advancement of equity.

Moreover, a democratic leader promotes transparency in decision-making processes, ensuring that staff members are well informed and understand the rationale behind equity-related initiatives. They encourage open dialogue and encourage staff to provide feedback, share concerns, and propose innovative solutions. By employing a democratic leadership style, principals can harness the collective wisdom and expertise of their staff to drive meaningful change and promote equity.

Affiliative Leadership

Affiliative leadership is a leadership style that prioritizes building strong relationships, fostering a sense of belonging and promoting harmony within the organization (Wynn, 2019). An affiliative leader can cultivate a sense of belonging, collaboration, and trust among staff members, all of which are crucial elements for fostering equity. An affiliative leader prioritizes building positive relationships and creating a supportive work environment. They value the emotional well-being of staff members and encourage open communication and empathy. By fostering a culture of inclusion and acceptance, the principal establishes a foundation for promoting equity.

Principals who embrace an affiliative leadership style actively listen to the concerns and perspectives of staff members. They create opportunities for dialogue and collaboration in which staff members feel comfortable sharing their experiences, challenges, and ideas. By creating a safe space for open discussions, the principal allows staff members to contribute their unique insights and collectively address equity concerns. Furthermore, affiliative leaders promote teamwork and encourage collaboration. They facilitate a sense of unity and shared purpose, emphasizing that everyone's contributions are essential for advancing equity goals. By encouraging staff members to work together, share best practices, and support one another, the principal fosters a culture of collective responsibility for equity.

Coaching Leadership

Coaching leadership focuses on developing and empowering individuals to reach their full potential (Ray, 2017). A coaching leader focuses on building individual and collective capacity by providing guidance, feedback, and resources to support staff members. They establish a trusting and collaborative relationship with each staff member, taking into account their unique strengths and areas for growth. By identifying professional development opportunities and offering coaching sessions, the principal helps staff members enhance their knowledge and skills related to equity.

Principals who adopt a coaching leadership style actively listen to the needs, concerns, and ideas of their staff. They create a safe and supportive environment where staff can openly discuss challenges and seek guidance. By asking powerful questions and actively engaging in reflective conversations, the principal helps staff explore various strategies and approaches that promote equity.

Furthermore, a coaching leader encourages self-reflection and self-directed learning among staff. They empower staff to take ownership of their professional growth by setting goals and supporting them in achieving those goals. By fostering a culture of continuous improvement and learning, the principal nurtures a sense of agency among staff members to proactively contribute to equity initiatives.

Now, let's take a look at the more popular and widely used leadership styles—*servant, authoritative,* and *transformational.* The following sections go into more depth, focusing on the attributes of these leadership styles that promote more equitable school environments.

Servant Leadership

At the heart of the matter, a servant leader embraces serving the needs of others. As the term *servant leadership* suggests, servant leaders prioritize serving first and leading second (Crippen & Willows, 2019). Their willingness to serve is genuine, and their desire to lead is an intentional decision. A servant leader listens actively, supports the growth and development of their staff, and fosters collaboration and empathy.

Robert K. Greenleaf first introduced the servant leadership philosophy in his seminal essay "The Servant as Leader" in 1970 (LEADx, 2022). The philosophy quickly gained traction with business and leadership audiences around the globe, and it remains popular because it is so effective. History shows that servant-led companies are more likely to outperform competitors, retain employees, and develop future leaders than companies that operate out of more traditional command-and-control leadership styles. In a school setting, that means making your teachers' and staffs' personal and professional growth your first priority (Tucci, 2018). Servant leaders put others' needs before their own and support them to meet goals.

Servant leaders prioritize establishing and maintaining a supportive community environment. They place a high value on relationships with students, teachers, staff, and parents. Servant leadership "emphasizes the values of respect, altruism, fairness, and honesty, creating a strong foundation for moral literacy and caring learning communities. Servant leadership combines the scholarship of teaching and instruction as well as serving and leadership" (Shkurina, 2018). Servant leaders are also known to be excellent forecasters and vision communicators. They are skilled at making predictions and setting and achieving goals. A lot of leaders are blessed with foresight, but servant leaders are especially skilled at leading people by collaborating with and supporting them. They accept people with open arms and demonstrate empathy (LEADx, 2022). While servant leaders embrace people, they also expect high performance. Notable pros and cons of servant leadership exist in terms of leading a school.

Some of the pros include:

- Increased trust and autonomy of teachers and staff in the school
- Teacher satisfaction and loyalty
- Higher staff engagement
- Improved teacher confidence in decision making
- Strong leadership pipeline

Some of the cons include:

- Time-consuming to implement within a school or district
- Confusing and uncomfortable for staff and administrators accustomed to other leadership styles
- Lack of clarity about formal authority, which can cause conflict and misalignment

Some teachers and staff may try to exploit or take advantage of principals who practice servant leadership (LEADx, 2022). *This style of leadership lends itself to equity enhancement because of its emphasis on taking responsibility for the needs and desires of others.* This is akin to ethical leadership, which urges leaders to show respect for the values and dignity of their subordinates and others.

Authoritative Leadership

Authoritative leadership involves setting clear expectations, providing guidance, and holding others accountable (Veale, 2010). An authoritative leader establishes a strong vision for equity, communicates it effectively, and ensures all members of the school community are aligned with this vision. By providing structure, direction, and necessary resources, authoritative leaders create a supportive environment where expectations for equity are upheld and progress is monitored. Their decisive actions and willingness to address inequities head-on inspire confidence and motivate others to actively engage in equity-focused initiatives.

Daniel Goleman (2002) defines the authoritative leadership style in his book *Primal Leadership: Realizing the Power of Emotional Intelligence*. He discusses it in comparison to a variety of leadership approaches, including coaching, affiliative, democratic, coercive, and pacesetting. "While [various] styles have the potential to be effective when deployed in the right situation, authoritative leadership is often viewed as one of the more positive and harmonious" (Stobierski, 2019).

The terms *authoritative* and *authoritarian* sound alike and are sometimes mistakenly used interchangeably, but they couldn't be more different. Authoritative leaders lead by example and are inspiring. Authoritarian leaders use rules, orders, and ultimatums; demand compliance; and do not allow questioning, opinions, or input from the people doing the work who are mostly affected by decisions (Stobeirski, 2019). There is no shared decision making in an authoritarian style of leadership. "Authoritative leaders say, 'Come with me'; authoritarian leaders say, 'Do what I tell you.' Authoritative leaders view success as something to be shared by the team; authoritarian leaders view success as something stemming from themselves" (Stobierski, 2019).

Authoritarian leadership is also referred to as *commanding leadership*. Even though it's viewed as a negative approach, it can be effective given the right circumstances (Stobierski, 2019). An authoritarian approach may be appropriate when a school needs major change and more of a turnaround than a school-improvement approach, or if a school or district needs firm guidance through a crisis or challenge.

Authoritative leaders are also referred to as visionary leaders. They approach leadership like a mentor teaching a protégé. They refrain from the urge to demand that their employees follow instructions and do as they are told. Instead, they place themselves in the situation and utilize a collaborative approach. Stobierski (2019) writes, "They have a firm understanding of the challenges to overcome and the goals to reach and have a clear vision for achieving success." This leadership style offers direction, guidance, and feedback to maintain enthusiasm and a sense of accomplishment from the inception to the conclusion and manifestation of a vision.

Principals who use this style are confident and enjoy inspiring change, which is crucial when establishing equitable practices. This leadership style is effective in schools when a new vision is necessary and change is required. The leader makes the decision about changes to be made and inspires staff to work to that end (Acquisitions International, 2020). One similarity that authoritative leadership has with servant leadership is a thoroughly developed sense of emotional intelligence. To be effective, authoritative leaders must demonstrate empathy to understand and anticipate the emotions team members feel at key junctures during a project (Stobierski, 2019). Another similarity it has with servant leadership is growing the capacity of other leaders within the organization by delegating tasks. The Indeed Editorial Team (2023) states:

> When you adopt an authoritative style, you establish a large-scale vision and the short-term goals needed to achieve it. You then delegate specific guidelines for how each person can help the organization reach those goals and then supervise your staff to closely monitor performance and progress.

Teachers appreciate this approach rather than an authoritarian approach where tasks are dictated and often micromanaged. The latter can create an unbearable work environment in which teachers feel that they are not respected as professionals.

> *One similarity that authoritative leadership has with servant leadership is a thoroughly developed sense of emotional intelligence.*

The outcomes of an authoritatively led school will vary, but there are pros and cons to every leadership style. The pros of an authoritative leadership style include the following.

- A sense of clarity
- Direction and vision
- Fostering of goodwill

Authoritative leadership has cons as well, such as the following.

- May appear overbearing
- Is highly demanding
- Has expectations of compliance
- May prioritize procedures over people (Iqbal, Abid, Arshad, Ashfaq, Ahsan Athar, & Hassan, 2021)

Stephen Dinham (2007) claims that "authoritative leaders exercise their authority in a timely fashion. They know when to consult and when to be decisive. They have the skills to work with others and the courage to act alone." *This combination is effective for enhancing equity because it requires collaboration while simultaneously allowing the leader to step in and make necessary decisions, even if they are unpopular.* Also, authoritative leaders keep student achievement the primary purpose for the work they do and solicit others to engage. They provide meaningful and balanced feedback, both positive and negative, so people are aware of their performance and where they meet expectations and fall short (Dinham, 2007). Authoritative leadership shares some qualities with transformational leadership, professional growth being the most prominent.

Transformational Leadership

Transformational leadership focuses on inspiring and motivating others to achieve higher levels of performance and personal growth (Li & Liu, 2020). Transformational leaders encourage innovation, creativity, and critical thinking, challenging the status quo and promoting equity-centered practices. They foster a shared sense of purpose, provide individualized support and mentorship, and actively advocate for equity-oriented policies and initiatives. Through their charismatic and inspirational approach, transformational leaders empower educators to become change agents, creating a culture of continuous improvement and equitable outcomes.

This leadership style has become increasingly popular in schools and businesses alike. James V. Downton, considered the founder of this leadership style, conceived the idea in 1973. James Burns might then be considered the godfather of this style since he built on it in 1978. In 1985, Bernard M. Bass further grew this concept for the purposes of quantifying the success of transformational leadership (White, 2022).

Some characteristics of this style include:

- Connecting the follower's sense of identity and self to the mission and the collective identity of the organization;

- Being a role model who inspires followers;

- Challenging followers to take greater ownership for their work; and

- Understanding the strengths and weaknesses of followers, so the leader can align followers with tasks that optimize their performance. (White, 2022)

Transformational leadership is also a style in which school leaders influence, inspire, and encourage staff to deliver positive change. Fontein (2022) identifies prominent transformational leaders, including Steve Jobs of Apple and Jeff Bezos of Amazon. These transformational leaders possess characteristics such as the following:

- They work with teams beyond their immediate self-interests to identify needed change and create a vision to guide that change.

- They set an example at the executive level and strive for a strong sense of organizational culture, employee ownership, and autonomy in the work community, while motivating individuals without micromanaging.

So how does transformational leadership work in schools when so much emphasis has been placed on the importance of principals as instructional leaders?

Instructional leadership is a style in which principals know the curriculum and best practices in teaching and support teachers to improve their instruction. This style grew in the 1980s, but transformational leadership became more popular than instructional leadership in the 1990s (Fontein, 2022). However, the benefits of transformational leadership aren't always as noticeable as those of instructional leadership, because transformational leadership isn't typically about finding innovative ways to teach the curriculum. Instead, it's about improving the culture to align with school goals, which leads to student achievement (Fontein, 2022). Now, transformational leadership is accepted as being more effective than instructional leadership at driving school improvement.

Transformational leadership has been shown to positively impact factors that lead to school improvement, such as professionalism, collaboration, and planning. Schools are constantly under the microscope and must show that they are getting the job done when it comes to meeting accountability measures and earning high ratings from their respective state. Therefore, transformational leadership is beneficial for schools because it emphasizes supporting employees to gain new skills, establishing organizational norms, deriving paradigm shifts, and helping leaders dismantle old, ineffective systems while implementing new ones that work more effectively (Anderson, 2017). *This seems like the perfect fit for promoting equity!*

To effectively transform school culture, principals must model those behaviors they would like their school leadership team to exhibit. Bernard Bass and Ronald Riggio derived the four pillars of leadership in 1985, which are (1) influence by charisma, (2) individualistic consideration, (3) empowerment, and (4) the ability to motivate the team through intellectual stimulation.

Transformational leaders hold themselves accountable for role modeling what they want to see from their staff. James Baldwin wisely said, "I can't believe what you say because I see what you do" (Baldwin, 1966). This would be the opposite of the transformational leadership principal because actions and behaviors line up with words and commitments.

> **To effectively transform school culture, principals must model those behaviors they would like their school leadership team to exhibit.**

It's usually easy for teachers to get behind principals who practice transformational leadership and fall in line with the vision. "Transformational leaders have high expectations for themselves and others, instead of laying down the law, these leaders 'walk the walk' and model the standards of behavior they expect from the team" (Thompson, 2019). That is one of the greatest strengths of this leadership style, and although it shows promising results, there are also some weaknesses to consider before deciding if it is the right leadership style for you and your school.

Some of the pros of transformational leadership include the following:

- Set clear and consistent goals
- Encourage others
- Lead through influence and charisma
- Model integrity and fairness
- Inspire others to rise to challenges
- Encourage people to look beyond their self-interest toward the greater good of the organization (Thompson, 2019)

Some of the cons of transformational leadership include the following:

- [It creates] too big of a picture. It's one thing to rally support for the big-picture vision, and quite another to actualize that vision with clear operational strategies on the ground.

- It can lead to teacher and staff burnout. While some will feel inspired by a transformational leader, others feel their presence as a constant pressure.

- It requires a continuous feedback loop. The other side of communication is that it really only works if there's continuous communication available.

- Leaders lose power if people don't agree with them. Transformational leadership relies on employees being intrinsically motivated to work hard, but if those employees are not hearing, feeling, and connecting with the vision, then intrinsic motivation will be lacking. (Thompson, 2019)

Transformational leadership shows great potential for enhancing equity in education because these leaders are quick to try innovative new technologies, teaching methods, or processes. They also are the change makers who ensure the adoption and success of these innovations within their schools. Because such a need for significant change exists in so many schools and districts, this leadership style—implemented by the right leaders—can help identify problems, encourage solutions, and drive the sort of monumental, far-reaching change that will reshape the education landscape.

What It Looks Like in the Real World

If there is one thing that I love studying more than building bridges—building relationships with students and teaching social-emotional learning—it's leadership and advocating for equity! Like you, I have read countless books, articles, and blog posts, and regularly listen to podcasts on leadership. When it comes to seeking knowledge from strong leaders, I do not discriminate. I take what I can from school leaders, business leaders, industry leaders, elite athletes, and leadership gurus from across the world. It is exciting to absorb words of wisdom and learn intentional actions that I can adopt to improve my skills as a leader while increasing my influence and impact. Excitement flows through me whenever I attempt a new leadership principle. I'm sure you have the same desire to be a stronger leader.

The Right Fit

Many different leadership styles are effective for leading schools and making an impact. You may find yourself having to be more authoritative when holding your staff accountable for agreed-on equity initiatives; or more transformational when the topic of equity is foreign to staff; or more of a servant leader when staff needs an example what equity looks like in action, and you have to model this for them. But just like the analogy I used at the beginning of the chapter about choosing a car that fits your style, principals who want to enhance equity must choose a leadership style that fits them *and* suits their school's needs.

Consider this scenario. My brother-in-law and I were in the store looking at suits. He saw one with a poster next to it showing the suit on a handsome, fit model.

"That ad is false advertisement," he said after trying it on. "This suit doesn't look that good on me."

"Bro, what did you expect?" I asked. "I'm sure he had the suit he is wearing in that picture perfectly tailored before the photo shoot. Once you get it tailored, it will look better on you. Not as good, but better!"

The point is that you, your personality, and your authentic self are what's going to make you a strong leader. You must tailor whatever leadership style you choose to your personality and to what your school, teachers, students, and community need in order to enhance equity and create an environment where everyone grows, feels welcome, and contributes in a positive fashion. Not all teachers and staff will always embrace the leadership style you use, while others may respond favorably. Therefore, building relationships is as key in this situation as it is in working with students in a classroom. Leaders who have solid relationships with staff will know what leadership style works best to motivate them to work toward promoting equity. The goal of any leadership style is to get your staff to perform at a level even higher than set expectations.

> *The goal of any leadership style is to get your staff to perform at a level even higher than set expectations.*

Leadership Style Agility

What it takes to motivate staff members to perform at a high level may be different for different groups and certain individuals. This principle was very clear to me when I was a high school basketball coach. At that time, I came to understand the different personalities of all my players. A large factor in my success as a coach was the time I devoted to building relationships with them. I knew what did and did not motivate them.

Some players responded to shouts, while others shut down and lost confidence. Some players responded well to me pulling them to the side and whispering in their ears, while others didn't take that approach seriously. Some players responded to the threat of losing playing time, while others seemed unaffected by this threat. One thing all my players knew was that I would work hard to support them and help them become better players. They also knew that I expected them to use their individual skills to contribute to the overall success of the team.

I found that encounters like this occurred with teachers too, and you have probably had similar experiences. Equity is about giving people what they need to be successful, and when working with teachers and staff, it's about supporting their growth by using the leadership style they respond to most. While effective leaders use an overall style when interacting with staff as a whole, they're agile and adept at changing their style when interacting with individual teachers and staff members.

> *While effective leaders use an overall style when interacting with staff as a whole, they're agile and adept at changing their style when interacting with individual teachers and staff members.*

In "The 7 Most Common Leadership Styles (And How to Find Your Own)," Sophia Demetriades Toftdahl (2020) suggests that leaders should be familiar with the repertoire of leadership styles that work best for a given situation. She shares seven different leadership styles and when they are most appropriately used. Knowing which leadership style works best for you is part of being a good leader.

Traditional leadership styles are still relevant today, but they should be blended with new approaches to answer the call for equity. The ultimate leadership style should be agile. Developing a signature style while maintaining the ability to stretch into other styles as the situation warrants is ideal (Toftdahl, 2020).

Educational leadership experts suggest that changing up leadership styles in educational settings is necessary and effective. Josep Maria Lozano and Ángel Castiñeira (2019) assert that "leadership is not something we do *to* other people, but something we do *with* other people. In the case of educational leadership, it is essential to know how to move from 'me to we,' and from 'me to us'" (p. 1). This requires replacing opacity with transparency and control with trust. Rarely do professionals like taking orders; they prefer collaboration and leadership that focuses on people, not tasks. To be more people-centered, Lozano and Castiñeira (2019) suggest that leaders should switch from an autocratic leadership style to a style that combines transformational and distributive leadership. *Distributive leadership* in K–12 schools refers to a collaborative approach where leadership responsibilities and decision-making authority are shared among multiple individuals, including administrators, teachers, and staff (Richards, 2020). It emphasizes the equitable distribution of leadership roles and encourages collective participation to foster a culture of shared responsibility and decision making.

The American University School of Education (2019) states that when it comes to leadership styles in education, there's no one right approach. Effective educational leadership means adapting one's leadership style to suit a situation. Learning about different leadership styles contributes to becoming a more effective leader.

"Different leadership styles produce different results, and certain people are suited to different styles of leadership" (Robinson, 2022). Your personality, where your school is situated in the change process, and the makeup of staff are all factors for consideration when deciding on which leadership style to adopt. Since strategic leaders make data-based decisions, leaders need to consider what style best fits their school. According to Christina Garibay (2021), "Many ways lead up a mountain and each one may suit different people at various points along the journey" (p. 2). As discussed previously, different institutions will need different leadership approaches.

Exceptional leaders share many of the same qualities, but this doesn't mean that they share the same leadership style. Some leaders' styles are fluid because they understand the necessity to adapt and change given the circumstances in any given moment. Robyn Benincasa, CEO of World Class Teams, states, "The most successful leaders are able to adapt their leadership style to the situation. They become the person their team needs them to be in that moment" (as cited in Gale, 2019). To be the driving force for promoting equity, principals and other school leaders should be well versed in the menu of leadership styles that best fit their situation.

> *To be the driving force of promoting equity, principals and other school leaders should be well versed in the menu of leadership styles that best fit their situation.*

I used a coaching style of leadership during one of my very first leadership positions in education. The coaching style of leadership is an approach where leaders act as coaches, focusing on developing the skills, knowledge, and potential of their team members. In this style, leaders provide guidance, support, and feedback to help individuals grow, learn, and maximize their performance. Rather than giving direct instructions or controlling every aspect, coaches empower their team members to take ownership of their work, problem solve, and make decisions independently. The coaching style emphasizes collaboration, active listening, and fostering a positive and developmental relationship between the leader and their team members.

After being a high school dean of students for five years, I became an assistant principal of culture and climate at a larger high school. In this position, I supervised the dean's office, attendance office, security team, and social workers, and worked with the guidance counselors to apply and monitor behavior and academic interventions for students. Since these were all my responsibilities in my previous position, I was able to coach and model for my staff. After researching leadership practices that work best for improving schools, coaching is one of the best styles to develop people over the course of time (Acquisitions International, 2020).

Coaching takes people from where they are to where they need to be. It also provides people with a sense of their strengths and weaknesses. They are encouraged to take advantage of what they do well while also focusing on opportunities for growth in areas that need improvement. "This leads to more self-awareness, which helps people focus on their strengths in a much more positive way" (Acquisitions International, 2020). This led me to modeling how to run peer mediations, parent meetings with students, and interacting with students so my deans would see how to turn students' behavior infractions into teachable moments. As I observed my staff performing these skills, I coached them to continue the things they did well and improve on the areas where they needed to grow.

During another one of my early leadership positions as an assistant principal of activities and athletics, I used an authoritative leadership style. In this position, I managed all the sports teams and athletic clubs, and the coaches and sponsors in charge. I also was the administrator for the physical education department, fine arts department, career technical education department, and the world languages department. The culture at this school needed much improvement and, of course, the culture of the overall school environment filtered into the departments I managed. Apparently, the school environment had been trending down for several years due to frequent changes in leadership in the principal position and a lack of accountability.

I used the authoritative style of leadership to drive people toward the vision I had for my departments. Research shows that people who use this style are self-confident leaders who like to inspire change. This leadership style is very effective whenever a new vision is required or when things need to change at a fundamental level (Veale, 2010). The leader decides what this change will be and then motivates others to work toward that change. This is exactly what I tried to do in this position. I motivated staff to improve their performance to provide students with a better education based on the subjects they taught, and an enriching extracurricular school experience based on the activity or sport they sponsored or coached. That was a reflection of my vision.

I worked at this school for several years, and agility in my leadership style was required. The base style was the authoritative style, but I also utilized the democratic leadership style with several of my teachers, activity sponsors, and coaches who already were effective and performing at a high level. The democratic leadership style was good for this group because they were already highly motivated to do a good job and they appreciated being included in the decision-making process. This leadership style encouraged them to use their creativity, and they willingly stayed highly engaged in projects and decisions. As a result, they had high job satisfaction and high productivity. I found this to be the case with high performers whenever I yielded to a collaborative approach. Since they had strong work ethics, high competence, and passion, the collaborative approach helped them feel respected, appreciated, and valued. The end result was their continual striving toward excellence. This is an example of how to consider equity when choosing your leadership approach because staff members were led in a way that motivated them to be highly successful.

Leaders will find that even in low- or average-performing schools, there are great teachers who bring it every day. Always, you'll find diamonds whose light may have been overshadowed by the school's poor reputation. This reminds me of a lot of sports teams that may have dismal records, but also have one or two players who are phenomenal. This was the case in my principal positions. In both positions, the superintendents who hired me told me that I was going to have a real challenge on my hands to improve the culture and climate of the school and enhance equity in the building. These were the things that I was told to focus on because the schools had numerous challenges when it came to student achievement, student behavior, and the overall climate of the school.

Coupled with an authoritative leadership style, I approached these jobs with a transformational style because transformational leadership focuses on role modeling. With this style, leaders influence, inspire, and encourage employees to deliver positive change. Transformational leaders work with teams beyond their immediate self-interests to identify needed change and create a vision to guide that change.

Although the transformational style was the base leadership style, I also employed others, including authoritative and affiliative, as needed. The affiliative leadership style works best during stressful circumstances to heal rifts in a team or motivate them to keep working. The main qualities of affiliative leaders are that they are more inclined toward building relationships and exhibiting empathy. This style puts people first and creates harmony and builds emotional bonds. Affiliative leaders also build teams in which their followers feel connected to each other. As the new principal of a school with a divided staff, and with performance and commitment to equity lacking, I knew it was crucial to build relationships, address the harm that had been done in the school, and unify the staff. My vision for my first principal's position was "We are one!" and at my second, it was "Above and beyond!"

Even though the culture at both schools had been damaged prior to my tenure, both schools boasted some really strong teachers and overall great staffs. I varied my leadership approaches depending on different situations, assessing the needs of different groups of teachers as well as individual teachers. All appreciated that the vision and expectations were clearly communicated and shared. Having the adaptability to use the correct leadership styles at the right time with the right people proved effective at improving student behavior and achievement while also improving the culture and enhancing equity at each respective school.

Taking Action to Select the Appropriate Leadership Style

In the pursuit of fostering equity within schools, principals play a critical role in selecting a leadership style that aligns with their values and aspirations. By understanding the impact of leadership style on promoting equity and embracing intentional strategies, principals can create an environment that nurtures inclusivity, fairness, and justice.

Consider taking some of the following action steps to select the appropriate leadership style for your school and situation.

ACTION 1: **Know yourself as a leader.** Start by learning your dominant leadership style. Do you prefer to delegate authority or give orders? Or do your preferences lie somewhere in between? Talk to a mentor about your strengths and weaknesses. Take the leadership survey at the end of this chapter to determine what leadership style best fits your personality and beliefs about leadership.

ACTION 2: **Become more familiar with the staff you lead.** Your leadership style should be dictated by your situation and especially the makeup of your staff. Leaders must learn to adjust to their staff's personalities and goals of the school (Doyle, 2022). Ask yourself, "What adaptations do you need to make that best fits my staff's needs?" Determine how your style might need to change depending on the individual teacher or staff members you are interacting with. To gain a deeper understanding of your staff and select the most effective leadership style to motivate them toward a schoolwide vision of equity, you can engage in various activities.

Begin by conducting one-on-one meetings with each staff member, fostering open and honest conversations to build trust and establish rapport. Organize team-building activities, such as retreats or professional development sessions focused on equity, allowing staff to collaborate, share their perspectives, and develop a sense of collective purpose. Additionally, create opportunities for staff to provide feedback and contribute to decision-making processes through surveys, suggestion boxes, or staff committees, empowering them to shape the school's equity agenda. By actively listening, valuing input, and investing time in getting to know your staff, you can gain valuable insights that inform your leadership style and create an environment conducive to collective growth and equity-driven outcomes.

ACTION 3: **Learn more about each leadership style.** As a school leader, you must cultivate a deep knowledge of the various leadership styles to effectively navigate the complexities of educational leadership. To enhance your understanding, commit to continuous learning and professional development. Read and research to explore scholarly works and case studies that examine different leadership styles and their applications in educational settings. Attend workshops, conferences, and seminars led by experts in the field to gain insights and practical strategies for implementing diverse leadership approaches. Seek out mentorship or coaching from experienced leaders who can provide guidance and support tailored to your growth as a leader.

By embracing a mindset of lifelong learning, exploring diverse resources, and seeking guidance from mentors, you can develop a comprehensive understanding of different leadership styles and discern when and how to deploy each one to best serve your school community and advance the cause of educational equity.

ACTION 4: **Learn how to use different aspects from various leadership styles.** Leadership styles are not one-size-fits-all. Therefore, you will be most effective, and your staff will likely perform better if you develop a wide set of styles and apply them appropriately. As a school leader striving to be the driving force to enhance equity at your school, the vision you have coupled with the personalities that exist on your staff will help you understand the kind of leadership style or styles you need to use.

Conclusion

This chapter discussed how leadership styles can play a crucial role in promoting equity. It explored ethical, democratic, affiliative, coaching, servant, authoritative, and transformational leadership styles and how each offers its own unique strengths and approaches.

Leadership styles are not one-size-fits-all, and effective leaders must be adaptable and flexible in their approach. While leaders may naturally gravitate toward a specific style that aligns with their personality and strengths, they must be open to utilizing a range of styles based on the needs of their school community. By understanding and employing different leadership styles strategically, leaders can motivate and inspire their teams, build trust, and create an environment that values diversity, equity, and fairness. Ultimately, the goal of leveraging diverse leadership styles is to foster an equitable and thriving learning environment where all students have the opportunity to succeed.

Questions for Reflection

Working individually or with a collaborative group, ask yourself the following reflective questions.

1. How can you determine which leadership style is most appropriate for promoting schoolwide equity, and what factors should you consider when making this decision?

2. In a situation in which some members of the school community resist supporting or promoting equity, which leadership style do you believe would be most effective in addressing and resolving the issue? Why?

3. When working with a team of educators who are not all committed to promoting equity, which leadership style do you think would be most effective in fostering collaboration and teamwork, and how would you use it to get this done?

4. When implementing a new equity program or initiative, which leadership style do you think would be most effective in ensuring all stakeholders are invested and committed to the success of the program? Why?

5. In what ways does your current leadership style inspire and motivate your staff toward achieving shared equity goals, and how might you adapt or refine your leadership approach to better support and empower them?

Leadership Styles Survey

For each item, circle the response that best describes your style as a school leader. Be as honest and reflective as possible.

1. I actively seek input and involvement from staff members in decision-making processes.

1	2	3	4	5
Strongly disagree	Disagree	Neutral	Agree	Strongly agree

2. I provide clear directions and guidelines for tasks and expectations.

1	2	3	4	5
Strongly disagree	Disagree	Neutral	Agree	Strongly agree

3. I strive to inspire and motivate others through my vision and enthusiasm.

1	2	3	4	5
Strongly disagree	Disagree	Neutral	Agree	Strongly agree

4. I prioritize ethical decision making and hold myself accountable to high moral standards.

1	2	3	4	5
Strongly disagree	Disagree	Neutral	Agree	Strongly agree

5. I frequently engage in coaching and mentoring conversations to support the growth of my staff.

1	2	3	4	5
Strongly disagree	Disagree	Neutral	Agree	Strongly agree

page 1 of 4

6. I value collaboration and foster a sense of teamwork and camaraderie among staff members.

1	2	3	4	5
Strongly disagree	Disagree	Neutral	Agree	Strongly agree

7. I prioritize the well-being and needs of others above my own.

1	2	3	4	5
Strongly disagree	Disagree	Neutral	Agree	Strongly agree

8. I encourage open and honest communication, allowing for diverse perspectives to be heard.

1	2	3	4	5
Strongly disagree	Disagree	Neutral	Agree	Strongly agree

9. I believe in empowering others by delegating responsibilities and fostering their professional growth.

1	2	3	4	5
Strongly disagree	Disagree	Neutral	Agree	Strongly agree

10. I actively promote a culture of inclusivity and respect for all individuals in the school community.

1	2	3	4	5
Strongly disagree	Disagree	Neutral	Agree	Strongly agree

11. I provide regular feedback and recognize the achievements of staff members.

1	2	3	4	5
Strongly disagree	Disagree	Neutral	Agree	Strongly agree

12. I lead by example and demonstrate the values and behaviors I expect from others.

1	2	3	4	5
Strongly disagree	Disagree	Neutral	Agree	Strongly agree

13. I encourage innovation and creative problem solving among staff members.

1	2	3	4	5
Strongly disagree	Disagree	Neutral	Agree	Strongly agree

14. I am adaptable and open to change, considering different approaches and ideas.

1	2	3	4	5
Strongly disagree	Disagree	Neutral	Agree	Strongly agree

15. I demonstrate empathy and understanding toward the challenges and needs of others.

1	2	3	4	5
Strongly disagree	Disagree	Neutral	Agree	Strongly agree

Survey Results:

Based on your survey responses, your leadership style aligns most closely with the following.

- If you chose higher numbers on statement 1–5, you are more of a transformational leader.
- If you chose higher numbers on statements 6–10, you are more of a servant leader.
- If you chose higher numbers on statements 11–15, you are more of an authoritative leader.

Statements 1–5: Transformational Leadership Style

Your results indicate a strong inclination toward transformational leadership. You prioritize inspiring and motivating others through your vision and enthusiasm. You actively seek input and involvement from staff members, encouraging innovation and fostering a sense of empowerment. Your focus on personal growth and development helps create a positive and forward-thinking environment that promotes equity and progress.

Statements 6–10: Servant Leadership Style

Your results suggest that you exhibit characteristics of a servant leader. You prioritize the well-being and needs of others above your own, and you actively promote a culture of inclusivity and respect within the school community. Your emphasis on collaboration, empathy, and supporting the growth of your staff creates an environment that values equity, teamwork, and shared responsibility.

Statements 11–15: Authoritative Leadership Style

Your results indicate a preference for an authoritative leadership style. You value providing clear directions and guidelines for tasks and expectations, ensuring that tasks are completed efficiently and effectively. Your confident and decisive approach sets a strong framework for the staff to follow, promoting accountability and a focus on achieving equity goals.

Note: These scores provide a snapshot of your leadership style based on the survey responses; effective leadership often combines elements from various styles. Reflect on your scores and consider how you can leverage your strengths and address areas for growth to further promote equity, collaboration, and positive outcomes within your school community. Leadership is a continuous journey of learning and development, and adapting your style to meet the evolving needs of your staff and students is crucial for sustainable success.

page 4 of 4

CHAPTER 4

CREATING THE VISION TO DESIRED DESTINATIONS

Developing a vision and mission for your school is an important part of being an effective school leader. It is one of the biggest contributors to a principal's success. In the same way that safe drivers maintain clear vision and regularly scan the road ahead, effective principals establish a clear vision for their schools—strategies that encompass short-term goals as well as incorporate the long view. The vision statement encompasses where a school wants to go, while the mission statement is the map showing how to get there.

*M*Y DAD COULD be pretty intense at times, especially when he was teaching me how to drive. The very first time he took me out for a driving lesson, we were on a busy street. From the passenger's side of his 1987 burgundy Chevy Caprice, he turned sideways in his seat and shouted, "What are you looking at?" I nervously told him that I was looking at the car in front of me and up the street. He then said, "Pull the car over right now." I quickly pulled the car over. He told me that I should always look as far down the road as possible, and stated, "Your vision is the most important tool you have while driving. Use it effectively!"

According to Defensive Driving (2020), many drivers focus on the road for about five to eight seconds ahead. Driving instructors advise that you should be looking a minimum of fifteen to twenty seconds ahead of your car, even farther if conditions allow. This gives you enough time to recognize and avoid most potential hazards before they become a problem. Keeping your focus down the road instead of just past the end of your car creates stability. Defensive Driving (2020) also highlights other important ways for drivers to use their vision as a defensive driving tool for safe driving:

> By looking ahead, drivers can see the entire picture. They're in a better position to react early, avoiding that last-minute lane change or sudden stop. Drivers should see, and be mindful of, everything around them on both sides and for several hundred feet ahead, about two blocks, and also to the rear.

This concept is also referred to as "aiming high in steering" (Owens, 2015). Being aware of the environment keeps drivers and passengers safe. Those who look ahead are more likely to stay alert and awake, and less likely to end up in a car crash. Vision is also an important tool for communicating with other drivers. Making eye contact helps ensure that your intentions are communicated, frequently bringing the desired response from other drivers and pedestrians. Eye contact, however, indicates only that people see you. It does not guarantee that they will do what you want. So, to stay safe, pay attention. To arrive at your destination safely, maneuver smoothly and monitor what other drivers are doing.

We can make many analogies between the importance of vision to safe driving and the importance of vision in effective school leadership. A clear vision, an essential part of moving safely from point A to point B, is required for a principal to move a school from a position of inequitable educational progress to a position of equitable progress for all students. Effective school leaders aim high, driving their schools toward more positive futures. They are always scanning the horizon, spotting potential hazards along the way, and communicating with others about who must do what to circumvent them. The point of driving is to safely get to where you need to go. Often, a road map or GPS is needed. The same is true in schools. A well-reasoned vision and mission, showing clear markers along the way, are the road maps to guide your school to its enhanced-equity destination.

> *A clear vision is required for a principal to move a school from a position of inequitable educational progress to a position of equitable progress for all students.*

This chapter discusses how principals and other school leaders play a crucial role in promoting equity within their schools and how they can develop a clear vision and mission statement that prioritizes equity as a key value. These statements should clearly communicate the school's commitment to ensuring *all* students have access to high-quality education and support, regardless of their background or circumstances. By emphasizing equity in their vision and mission statements, leaders set the tone for the school culture and guide stakeholders toward the same goal. This can help create a sense of safety among staff, students, and families, which is essential for promoting equity in all aspects of school life.

What the Research Says

Establishing school vision and mission statements, or revising existing ones, is a task that must be accomplished early in one's tenure. Leaders have to go beyond prioritizing the day-to-day responsibilities and place more time and energy into planning for the future. Principals must have visionary leadership with a strong equity orientation, a clear sense of purpose, and the ability to mobilize people in their communities in an aligned direction to effectively address the deep, persistent disparities in today's schools. They are "a fundamental measure of how schools are doing with regard to pursuing strategic direction and strategic initiatives aimed at advancing equity" (Pierce, 2020). Administrators and faculty should design a creed that identifies the goals, policies, and aspirations their school communities seek to achieve (Education World, 2015).

Kelly-Ann Allen and Peggy Kern (2018) write:

> A school's vision and mission statement make a public statement about what the school sees as the purpose of education and how students should learn. Vision statements outline a school's objectives, and mission statements indicate how the school aims to achieve that vision.

According to the National School Boards Association (2017), a school *vision statement* is a concise, focused expression of the school's purpose and aspirations. It should reflect the school's core values and beliefs and provide direction for the school community to achieve its goals. A well-crafted vision statement can help create a sense of shared purpose among stakeholders and inspire them to work toward a common vision for the school. The most effective school leaders inspire their staff to reach for ambitious goals (SHRM, 2012).

John Gabriel and Paul Farmer (2009) write that a *mission statement* "provides an overview of the steps planned to achieve that future" vision and includes lengthier "'how-to' statements . . . that help schools achieve their vision" (pp. 45, 54). The mission statement acts as a compass and map to keep the organization on course in a constantly changing environment, avoiding the *activity trap*, which is a situation in which an organization commits to engaging in specific activities rather than producing specific results (Odiorne, 1974, as cited in Slate, Jones, Wiesman, Alexander, & Saenz, 2008).

Figure 4.1 shows examples of ineffective and effective, equity-based vision statements. These examples illustrate the difference between simply stating a commitment to equity and actively working to create an environment that promotes equity and ensures all students have an equal opportunity to succeed. While some schools are truly working to be equitable and matching their activities to achieve their goals, others are falling victim to the activity trap. John R. Slate, Craig H. Jones, Karen Wheeler Wiesman, Jeanie Alexander, and Tracy Johnson Saenz (2008) write that the *activity trap* allows members of an organization to believe they are accomplishing the mission regardless of how well it is actually performing. The activity trap usually involves having students complete a system of courses and teachers assigning grades without much concern for the quality of students' educational experiences or the actual academic achievements symbolized by those grades (Slate et al., 2008).

To avoid the activity trap, new principals should familiarize themselves with the vision and mission statements that are in place and review them with staff to

Ineffective Equity-Based Vision Statements	Effective Equity-Based Vision Statements
Our school promotes diversity and inclusivity.	Our school celebrates diversity and values the unique experiences and backgrounds of all students, families, and staff.
We strive to treat everyone equally.	We strive to recognize and address systemic inequities that have created disparities in educational opportunities and outcomes for historically marginalized groups.
Our school welcomes all students regardless of race, gender, or socioeconomic status.	Our school actively works to create a safe and inclusive environment where all students feel seen, heard, and supported to reach their full potential.
We believe that every student has the potential to succeed.	We are committed to providing equitable access to high-quality instruction, resources, and support that ensures every student has the opportunity to thrive academically and socially.
Our school is committed to providing a level playing field for all students.	Our school recognizes and addresses the barriers that prevent historically marginalized students from accessing and benefiting from essential educational opportunities and resources.

FIGURE 4.1: Ineffective and effective equity-based vision statements.

determine if they want to keep, revise, or change them altogether. Principals who have been in their schools for a few years may want to revisit these statements and compare them to where the school is now as it relates to student achievement, school culture and climate, and student population.

When navigating parental and community interests, district and state developments, and the trends and progress in education, a vision statement acts as a natural checks-and-balances system for the school that reflect, for example, demographic shifts in the student and community population. Since 2020, in particular, many districts experienced increasing diversity of student populations, and this trend is expected to continue in the years to come. According to the National Center for Education Statistics (2021b):

> Between 2000 and 2017, the percentage of students who were white decreased from 61 to 48 percent, and the number of white students decreased from 28.9 million to 24.1 million. Similarly, the percentage of students who were Black decreased from 17 to 15 percent, and the number of Black students decreased from 8.1 million to 7.7 million. In contrast, the percentage of students who were Hispanic increased from 16 to 27 percent during the same period, and the percentage of students who were Asian/Pacific Islander increased from 4 to 6 percent. Between 2017 and 2029, the percentage of public elementary and secondary students who are white is projected to continue decreasing

from 48 to 44 percent. In contrast, the percentage of students who are Asian/Pacific Islander is projected to continue increasing from 6 to 7 percent, and the percentage of students who are Hispanic is projected to be higher in fall 2029 than in fall 2017.

This increase in student diversity, including more students from varying socioeconomic backgrounds, demands a response from schools to increase their equitable practices. What better place to make a public statement that your school is committed to enhancing equity than in the vision and mission statements? Vision and mission statements are supposed to be trustworthy representations of what schools stand for, helping to keep the values of the school central to how it operates (Allen & Kern, 2018). *If equity is a goal for your school, it should be part of your vision and mission.*

> **What better place to make a public statement that your school is committed to enhancing equity than in the vision and mission statements?**

By using vision and mission statements as vehicles to show a schoolwide commitment to diversity and equity, schools aiming to improve equity and remove barriers to historically marginalized students' achievement make the environment more welcoming for all students, no matter their socioeconomic status, racial or cultural heritage, or gender identity. Never forget that, as principals and educational leaders, we are tasked with supporting *all* students in mastering grade-level standards. It is our responsibility to teach in a way that reaches every student, regardless of their background (Clash, 2020). To ensure your vision and mission statements send a clear message that diversity is celebrated, consider how you will approach this work in collaboration with other stakeholders, the statement drafting process, and the implementation process.

Collaborating With Stakeholders

To be the most effective, vision and mission statements should be created in collaboration with all relevant parties, such as teachers, parents, community members, and school leaders. People will be more committed and supportive of something they helped create (Allen & Kern, 2018), and they function as the guideposts for how students and families are treated, how resources are allocated, curriculum decisions, discipline issues, and other important issues that take place in schools daily. Further, if the statements are unclear and put into place without consensus, they can lead to continuing conflicts, the hallmark of a school that has difficulty identifying priorities (Center for School Change, 2022). Leaders who want to enhance equity in their schools and districts ensure that all key stakeholders are represented.

A diverse and effective team of school stakeholders can include individuals from different racial, ethnic, cultural, and socioeconomic backgrounds, as well as varying ages, genders, and abilities. This team can consist of educators, parents, students, community members, and other stakeholders who bring unique perspectives, experiences, and expertise to the table. It is important to have a team that represents the diversity of the school community to ensure that all voices are heard and considered in decision-making processes. An effective team works collaboratively toward a common goal, recognizes and values diversity, and encourages open communication and constructive feedback. Equity and inclusion mean considering different thoughts and ideas (Hein, 2013).

The Georgia Leadership Institute for School Improvement for the Principal Professional Learning Community (2014) suggests:

> Casting an effective vision requires principals to solicit input from school stakeholders about what the community values and what the hopes and dreams are for the students the school serves. These shared values, hopes and dreams are the foundation upon which the school vision statement should be built. Without them, the statement has little hope of being either inspirational or aspirational.

Everyone knows the Golden Rule, "Do unto others as you would have them do unto you." But we might upgrade this to the Platinum Rule, "Do unto others as they would want done to them" (Economy, 2016). School leaders attuned to their teachers, parents, students, and communities listen and provide opportunities for these key stakeholders to state what they need. They plan inclusive processes that let them know they are valued.

Laura Hill (2022), former teacher and now school principal, discusses the effectiveness of schools that have a clear vision and mission to equitably involve parents in their children's education, and how this has a positive effect on student outcomes. Her article "How Schools Can Overcome the Barriers of Family Engagement and Inspire Success" states that higher-performing schools were more likely to include community engagement and collaboration in their mission statements, and schools can establish a shared vision for family engagement that includes the values of trust, relationships, partnership, collaboration, inclusion, and equity (Hill, 2022). From this, expectations and goals are created.

Hill (2022) further suggests that involving stakeholders and community members in the school's mission statement can lead to greater support and engagement, which can contribute to improved academic outcomes. Successful schools are more likely to incorporate the voices of stakeholders and community members and mention them in their mission statements, compared to schools that are not as academically successful.

Drafting Vision and Mission Statements

In addition to the research and academic literature supporting how vital it is to collaborate with stakeholders as you update your school's vision and mission statement, an abundance of research exists on best practices for writing school vision and mission statements. You will have considerable expertise in the room with you as you do this work, but as the principal, you need to be familiar with the process. Gabriel and Farmer (2009) share an effective process for developing mission and vision statements in their book *How to Help Your School Thrive Without Breaking the Bank*. Following is an abridged version of this process (as cited in College and Career Alliance Network, 2022).

1. Explore the purpose of a mission statement. This is how the school will work collaboratively to achieve the vision. Then discuss the essential practices school staff must prioritize to work toward the vision.

2. Examine the school's previous mission statement and the district's strategic plan.

3. Break the teams into groups of three to four to discuss what it is they truly want from their students and school.

4. Review the school's existing vision statement and other documents that describe the school's vision and any vision statements that exist, and the district's strategic plan. The design team should discuss their impression as an entire team.

5. Draft a vision statement. The vision design team should break into small groups, with one person serving as a scribe who will record responses, ideas, key terms, and phrases and write a two- to three-sentence vision statement.

Another way to accomplish revising your school vision and mission statements is by looking at other schools' statements and seeing if they align with your school's values and beliefs. The statements can be adjusted and revised to the committee's liking and tailored to fit your school's philosophies. Remember, you don't have to reinvent the wheel. Many great vision and mission statements are out there that encompass the beliefs of school leaders, teachers, parents, community members, and students.

Coming to a Consensus

Conceptualizing a vision and mission statement is one thing, but coming to a consensus with stakeholders is something else entirely. Begin by creating a committee consisting of a diverse group of stakeholders, and gather data on the school's strengths, weaknesses, and areas for improvement. These data can come from surveys, focus groups, and other sources. The committee should then analyze the data and identify common themes and priorities. Using the data, the committee can develop draft vision and mission statements that reflect the school's values, priorities, and goals. The committee can then seek feedback on the draft statement from all stakeholders, including students, parents, and community members. Based on the feedback, the committee can then revise the draft statements as needed and finalize them (Ma, Yao, & Mu, 2020).

Once the committee members agree on the vision and mission statements, you must decide how and where to share them with stakeholders. More importantly, school staff must decide how they will bring the vision and mission to fruition. Without aligned daily practices, vision and mission statements are no more than words on paper.

Implementing Your Vision and Mission Into Daily Practice

How will school personnel and stakeholders walk the walk and not just talk the talk? How will they manifest the vision and mission? How will schools keep these statements alive once they are written? Ben Owens (2017) asks school leaders if their vision statement would pass the "red face" test:

> If you gave your vision to an outside observer and asked her to tour your school for a day, could she identify examples that match the words in the statement to the actions of members of your learning community? Or would she come up blank, leaving you embarrassed with a red face?

Reflecting on this question should cause a leader to constantly monitor the actions and behaviors of those within the organization. The best leaders consistently have that vision in their mind and model it faithfully.

Repeatedly communicating the vision and mission to everyone is an effective way of putting words into action. Communicating the school's vision and mission in a positive, enthusiastic manner ensures that staff and students engage positively with what you have set out for the school to achieve. Taking internal measures helps ensure everyone speaks with a unified voice about the vision and mission (Monteith, 2018). Consider doing the following to be sure your vision and mission are visible to everyone.

- Place them in internal and external documents to regularly remind school staff and stakeholders of what the school is working toward and how the school plans to get there.
- Post them on the school's website, recruitment literature, press releases, social media, and community newsletters.
- State the vision and mission at the start of staff meetings. Periodically invite faculty and staff to discuss what the vision and mission mean to them. Ask what daily habits they have adopted toward achieving them.

All these things help keep the vision and mission statements on everyone's minds.

> *Communicating the school's vision and mission in a positive, enthusiastic manner ensures that staff and students engage positively with what you have set out for the school to achieve.*

What It Looks Like in the Real World

During the vision and mission statements revision process at my school, I held a series of staff meetings focused on the school's goals and future aspirations. Recruiting staff, parents, community stakeholders, and students to be present at the table, I gave everyone a voice and created an inclusive culture. This approach reduced the fear of change. It also improved buy-in, especially among teachers. Educators who are consulted on changes to their school's vision and mission statements are more likely to support them in the classroom and throughout their daily practices at school. A principal who is aware of what staff members think and has collaborated with them in adjusting the new vision statement is far more likely to receive their support when it comes time to implement the new vision and mission.

Building Relationships to Set the Foundation

Significant work is hard to achieve without supportive, trusting relationships between teachers and students. The same holds true in the staff-principal equation. A significant relationship must exist between the principal and the teachers if the work of advancing a new vision and mission statement is going to succeed. Of course, we all typically believe what our school vision and mission statements say. But people are more likely to get behind a person than a cause. Teachers will not buy into the vision or devote themselves to the mission if they do not buy into the principal's leadership. School leaders must win the hearts of their teachers and staff to start the momentum of bringing the school vision and mission to fruition.

> **Teachers will not buy into the vision or devote themselves to the mission if they do not buy into the principal's leadership.**

Promoting Equity as the Core Value

After building relationships with teachers and introducing the idea of revising our school's vision and mission statements, I met with my school's administrative team to discuss how we needed to promote equity in our school's statements during the revision process. We entertained questions like:

1. Where do we think the school is presently in general and in regard to equity?

2. Where do we see the school in the future?

3. What part of the school's identity should be accentuated?

My two assistant principals and school leadership team also posed these questions to our staff during meetings and took deep dives into exploring the answers.

We divided teachers into small groups to discuss the questions as they related to school equity. Each small group then shared their consensus with the larger group. Many similarities arose.

We also engaged parents in the discussion during our Parent-Teacher Organization meetings, asking them these same questions. The parents were passionate about what they expected and wanted from the school for their children. They discussed their thoughts, listed them on chart paper, and looked for themes. They enjoyed the opportunity over several monthly meetings to discuss topics important to them regarding equity and share what they viewed as the school's chief strengths and weaknesses. We visited classrooms and held discussions about equity with students and recorded how they felt in response to the questions we asked.

Comparing Vision and Mission Statements

After gathering data on teachers', students', and parents' thoughts, we compared the information with the school-improvement plan and reviewed the existing school vision and mission statements. During a school-improvement day, we broke teachers into several groups and gave each group a list of twenty to thirty school vision statements from different schools. We asked them to highlight the statement aspects that they considered to be most potent—culling words or phrases we might adopt as part of our new vision and mission statements. We tasked each group with coming back to the larger group meeting with their own vision and mission statements, plus a summary of their key components and why they believed they would work best for our school. Interestingly, most group statements were very similar. At the end of the meeting, we fused together pieces from each group to form our school's vision and mission statements.

Presenting Vision and Mission Statements to the School Community

After much research, discussion, and collaboration, we constructed our new vision and mission statements. And now, it was time to present them to our school community! Kampen (2019) suggests several ways to accomplish this important task:

> Put the vision and mission statement everywhere: on the wall, in your office, in your weekly newsletter, and on your website. Make sure it's visible to the entire community. This could be through a meeting with district leaders, a parent evening, or through the school newsletter.

Furthermore, to keep it on the minds of teachers, I put it on every staff meeting agenda. My administrative team adopted a short motto that summarized our vision and mission statements. One year, the motto was "Above and beyond," which served as a reminder of the commitment the staff made to go above and beyond for our students. A couple of years later, we changed the motto to "Striving for excellence" to align with the district's focus. Each time we changed the motto, we ordered school spirit T-shirts with our school logo on the front and our motto on the back. Each staff member received a complimentary T-shirt that we all wore on spirit days, and we also made the T-shirts available for sale to students and parents. This turned out to be a great fundraiser, but most importantly, it was an effective way to keep our school vision and mission statements alive.

Taking Action to Create or Revise Vision and Mission Statements

Establishing school vision and mission statements, or revising existing ones, is a task that school leaders must accomplish early in their tenure. Leaders have to go beyond prioritizing the day-to-day responsibilities and place more time and energy planning for the future to enhance equity and continue school-improvement efforts. Consider taking some of the following steps to create or revise your school vision and mission statements.

ACTION 1: **Assemble a school vision and mission committee or team that consists of school administrators, staff, students, parents, community members, and other stakeholders.** Schedule a series of meetings around the school vision and mission statements and how the school will practice them and bring them alive.

ACTION 2: **Review your current vision and mission statements and determine if they encompass equity and the vision of school leaders and stakeholders.** School leaders can determine if the school's statements encompass equity by assessing whether they align with the school's policies, practices, and actions. They should also check if the statements reflect the diversity of the student population and address their unique needs and challenges.

ACTION 3: **Facilitate discussions about where the school is now and where you would like it to be three years from now related to enhancing equity and providing students with what they need to be successful.**

Pose questions to stakeholders on the committee that lead to a consensus about what the community wants their school to represent and how they want to be viewed.

ACTION 4: **Seek out resources from other schools and online to help you develop vision and mission statements that work for your school.** There are great vision and mission statements available on the internet. Print out several of them, share them with the committee, and decide which ones contain the same thoughts and beliefs as the committee and most closely fit the kind of vision and mission statements the committee wants for their school.

ACTION 5: **Adjust the mission and vision statements to make them your own; write them out and tweak them so they reflect what the committee agreed on.** The committee should agree on what the statements say and the message they communicate about how the school will ensure equity.

ACTION 6: **Share the new vision and mission statements in as many ways as you can with the school community and all stakeholders.** Share them on the school and district website, put them on all the school letterhead and on meeting agendas, make special announcements, have teachers post them in their classrooms, post them on school bulletin boards, and recite them at meetings and school and community events. This action item is important to ensure the vision and mission statements become a driving force for the school, stay alive, and have a positive impact.

Conclusion

Establishing up-to-date, actively applied vision and mission statements paves the way for where the school is going and how it will arrive at a place of enhanced equity. School vision and mission statements should promote equity and equitable practices because they set a clear direction for the school, ensure all students receive a fair and inclusive learning environment, and provide a framework for the school's goals and objectives. Revising your vision and mission statements is like cleaning your windshield. Removing things that may block your view provides you with a long look down the road, bringing the sought-after destination that much closer.

Questions for Reflection

Working individually or with a collaborative group, ask yourself the following reflective questions.

1. What do you believe your community, school, staff, and students can accomplish toward equity?

2. What do you want parents, students, and the community to say about your school regarding equity?

3. Where do you see your school in the next three years regarding the equity goals stated in your vision and mission statements, and how will you get there?

4. As a school, how do you go beyond prioritizing day-to-day responsibilities and investing more time and energy into enhancing equity?

5. What are some ways your school can improve on your school vision and mission statements to reflect your goals for equity?

School Vision and Mission Survey

For each item, circle the response that best describes the vision and mission statements at your school.

1. My school has a big-picture vision and definition for what equity means to the community.

1	2	3	4	5
Strongly disagree	Disagree	Neutral	Agree	Strongly agree

2. My school or district's vision and mission statements speak to tailoring resources and opportunities to each student's individual needs.

1	2	3	4	5
Strongly disagree	Disagree	Neutral	Agree	Strongly agree

3. Part of my school's vision and mission is to provide high-quality instruction and opportunities for each student.

1	2	3	4	5
Strongly disagree	Disagree	Neutral	Agree	Strongly agree

4. My school's vision and mission statements communicate clear equity goals and how the school will measure them.

1	2	3	4	5
Strongly disagree	Disagree	Neutral	Agree	Strongly agree

5. My school examines student survey data to determine how diverse, integrated, and fair students consider it to be and uses the results to focus goals and priorities for its vision and mission statements.

1	2	3	4	5
Strongly disagree	Disagree	Neutral	Agree	Strongly agree

page 1 of 3

6. My school uses student survey data to determine whether students feel like they belong and if we are living out the school vision and mission statements.

1	2	3	4	5
Strongly disagree	Disagree	Neutral	Agree	Strongly agree

*Disaggregate the results by demographics—such as by race or ethnicity, free and reduced-price lunch (FRPL) status, and English learner (EL) status—to see how specific student groups reflected on their experiences of safety and belonging.

7. My school includes staff, students, parents, community members, and other stakeholders in the process of drafting its school vision and mission statements.

1	2	3	4	5
Strongly disagree	Disagree	Neutral	Agree	Strongly agree

8. My school updates its vision and mission statements regularly as new families move in and as students move on.

1	2	3	4	5
Strongly disagree	Disagree	Neutral	Agree	Strongly agree

9. My school's vision and mission statements are trustworthy representations of what the school stands for and how it operates.

1	2	3	4	5
Strongly disagree	Disagree	Neutral	Agree	Strongly agree

10. Staff feel that the school vision and mission is to teach in a way that reaches every student, regardless of background, socioeconomic status, or racial or gender identity.

1	2	3	4	5
Strongly disagree	Disagree	Neutral	Agree	Strongly agree

page 2 of 3

11. My school's vision and mission statements reflect how students and families are treated.

1	2	3	4	5
Strongly disagree	Disagree	Neutral	Agree	Strongly agree

12. My school's vision and mission statements collectively work together as the driving force to guide the direction of the school.

1	2	3	4	5
Strongly disagree	Disagree	Neutral	Agree	Strongly agree

Survey Results:

12–18	The school vision and mission are not alive.
19–24	The school vision and mission need to be revived.
25–36	The school vision and mission may be alive but need more purpose.
37–46	The school vision and mission are alive and purposeful.
47–60	The school vision and mission are alive in the hearts and minds of the school community.

CHAPTER 5

ADJUSTING THE SCHOOL CLIMATE

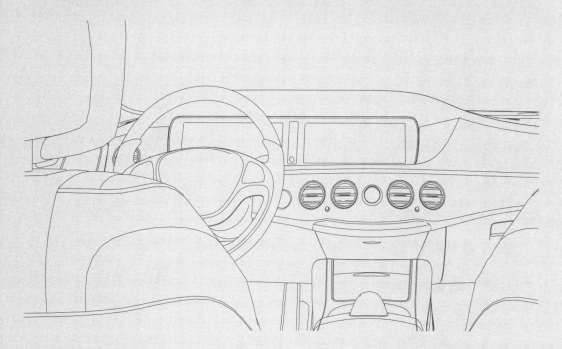

A car with dual temperature controls accounts for the differences between the needs of passengers in one sitting area and those in another. Similarly, schools must adopt multifaceted approaches to achieve a climate benefiting all. To effect real change and enhance equity, leaders must be aware of underlying assumptions and beliefs among teachers and staffs, which have a profound effect on the school climate. Leaders can take steps to establish a warm, inclusive climate, making their school a place where everyone feels like they belong.

*I*T NEVER FAILS! Whenever my wife and I get in the car to go anywhere, she always adjusts the temperature. The first thing she does, even before strapping herself in, is turn the temperature to the setting where she is most comfortable. If it's winter, up goes the heat. If it's summer, down goes the air conditioning.

Can you relate? How often have you had to adjust the temperature in your car to accommodate your passengers, even though it made you uncomfortable? Thank goodness car manufacturers now equip cars with dual temperature controls. This invention has made it easier to accommodate both me and my wife when we travel in the car together.

This innovation works in cars, but achieving the right climate in a school is not nearly as easy to fix, and I'm not talking about the temperature. To obtain growth in the performance of students, teachers, and school leaders, the school climate must be right for everyone. This cannot be accomplished by adjusting a dial to the appropriate setting. It is the very beliefs, attitudes, and behaviors of the adults in the building that often require adjusting. Shared mission and vision statements are good starts, but a principal cannot simply reach over and adjust staff's mindset dials. However, by adjusting their own beliefs, attitudes, and behaviors, school leaders can set the tone for a climate in which staff steadily improve their instructional methods, empowering students to grow academically and socially.

> *To obtain growth in the performance of students, teachers, and school leaders, the school climate must be right for everyone.*

Creating an equitable school climate is essential for ensuring all students feel valued and safe and receive access to a high-quality education. A school environment that values diversity, inclusivity, and equity not only benefits historically marginalized students, but also creates a sense of belonging for *all* students. This chapter explores how to foster and support an equitable school climate, including hiring diverse teachers, offering professional development on equity issues, and practicing strategies for implementing these practices in schools.

What the Research Says

When researching the definition of school climate or discussing what it means, you will discover many different interpretations. However, you'll find a widely accepted definition among education experts in a study by Sophie Maxwell, Katherine J. Reynolds, Eunro Lee, Emina Subasic, and David Bromhead (2017). They describe *school climate* as the social characteristics of a school in terms of relationships among students and teachers, learning and teaching emphasis, values and norms, and shared approaches and practices. Among all factors, empirical evidence confirms that school climate is one of the most powerful influences affecting student academic achievement and teacher job satisfaction (Osher & Kendziora, 2020).

So, how do you establish a school climate that breathes equity, one in which each student, teacher, and school leader feels valued, accepted, and inspired to perform at optimal levels? This question is not easy to answer. Much like the temperature setting you need out of your car's heating and cooling system, the answer depends on your school's environment. Principals must decide what setting makes for the most positive climate for their school's conditions, homing in on what is relevant to their community and the needs of students and teachers.

While each school team must determine what that looks or feels like, many child development and school leadership experts find it is vital that school principals understand that their single most important job is creating a school environment where students feel safe, supported, engaged, and accepted (Prothero, 2020). The same can be said of teachers who long for autonomy, appreciation, respect, empathy, and trust. The way teachers feel about their work environment, their relationship with their coworkers and administrators, and the level of support they receive all affect school climate.

Creating an Equitable School Climate

Equity is paramount to establishing, improving, maintaining, sustaining, and enhancing school climate. This is because students and staff need to feel a sense of belonging to strive and perform at high levels. Meeting the primary needs, learning needs, and social-emotional needs of each student and teacher is an example of equity. Supporting students and staff to be successful is a major component of a healthy school climate, and educational equity is necessary to meet the needs of each individual.

Equity in schools means that each student receives what they need to develop to their full academic and social potential. This involves ensuring equally high outcomes for each student in your school by removing the predictability of success or failures that currently correlate with social or cultural factors (Edmonds, 2022). With schools becoming ever more diverse across racial and ethnic lines, socioeconomic classes, gender and sexual identity preferences, different religions and cultural practices, schools are charged with creating inclusive environments. Staff also need support and a welcoming, inclusive environment to be at their best.

One of the major challenges to reinforcing equity through school climate is outdated school systems that have been in place for years, producing educators with antiquated mindsets who are resistant to change. And it's understandable. While some people find change exciting and full of possibilities, others experience fear—fear of losing power; fear of not knowing where or if they fit in a changed environment; or fear of acknowledging that the work they've always done hasn't supported students well (or has even harmed them). Individuals who operate these systems or hold fast to these beliefs may even realize they are hurting and holding students back but still be resistant to change. What they may fail to understand is that they, too, are hurt by their own locked-in perception of how schools "should" work.

In his book *Way of the Peaceful Warrior*, Dan Millman (1984) says that "the secret of change is to focus all your energy not on fighting the old, but on building the new" (p. 113). Equity is the new way in education, and instead of fighting against it, schools need to be fighting for it.

> **Equity is the new way in education, and instead of fighting against it, schools need to be fighting for it.**

Equity in the school climate means administrators and principals get together and discuss school issues in settings where everyone has the opportunity to share thoughts and suggestions. It means teachers and staff are free to respectfully express themselves without fear of retaliation, isolation, or rebuke. It means staff members of different races and cultures are valued, appreciated, and celebrated as opposed to being simply tolerated. Conversations take place about how the school can celebrate the different cultures represented within it, as well as how to create inclusive environments for LGBTQ+ staff members and students and recruit diverse teachers.

Hiring Diverse Staff

In a school with a climate of equity, school and district leaders understand the importance of having a diverse staff, and they work earnestly to put staff members in front of students who look like them, relate with them, and understand their lives. They understand that the impact of teachers who have cultural similarities with their students is powerful in closing the achievement gap. Researcher Hua-Yu Cherng (2017) writes:

> For young people, academic expectations and achievement are more than measures of academic outcomes but reflect facets of hope in their futures. A large body of literature has focused on the academic expectations and performance of racial/ethnic students of color, particularly given persistent achievement gaps. (p. 170)

While many White or affluent teachers are empathetic toward and effective teachers of students from marginalized communities, teachers who have experienced racial discrimination, low socioeconomic backgrounds, or both are likely to relate more readily with these students' struggles. They can also serve as living proof to students that high expectations for behavior and student achievement are obtainable, and the results are worth it. Do not take this impact for granted. A culture of high expectations has been identified as a chief characteristic of schools that maintain a thriving climate (Staats, Bohan-Baker, & Meyers, 2018).

Furthermore, the evidence is mounting that same-race teachers benefit students and demonstrate positive outcomes for Black students in particular, with this role-model effect lasting into adulthood and potentially shrinking the educational attainment gap (Rosen, 2018). Because they have similar cultural and life experiences, teachers of color or from other marginalized groups can authentically invoke belief in their students that they, too, can achieve at high levels. They demonstrate daily, as someone who once was similarly situated, that success is within these students' reach.

Research provides concrete evidence that a teacher's expectations, whether high or low, significantly affect students' educational outcomes. It shows that Black teachers usually have higher expectations of Black students than White teachers (O'Donnell, 2018). In their article "Who Believes in Me? The Effect of Student-Teacher Demographic Match on Teacher Expectations," Seth Gershenson, Stephen B. Holt, and Nicholas W. Papageorge (2016) analyze data from a nationally representative survey of high school students and their teachers to examine the relationship between student-teacher demographic match and teacher expectations. They found that Black students who had a Black teacher experienced higher expectations by that teacher than Black students who had a non-Black teacher. In addition, they found that the positive effect of race matching was most pronounced for Black male students.

> *Research provides concrete evidence that a teacher's expectations, whether high or low, significantly affect students' educational outcomes.*

This study provides empirical evidence to support the idea that Black students can benefit from having Black teachers, particularly in terms of teacher expectations. The authors suggest that the positive effects of race matching may be due to increased cultural understanding and trust between students and teachers who share the same racial or ethnic background.

Additional research supports these claims, as noted by Paulette Parker (2016) in her article "White Teachers Are More Likely to Expect Their Black Students to Fail":

> When a Black teacher and a white teacher evaluate the same Black student, the white teacher is about 30 percent less likely to predict the student will complete a four-year college degree. White teachers also are almost 40 percent less likely to expect their Black students will graduate high school, and when [evaluating the same] Black student, white teachers expect significantly less academic success than Black teachers.

It would be unfair to generalize and not acknowledge the many excellent and distinguished White teachers who diligently serve *all* their students. White teachers are highly capable of educating Black students and other students of color and holding them to high expectations, and it's your job as principal to see that this happens.

However, the teaching profession should note the additional positive effects and added inspiration that a teacher who is from the same culture or similar background as their students adds to their school experience. When students can identify with their teachers, this undoubtedly can have a positive effect on school climate. Still, according to Katherine Schaeffer (2021), elementary and secondary public school teachers in the United States are significantly less racially and ethnically diverse as a group than their students. While the number of Black, Hispanic, and Asian American teachers has increased since the 1980s, it has not kept up with the rapidly growing racial and ethnic diversity of students.

According to the National Center for Education Statistics (2021a):

- The number of Black teachers has increased steadily since the 1980s, but there was a notable increase between 2011 and 2016, when the number of Black teachers in public schools increased from 240,000 to 267,000, representing an increase from 6.5 percent to 7.0 percent of the teaching workforce.

- The number of Hispanic teachers has also been increasing steadily since the 1980s, and between 2011 and 2016, the number of Hispanic teachers in public schools increased from 185,000 to 219,000, representing an increase from 5.0 percent to 5.8 percent of the teaching workforce.

- The number of Asian American teachers has been increasing gradually since the 1990s, and between 2011 and 2016, the number of Asian American teachers in public schools increased from 68,000 to 78,000, representing an increase from 1.9 percent to 2.1 percent of the teaching workforce.

- During the 2017–2018 school year, about eight in ten U.S. public school teachers identified as non-Hispanic or White. That comprises 79 percent of public school teachers. Additionally, fewer than one in ten teachers were either Black (7 percent), Hispanic (9 percent), or Asian American (2 percent). Finally, less than 2 percent of teachers were either American Indian or Alaska Native, Pacific Islander, or of two or more races.

The chart in figure 5.1 (page 104) shows how the racial percentage of the student population compares to the racial percentage of the teacher population, as noted by the National Center for Education Statistics (2021a).

These data demonstrate that there is a need to increase the diversity of teachers as diversity increases in the student population. Research shows that White students who have diverse teachers are more likely to be equity-minded and demonstrate positive attitudes toward diversity and inclusion. Anna Egalite, Brian Kisida, and Marcus Winters (2015) found that White students who had a non-White teacher in elementary school were more likely to score higher on mathematics and reading tests than White students who did not have a non-White teacher. The authors suggest that having a non-White teacher may have exposed White students to different perspectives and experiences that improved their academic performance.

Race	Percentage of Students in U.S. Schools by Race in 2018–2019	Percentage of Teachers in U.S. Schools by Race in 2017–2018
White	47%	79%
Black	14%	7%
Hispanic	27%	9%
Asian and Pacific Islander	6%	2%
American Indian or Alaska Native	1%	1%

Source: National Center for Education Statistics, 2021a.

FIGURE 5.1: Racial percentage of student population compared to racial percentage of teacher population.

Another study conducted by David Blazar (2021), associate professor of education policy at the University of Maryland, found that White students who had a teacher of color were more likely to have positive attitudes toward diversity and inclusion than White students who did not have a teacher of color. Blazar (2021) suggests that having a teacher of color may provide White students with opportunities to learn about and appreciate different cultures. The same may be true with White teachers who are culturally proficient—they may be better at relating content to diverse students' real lives. Professional development on cultural proficiency can aide teachers' ability to improve in this area.

Offering Professional Learning About Equity Issues

A school with an equitable climate offers professional development depending on the needs of the staff, including becoming proficient at *culturally responsive teaching*, meeting the social-emotional needs of students, delivering sound instruction, and creating or sustaining effective teacher collaboration. As leaders, we want teachers to differentiate the instruction they give to students, so why is it that we mandate that all teachers experience the same professional learning? Teachers should have a voice regarding the kind of professional development they feel would benefit them most.

Teachers should have a voice regarding the kind of professional development they feel would benefit them most.

Given the data in figure 5.1, which compare the racial population between students and teachers, it's clear that no matter the makeup of your staff, there is a need for professional development on culturally responsive teaching for teachers who work with diverse student populations. (Learn more about culturally responsive teaching and practices in chapter 9, page 203.) Culturally responsive teachers and leaders may suggest professional development on culturally responsive teaching and practices because it helps participants gain a deeper understanding of themselves and how they affect others, leading to more cohesive and productive academic and social-emotional development of students.

Furthermore, they understand and value the notion that different people possess different lived experiences. There is no single way of doing or understanding something. What is seen as "correct" most often is based on personal experiences. Principals and teachers both should know about their students' lives outside of school. This understanding is invaluable in building instructional plans that leverage students' prior knowledge and skills. Including representative, familiar content in the curriculum validates and legitimizes students' backgrounds, while also exposing students to ideas and worldviews different from their own.

Recognizing how students' identities (race or ethnicity; national origin; language; sex and gender; gender identity; sexual orientation; physical, developmental, or emotional ability; socioeconomic class; religion; and so on) affect their perspectives about pedagogy and students, can help educators evaluate and understand how their biases affect their practice, and how they might modify their behavior regarding these issues (including racism, sexism, homophobia, unearned privilege, Eurocentrism, and so on; Joint Committee on Administrative Rules, n.d.). Constantly seeking to increase equity and improve the school climate and experience for each student, effective principals and leaders critically think about the institutions they lead, working to reform them whenever and wherever necessary.

What It Looks Like in the Real World

As a school principal, I always thought about how to actively pursue an improved and equitable school climate. Though it was never as simple as turning those dual-zone temperature control knobs in the car, the activities our administrative team planned had, at their heart, the idea of establishing an equitable climate to meet the needs of—and empower—both students and teachers.

Acknowledging Students' Lived Experiences

The school I led had a student population of 1.8 percent White, 34.5 percent Black, 1.7 percent Asian or Asian/Pacific Islander, and 60.9 percent Hispanic/Latino. My school team was conscientious about recognizing the cultures represented in the school and seeing each student as an individual with endless potential. The staff agreed: our mutual aim was an equitable school climate that fostered critical thinking, creativity, and student motivation.

Working toward this goal in any school setting starts by acknowledging that many students arrive in need of the sorts of social-emotional support that makes them feel valued and noticed. This places them in the best possible mindset for academic progress. Administrators who welcome each student by name as they enter the building establish a sound footing.

In my school, collecting student health certification forms and checking students in on a tablet during the COVID-19 pandemic helped us learn their names even faster. Teachers were outside their doors greeting students in the morning as well as during transitions, always welcoming them into class. Another small thing that made a big difference was our birthday board. Just inside the main entrance, a staff-decorated bulletin board brightly proclaimed the names of every student celebrating a birthday that month. We also acknowledged each student with a special birthday wish over the intercom the morning of their birthday, during morning announcements. Teachers, too, received a shout-out on their birthday. This was a quick, fun, and easy way to make the school climate a little warmer for every student and staff member.

Going deeper into enhancing equity through school climate and being aware of students' educational needs, principals who are the driving force help teachers understand that their students' backgrounds and lived experiences influence how they experience school. They support teachers to put best practices at the forefront and equip them with a range of tools for welcoming all students in their classroom.

Principals who are the driving force help teachers understand that their students' backgrounds and lived experiences influence how they experience school.

During teacher institute days, my administrative team reserved time to focus on teacher mental health. In addition to providing professional development, we included activities aimed at decreasing stress and promoting wellness. Certainly, the COVID-19 pandemic placed additional stress on teachers, whose struggles mirrored those of teachers across the United States and around the world.

Jennifer Curry and Imre Csaszar (2021) share similar sentiments among teachers in their article "Mitigating Teacher Stress and Burnout From the Pandemic." They found that the results of the State of the U.S. Teacher Survey were grave. The article says, "The pandemic was increasing job-related stress to a degree that threatened the long-term viability of the U.S. teaching workforce." Elizabeth Steiner and Ashley Woo (2021), policy researchers at RAND Corporation, found that a greater percentage of teachers reported stress and depression during the pandemic compared with the general U.S. population. Teachers identified major stressors such as teaching in person and online at the same time, technology glitches during remote instruction, and health issues with themselves and their family members (Steiner & Woo, 2021). Teacher stress during the pandemic also centered around instructional anxiety, communicating with parents, and administrative support (Pressley, 2021).

Addressing Staff Perceptions of School Climate

Leaders must be attuned to the importance of not only seeing and valuing students, but also seeing and valuing staff, especially when they are struggling. In my experience as a principal working with many different groups of teachers, a teacher's propensity for stress and burnout correlates with the teacher's perception of the school climate. Asking teachers to leave their baggage at the door and just report to work and focus on their job is like asking a student who has experienced trauma to just show up at school and learn. Both scenarios are unreasonable. Emotional support is necessary for productivity to flourish. Bottom line: Stressed-out teachers lead to stressed-out students, and healthy teachers make way for healthy students.

School equity involves providing students and teachers what they need to be successful and strive. Providing my staff with the kind of professional development they needed to better support their students and their own social-emotional well-being was a schoolwide equity initiative. In response to the unprecedented stressors of the pandemic, we included yoga, meditation, leadership training, physical activity, mental health training, and discussions of best paths forward during staff meetings and school-improvement trainings.

> *Asking teachers to leave their baggage at the door and just report to work and focus on their job is like asking a student who has experienced trauma to just show up at school and learn.*

We designed our professional activities based on suggestions made during collaborative meetings, yielding positive emotional responses from our staff. Inviting input and showing that it is valued builds relationships and bridges the divide that often exists between teachers and administrators. It builds the trust that allows teachers to feel safe communicating about anything from the personal events driving their emotions to shared on-the-job challenges. Trust-based relationship building is a major part of establishing an equitable climate. This "family feel" will filter into classrooms, to the benefit of all.

Effective educators long have provided emotional *and* academic support. The need to incorporate both is only ramped up as we continue to navigate the pandemic and its aftermath. Knowing and understanding how inequitable systems have affected certain populations during the pandemic, including student population subsets, provide a sense of urgency. Throughout the pandemic, our team grew more intentional, adopting a social-emotional curriculum from which team members taught lessons twice a week. Momentum continues to build for the practice and promotion of emotional intelligence.

Encouraging Culturally Responsive Practices

To encourage staff to adopt culturally responsive teaching schoolwide, I met with a textbook representative who sells culturally diverse books and classroom novels. She visited the school regularly to update my team on the latest culturally responsive teaching materials. We purchased these for teachers to use and placed many in our school media center. The books and curriculum introduce stories and materials that act as mirrors, windows, and sliding glass doors. In "What Are Mirrors, Windows, and Sliding Glass Doors?" the We Are Teachers (2018) staff describe this concept in more detail:

> A window is a resource that offers you a view into someone else's experience. A sliding door allows the reader to enter the story and

become a part of its world. A mirror reflects your own culture and helps you build your identity. It is critical to understand that students cannot truly learn about themselves unless they learn about others as well. When students read books where they see characters like themselves who are valued in the world, they feel a sense of belonging.

Teachers utilized culturally responsive teaching practices that connected students both to the content and to themselves. My team met regularly and planned events around national celebrations of our students' culture. Progressing on the scale of cultural competence requires that school personnel hold various cultures in high esteem and use this as a foundation to guide all endeavors. Schools that achieve cultural competence understand how to include students' cultures in everything they do on a daily basis. Celebrating cultures and students' identities—and being sensitive to them—becomes second nature.

As the leader of a school with an equitable culture, you want everyone who enters your doors to feel a sense of belonging, including students' parents. Annually, at the beginning of the fall term at my school, I met with my office staff to review job duties, expectations, and the school calendar of events. I stressed, above all else, that the manner in which we greet parents and visitors, either in person or on the phone, is key. Parents met with professionalism and courtesy feel valued and sense that their children, too, are highly valued. Recruiting parents to participate in the Parent-Teacher Organization becomes easier and results in a more highly engaged group offering a freer flow of school-improvement ideas.

Maya Angelou said, "I've learned that people will forget what you said, people will forget what you did, but people will never forget how you made them feel" (as cited in Tunstall, 2014). The way you make people feel when they come to your school says a great deal about the climate. Either your school climate will be inviting and comfortable for students, staff, and parents, or it will leave them reaching for the control knobs. Or worse—it will make them prefer not to be there at all.

> *Either your school climate will be inviting and comfortable for students, staff, and parents, or it will leave them reaching for the control knobs.*

Taking Action to Adjust the School Climate to Promote Equity

Consider taking some of the following action steps to ensure your school climate embraces and promotes equity.

The following are student-focused actions.

ACTION 1: **Greet each student as they enter the school doors, and ask teachers to greet each student as they enter their classrooms.** When teachers greet students at the door, it creates a positive and inclusive classroom climate where students feel comfortable and safe. This small gesture can also help build positive relationships between teachers and students, which can lead to improved academic and behavioral outcomes.

ACTION 2: **Find unique ways to acknowledge and celebrate students' birthdays.** Display a birthday bulletin board and post the names or pictures of students born during the current month. Give a birthday "shout-out" to students during morning announcements. Acknowledging students on their birthday can make them feel valued and appreciated, create a sense of community in the classroom, and help foster positive relationships between teachers and students. It also can provide a sense of belonging, which can be especially important for students who may not feel connected to their school or peers. Overall, these activities can help create a positive and inclusive classroom environment that supports students' social-emotional well-being.

ACTION 3: **Distribute school climate surveys to students two to three times per year to assess your school climate from students' point of view.** You might have students complete surveys about the school climate because it can provide valuable insights into students' perceptions of their school environment. By gathering feedback directly from students, you can better understand the strengths and challenges of the school climate and identify areas for improvement. Surveys can also help you assess the effectiveness of policies and programs designed to improve the school climate. Involving students in this way can promote a sense of ownership and engagement in the school community, which contributes to a more positive and inclusive school culture.

ACTION 4:   **Host a student focus group to discuss school climate and discover areas in need of improvement and what to continue doing that students appreciate.** Here are three reasons why this is important: (1) students are the primary stakeholders in the school community, and their perspectives and experiences can provide valuable insights into the school's strengths and weaknesses; (2) involving students can promote a sense of ownership and engagement, leading to greater buy-in and support for changes; (3) focus groups can help ensure that the school is meeting the needs of all students and creating a positive, inclusive, and welcoming environment for everyone.

ACTION 5:   **During morning announcements, give a pep talk or inspirational message to students and staff, assuring them that it's going to be a great day at school and that they are valued and appreciated.** Morning announcements that include positive and uplifting messages can help create a positive school culture by setting a tone of optimism and kindness for the day ahead. When students are greeted each morning with messages of encouragement, they are more likely to feel valued and appreciated by the school community, which can contribute to a sense of belonging and connection.

Moreover, morning announcements that feature messages about kindness, respect, and empathy can help promote social-emotional learning and support students' mental health and well-being. By starting the day with positive messages and reminders of important values, students can feel more prepared and motivated to engage in their learning throughout the day.

ACTION 6:   **Celebrate students' cultures throughout the entire year, not just on certain holidays.**

a.   *Create a cultural showcase*—Organize a cultural showcase that allows students to share their cultural traditions, food, music, and dance with the school community. This can be done through a cultural fair or a talent show that features performances and presentations from students of diverse backgrounds.

b.   *Incorporate diverse literature*—Introduce diverse literature into the curriculum, including books, poems, and stories that reflect students' cultural backgrounds. This can help students feel seen, valued, and represented in the classroom.

c. *Host a cultural exchange program*—Organize a cultural exchange program that allows students to learn about the cultures and traditions of their peers from different backgrounds. This can involve partnering with a school or community group from a different cultural background to share experiences and learn from each other.

d. *Celebrate cultural heritage months*—Highlight cultural heritage months throughout the year, such as Black History Month, Asian Pacific American Heritage Month, or Hispanic Heritage Month. This can involve classroom activities, guest speakers, and cultural events that recognize and celebrate the contributions of different cultural groups.

e. *Create a multicultural club or committee*—Form a multicultural club or committee where students can come together to celebrate and promote diversity and inclusion in the school community. This can involve planning events, organizing service projects, and promoting cultural awareness and understanding.

f. *Feature different cultures in classroom décor and activities*— Decorate bulletin boards with information, pictures, and photos of various cultures represented in the school all year round. Read the biographies of prominent people from each culture represented in the school throughout the year, not just during the month or day that the national calendar tells us to recognize it. This instills a sense of pride in students' cultures and helps them to feel celebrated, unique, and significant.

The following are staff-focused actions.

ACTION 1:   **Provide professional development on cultural competence.** Provide professional development opportunities for teachers that focus on building cultural competence and understanding. This training can help teachers understand and appreciate the cultural backgrounds of their students, which can help them be more effective in the classroom.

ACTION 2: **Create a safe and supportive environment.** Create a safe and supportive environment for teachers by promoting open communication, collaboration, and trust. This can involve regular check-ins with teachers, creating opportunities for teacher feedback, and providing support and resources for teachers who are struggling.

ACTION 3: **Address bias and stereotypes.** You should be aware of and address any biases or stereotypes that may exist within the school community. This can involve creating a culture of openness and transparency, promoting diverse hiring practices, and addressing any incidents of discrimination or bias.

ACTION 4: **Provide adequate resources.** Ensure teachers and staff have access to the resources they need to be successful in the classroom. This can involve providing funding for classroom supplies, technology, and other materials, as well as offering professional development opportunities that promote equity.

ACTION 5: **Promote a work-life balance.** Be mindful of the demands placed on teachers and staff, and promote a healthy work-life balance. This can involve setting realistic expectations for workloads, providing opportunities for self-care and stress management, and creating a supportive culture that values teacher and staff well-being.

ACTION 6: **Acknowledge and celebrate teacher and staff diversity.** Acknowledge and celebrate the diversity of teachers and staff, and create opportunities for them to share their backgrounds and experiences. This can involve hosting teacher-led cultural events or professional development sessions that highlight different perspectives and experiences.

ACTION 7: **Foster a culture of continuous learning and improvement.** You can foster a culture of continuous learning and improvement by encouraging teachers and staff to reflect on their practice, share their successes and challenges with colleagues, and engage in ongoing professional development. This can help them stay engaged and motivated, and ensure they are always improving their practice to better serve students.

Conclusion

As caring, well-trained principals, our eyes should always be focused on an equitable, welcoming, supportive school climate where high academic standards are set and the tools for meeting them are accessible. Creating an equitable, welcoming, and supportive school climate for both staff and students is essential for promoting a positive learning environment. School leaders can take several steps to achieve this goal. They can work to create a culture of inclusivity and respect within the school community by promoting open communication, collaboration, and trust among staff and students, as well as addressing any incidents of discrimination or bias that may occur. They can also focus on providing resources and support for staff and students. This can involve providing access to professional development opportunities that promote cultural competence and understanding, as well as providing resources for teachers such as adequate funding for classroom supplies and technology.

School leaders should support teachers and staff by promoting a healthy work-life balance and providing opportunities for self-care and stress management. More importantly, principals can work to celebrate and honor the diversity of their staff and students by hosting cultural events, promoting the use of inclusive language and practices, and providing opportunities for staff and students to share their experiences and perspectives. By fostering a culture of inclusivity, providing resources and support, and celebrating diversity, leaders can create an equitable, welcoming, and supportive school climate that benefits everyone. Remember, like the dual temperature controls on modern-day cars, a multifaceted approach is best-suited to achieving a climate that takes individual needs to account while benefiting all.

Questions for Reflection

Working individually or with a collaborative group, ask yourself the following reflective questions.

1. What activities can you and your staff engage in every day to improve the school climate and enhance equity at your school?

2. How are you supporting the academic and social-emotional needs of each student to ensure that they thrive?

3. How are you encouraging and supporting the professional development of teachers around issues of equity, diversity, and inclusion?

4. What steps are you taking to ensure all students, regardless of their background or identity, feel safe and welcome in your school?

5. How are you addressing incidents of bias or discrimination that occur in your school, and what are you doing to prevent them from happening in the future?

School Climate Survey for Students

For each item, circle the response that best describes your school climate.

1. Overall, this is how I would rate my experience at school so far this year.

4	3	2	1
Excellent	Good	Fair	Poor

2. I feel safe at school.

4	3	2	1
Always	Sometimes	Rarely	Never

3. I feel respected by teachers and staff.

4	3	2	1
Always	Sometimes	Rarely	Never

4. I feel respected by my peers.

4	3	2	1
Always	Sometimes	Rarely	Never

5. I feel like my teachers and staff care about my well-being.

4	3	2	1
Always	Sometimes	Rarely	Never

6. I feel like I am challenged academically.

4	3	2	1
Always	Sometimes	Rarely	Never

7. There are adults at school who I feel comfortable talking to if I have a problem.

4	3	2	1
Yes, many	Yes, a few	Just a couple	No, none

8. I feel like I belong at my school.

4	3	2	1
Yes, completely	Yes, somewhat	No, not really	No, not at all

9. I am satisfied with the level of diversity and inclusion at my school.

4	3	2	1
Completely satisfied	Somewhat satisfied	Not very satisfied	Not at all satisfied

10. I feel school policies and rules are fair.

4	3	2	1
Yes, definitely	Yes, somewhat	No, not really	No, not at all

11. I feel like I have enough opportunities to be involved in school activities or clubs.

4	3	2	1
Yes, definitely	Yes, somewhat	No, not really	No, not at all

12. I feel like my school provides enough support for students with academic or personal challenges.

4	3	2	1
Yes, definitely	Yes, somewhat	No, not really	No, not at all

13. I feel like my school provides enough resources and support for students' mental health and well-being.

4	3	2	1
Yes, definitely	Yes, somewhat	No, not really	No, not at all

14. This is how I would rate the level of communication between students, teachers, and staff at my school.

4	3	2	1
Excellent	Good	Fair	Poor

15. Overall, this is how I would rate the climate at my school.

4	3	2	1
Excellent	Good	Fair	Poor

Survey Results:

15–25	The school climate is poor.
26–35	The school climate is fair.
36–45	The school climate is good.
46–60	The school climate is excellent.

Note: While the survey results provide an assessment of the school climate, it is important to recognize that creating an optimal and inclusive school environment is an ongoing process. The ratings of poor, fair, good, or excellent derived from this survey serve as a starting point for evaluation. It is essential for schools to continually assess their school climate, seeking feedback from students, staff, and stakeholders, and implementing improvements to ensure all students feel appreciated, valued, and significant. This includes fostering a climate where students' cultures are respected, cultivating caring relationships with teachers and staff, providing rigorous academics, and offering appropriate support to help students succeed academically and in life. Use these survey results as a means to inform the school's efforts in enhancing the school climate, rather than a definitive measure of its current state.

School Climate Survey for Teachers and Staff

For each item, circle the response that best describes your school climate.

1. The principal listens to and values diverse perspectives from staff.

1	2	3	4	5
Strongly disagree	Disagree	Neutral	Agree	Strongly agree

2. The principal demonstrates a commitment to equity and inclusion in school policies and procedures.

1	2	3	4	5
Strongly disagree	Disagree	Neutral	Agree	Strongly agree

3. The principal effectively communicates with staff about issues related to equity and inclusion.

1	2	3	4	5
Strongly disagree	Disagree	Neutral	Agree	Strongly agree

4. The principal provides opportunities for professional development related to equity and inclusion.

1	2	3	4	5
Strongly disagree	Disagree	Neutral	Agree	Strongly agree

5. The principal fosters an environment of trust and respect among staff.

1	2	3	4	5
Strongly disagree	Disagree	Neutral	Agree	Strongly agree

6. The principal provides resources and support to staff to create an equitable and inclusive classroom environment.

1	2	3	4	5
Strongly disagree	Disagree	Neutral	Agree	Strongly agree

page 1 of 3

7. The principal effectively addresses issues of discrimination or bias when they arise.

1	2	3	4	5
Strongly disagree	Disagree	Neutral	Agree	Strongly agree

8. The principal values and supports diversity among staff.

1	2	3	4	5
Strongly disagree	Disagree	Neutral	Agree	Strongly agree

9. The principal encourages and supports staff to use diverse teaching strategies and curriculum.

1	2	3	4	5
Strongly disagree	Disagree	Neutral	Agree	Strongly agree

10. The principal fosters an environment that is welcoming and supportive for all staff.

1	2	3	4	5
Strongly disagree	Disagree	Neutral	Agree	Strongly agree

11. The principal actively seeks feedback from staff about school climate and culture.

1	2	3	4	5
Strongly disagree	Disagree	Neutral	Agree	Strongly agree

12. The principal is accountable for creating an equitable and inclusive school climate.

1	2	3	4	5
Strongly disagree	Disagree	Neutral	Agree	Strongly agree

13. The principal takes action to address any disparities or inequities in school policies or practices.

1	2	3	4	5
Strongly disagree	Disagree	Neutral	Agree	Strongly agree

14. The principal works collaboratively with staff to create a shared vision of equity and inclusion for the school.

1	2	3	4	5
Strongly disagree	Disagree	Neutral	Agree	Strongly agree

15. The principal acknowledges and celebrates the diverse backgrounds and experiences of staff.

1	2	3	4	5
Strongly disagree	Disagree	Neutral	Agree	Strongly agree

Survey Results:

15–30	The school climate is poor.
31–45	The school climate is fair.
46–60	The school climate is good.
61–75	The school climate is excellent.

Note: While the survey results provide an assessment of the school climate, it is important to recognize that creating an optimal and inclusive school environment is an ongoing process. The ratings of poor, fair, good, or excellent derived from this survey serve as a starting point for evaluation. It is essential for schools to continually assess their school climate, seeking feedback from students, staff, and stakeholders, and implementing improvements to ensure all students feel appreciated, valued, and significant. This includes fostering a climate where students' cultures are respected, cultivating caring relationships with teachers and staff, providing rigorous academics, and offering appropriate support to help students succeed academically and in life. Use these survey results as a means to inform the school's efforts in enhancing the school climate, rather than a definitive measure of its current state.

School Climate Survey for Principals

For each item, circle the response that best describes your school climate.

1. As the school leader, I am aware of teachers' and staff's underlying assumptions and beliefs about students.

1	2	3	4	5
Strongly disagree	Disagree	Neutral	Agree	Strongly agree

2. School administrators meet with teachers regularly to discuss school climate issues related to equity, where everyone has a voice and an opportunity to share thoughts and suggestions.

1	2	3	4	5
Strongly disagree	Disagree	Neutral	Agree	Strongly agree

3. Teachers and staff are free to respectfully express themselves without fear of retaliation.

1	2	3	4	5
Strongly disagree	Disagree	Neutral	Agree	Strongly agree

4. Teachers and staff often celebrate the different cultures represented in the school.

1	2	3	4	5
Strongly disagree	Disagree	Neutral	Agree	Strongly agree

5. School and district leaders understand the importance of having a diverse staff and work earnestly to hire staff members who look like the student population.

1	2	3	4	5
Strongly disagree	Disagree	Neutral	Agree	Strongly agree

page 1 of 3

6. School leaders and teachers have high behavioral and academic expectations for students.

1	2	3	4	5
Strongly disagree	Disagree	Neutral	Agree	Strongly agree

7. School staff regularly receive professional development on meeting the social-emotional needs of students.

1	2	3	4	5
Strongly disagree	Disagree	Neutral	Agree	Strongly agree

8. School leaders and teachers are reflective and gain a deeper understanding of themselves and how they impact students.

1	2	3	4	5
Strongly disagree	Disagree	Neutral	Agree	Strongly agree

9. Principals and teachers both know about students' lives outside of school and use this knowledge to build instruction that leverages prior knowledge and skills.

1	2	3	4	5
Strongly disagree	Disagree	Neutral	Agree	Strongly agree

10. School leaders and teachers assess how their biases and perceptions affect their practice and access tools to mitigate their own behavior.

1	2	3	4	5
Strongly disagree	Disagree	Neutral	Agree	Strongly agree

page 2 of 3

11. Administrators and staff welcome each student by name as they enter the building.

1	2	3	4	5
Strongly disagree	Disagree	Neutral	Agree	Strongly agree

12. School staff acknowledge that many students arrive at school in need of more academic and social-emotional support, and they provide it and help them feel valued.

1	2	3	4	5
Strongly disagree	Disagree	Neutral	Agree	Strongly agree

Survey Results:

12–18	The school climate is not supportive of students' academic or social-emotional (SEL) growth.
19–24	The school climate is barely supportive of students' academic or SEL growth.
25–36	The school climate is moderately supportive of students' academic and SEL growth.
37–46	The school climate is supportive of students' academic and SEL growth.
47–60	The school climate is highly supportive of students' academic and SEL growth.

Note: While the survey results provide an assessment of the school climate, it is important to recognize that creating an optimal and inclusive school environment is an ongoing process. The ratings of not supportive, barely supportive, moderately supportive, supportive, or highly supportive derived from this survey serve as a starting point for evaluation. It is essential for schools to continually assess their school climate, seeking feedback from students, staff, and stakeholders, and implementing improvements to ensure all students feel appreciated, valued, and significant. This includes fostering a climate where students' cultures are respected, cultivating caring relationships with teachers and staff, providing rigorous academics, and offering appropriate support to help students succeed academically and in life. Use these survey results as a means to inform the school's efforts in enhancing the school climate, rather than a definitive measure of its current state.

CHAPTER 6

GROWING EQUITY FROM INTEGRITY

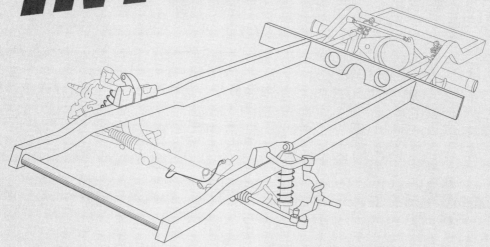

Inevitably, we ask teachers to do new things, take risks, and innovate. However, unless we have first established a relationship built on trust, the answers to your asks might be underwhelming. Such relationships do not simply materialize. You must nurture them. Think of a car's chassis, the framework that holds together all the key running gears. A chassis with integrity keeps the car running strong. School leaders also require integrity, exhibiting the strength to maintain the equitable, positive relationships that keep the staff, and the school, running strong.

*I*RECALL A TIME during the spring of 1987, right as the weather was breaking and spring was springing, when my dad wanted to spend some father-and-son time with me. I was twelve years old. We hopped into his blue 1975 Chevy Caprice. This car was also twelve years old, but for a car, twelve was not youthful.

My dad drove us to downtown Chicago, where we walked around and looked at the skyscrapers. We had a great time. For the ride home, my dad decided to take the scenic route along Lake Shore Drive where, as luck would have it, we struck a pothole—a common occurrence. The frequent use of salt to melt winter snow and ice, coupled with the heaving of the earth below from freezing and thawing, damages the asphalt and creates potholes.

As my dad continued to drive, squeaks, squeals, and grinding noises emanated from the car. I asked him what was wrong. He said that given the speed that he was driving and the jarring force the pothole delivered, the Chevy's chassis might be damaged.

A damaged chassis is serious trouble. This is the car's framework. It houses or supports the engine, transmission, driveshaft, differential, running gear, and suspension. Just as with other parts of a vehicle, the chassis and its various components can wear out over time or become damaged in an accident. If a chassis is bent, the car's moving parts no longer operate smoothly. Instead, they may bump or rub noisily together (Zientek, 2019). Besides forming the base for literally everything attached to it, the chassis plays a distinct part in determining how the car rides and can make or break a vehicle's ability to handle and perform well in a variety of situations.

Just like the chassis' integrity is the foundation for every other major part of a vehicle, a leader's integrity is their make-or-break feature for the school, its teachers and staff, and its students. Some leaders start with strong integrity, but poorly maintain it, allowing it to weaken over time. The difference, though, is that while outside forces deliver the blows that may weaken a car chassis' integrity, weak human integrity delivers the blows that damage schools. Just as a damaged chassis disrupts the smooth operation of a vehicle's moving parts, a leader's damaged integrity disrupts the smooth operation of their school's moving parts.

Leaders often are faced with the choice of doing what they know is necessary to increase equity or succumbing to the pressure of those who prefer the status quo. Suppressed equity in a school can bleed into the community, affecting industries, work opportunities, and more. Leadership integrity—a strong and principled human chassis, if you will—is vital if you are to be the driving force that not only aspires to but also achieves educational equity.

> *Just like the chassis is the integrity and foundation for every other major part of a vehicle, a leader's integrity is their make-or-break feature.*

In the diverse and rapidly changing educational landscape, the role of school leaders in promoting equity has never been more critical. Within this context, leader integrity emerges as a powerful force that shapes the very essence of equitable practices and outcomes. Leader integrity serves as the foundation on which equitable practices are built. When school leaders possess integrity, they demonstrate a deep commitment to ethical principles and values, fostering an environment where fairness and justice prevail. Their unwavering commitment to doing what is right, even in the face of challenges, inspires and emboldens others. The presence of leader integrity cultivates courage, enabling teachers, staff, and students to stand up for equity, challenge inequitable practices, and promote inclusivity.

In addition, leader integrity influences ethical behavior within the school community. Ethical leaders serve as role models, guiding others to make principled decisions that prioritize equity and fairness. By consistently aligning their actions with their values, leaders foster a culture of ethical conduct among staff and students. This culture, in turn, enhances trust, cooperation, and a shared sense of responsibility, creating a fertile ground for collaboration and collective action in pursuit of equity goals.

This chapter explores the multifaceted ways that leader integrity impacts school equity. Drawing on research, real-world examples, and practical insights, it examines the dynamic interplay between leader integrity, courage, ethical behavior, collaboration, and actions. By understanding the pivotal role of leader integrity, school leaders can harness its transformative power to create inclusive, just, and equitable educational environments for all learners.

What the Research Says

Leader integrity plays a crucial role in enhancing school equity because it establishes trust, promotes fairness, and guides decision-making processes. When school leaders demonstrate integrity, they align their actions and decisions with ethical principles and values. This consistency builds trust among staff, students, and the broader school community, which is fundamental for fostering an equitable environment.

A study by Anthony S. Bryk, Penny Bender Sebring, Elaine Allensworth, Stuart Luppescu, and John Q. Easton (2010) found that school leaders with integrity positively impacted the school climate and contributed to improved student outcomes, particularly for marginalized and disadvantaged students. The study emphasized the significance of ethical leadership in creating equitable educational opportunities.

Furthermore, leader integrity influences fairness in the distribution of resources, opportunities, and support within a school. By upholding ethical standards and values, school leaders are more likely to make decisions that prioritize equity and avoid favoritism or bias. This commitment to fairness can lead to the allocation of resources and support that address the diverse needs of students and ensure equal access to quality education. A study by Kenneth Leithwood and Carolyn Riehl (2003) highlights the role of ethical leadership in promoting equity in schools. The researchers emphasize that leaders who prioritize fairness and equity are more likely to create inclusive environments that value diversity, challenge inequitable practices, and foster academic success for all students.

Regarding the significance of leadership integrity, Kenneth Leithwood, Alma Harris, and David Hopkins (2020) state:

> The longstanding nature of matters about inequity demonstrate how intricate the problem has been to address. Evidence amassed over the past several decades, however, has provided key insights into promising elements of the solution. One of these thoughts is just how pivotal principals are to the success of most significant changes in schools.

To make transformational changes to increase equity in schools, principals must recognize and make meaning of the historical and ongoing impacts of discrimination and inequities in school systems.

A majority of K–12 public school students in the United States are students of color (National Center for Education Statistics, 2015). Expectations about the responsibility of principals to create an inclusive culture are constantly evolving, identifying new tasks for a job already loaded with responsibilities. In 2020 and beyond, protests over police violence against people of color brought heightened awareness to a centuries-long issue of racial inequality in the United States. Schools can be part of the solution, making it vital that they not only welcome diversity in the classroom but also demonstrate to students how to navigate an increasingly racially, ethnically, and socioeconomically diverse society (Texas Elementary Principals and Supervisors Association, 2020). The good news is that equity efforts are on the rise in schools. It is exhilarating to see the results of the efforts of equity advocates. Increasing equity is changing the trajectory of students' futures.

School leaders with integrity take responsibility for their actions. They practice seeing, engaging, and acting in ways that build empathy and commitment. They foster healing and increased agency. They activate equity, justice, and belonging. Instead of turning a blind eye, they make inequities visible and disrupt unproductive discourse along with unjust practices and policies. These actions require discovering new ways to engage and build equity within their communities (National Equity Project, 2022). It takes courage.

The following sections focus on the four crucial characteristics of leaders of integrity: (1) courageous, (2) ethical, (3) collaborative, and (4) action oriented, as it relates to fostering a more equitable educational environment. Courage emerges as a significant aspect of school leader integrity as it empowers leaders to challenge inequitable systems, confront biases, and advocate for marginalized students. Ethics also play a vital role in school leader integrity, guiding their decision-making processes to ensure fairness, justice, and inclusivity in educational practices. Collaboration becomes a significant factor as school leaders actively engage stakeholders, including teachers, students, and families, to collectively address equity issues and co-create solutions that promote a more equitable school community. Lastly, the intentional actions school leaders take can demonstrate their commitment to dismantling barriers, implementing inclusive policies, and fostering equitable practices for the benefit of all students.

Courageous

Doing this work is not easy; it often goes against the grain. Many people work in environments where they see inequities but must "go along to get along." Lynch (2015) explains that school leaders must show personal courage, which is one of George Marshall's eight principles of ethical leadership. He writes:

> While it seems that the challenges that schools are facing increase by the day, it's still the case that in order to create a positive educational environment, administrators must be willing to stand up against policies that they feel are not helpful for their students, rising against both local, state, and national interests as needed. Dissenting opinions must essentially be expressed, even in the face of the administrators' own superiors.

Many people work in environments where they see inequities but must "go along to get along."

Most school leaders would agree with this sentiment in principle. But in practice, it is difficult and even daring to go against your boss or your superiors when the fate of your evaluation and sometimes your career is at risk. The fear of losing your job for doing something unpopular, even though it's the right and ethical thing to do, is a real challenge to a leader's integrity. Some districts, communities, states, and municipalities do not embrace equity and take solace in their position of power and privilege.

It sounds easy when someone says, "Just do the right thing," but inequity is layered at so many levels that it can be physically and mentally draining. School leaders who lead with integrity spend countless hours figuring out how to address others' dispositions while maintaining positive regard from those they work with and for. Lynch (2015) writes:

> What is best for students and staff must be placed ahead of the needs of the individual leader. In this case, the public interest is understood to be the interest of the school community and the stakeholders therein. Their opinions and needs should always precede the self-interests of the school leader.

School leaders who lead with integrity spend countless hours figuring out how to address others' dispositions while maintaining positive regard from those they work with and for.

In her article "Future of Education: Leading for Equity," Emily Boudreau (2020) gives advice to school leaders on how to be bold in leading for equity and summarizes an interview that was a part of the Harvard Graduate School of Education's Future of Education series. During this panel discussion, senior lecturer Jennifer Cheatham, a former superintendent in Madison, Wisconsin, and now co-chair of the Public Education Leadership Project, moderated a conversation between superintendents Brenda Cassellius of Boston Public Schools; Joseph Davis, superintendent of the Ferguson-Florissant School District; and Chicago Public Schools CEO Janice K. Jackson. They all offer insights and inspiration on how to keep working toward racial equity.

Brenda Cassellius advises leaders to be bold, saying, "We have to stop waiting and putting it to the next generation. Someone has to stand up and be courageous. We need to rally everybody. This is coordinated, all-hands-on-deck work, because schools can't do it alone" (as cited in Boudreau, 2020). She encourages leaders to step up and take on the responsibility of moving equity work forward. Cassellius adds:

> Kids aren't going to get what they need if you don't stand in the gap for them and if we don't put together the connections for their families. We allow this to happen generation after generation for poor children, especially for poor children of color, and poor Black children. (as cited in Boudreau, 2020)

Speaking on this same issue, Janice Jackson asserts that leaders need to call out equity explicitly:

> If leaders want to advance racial justice and eliminate systemic inequities, they need to make that a clear goal, one that educators at all levels are working toward and using to guide decisions. What I've done in my role is not only name equity as a focus explicitly because, although it's always been a part of the work we've done here in CPS, it wasn't called out explicitly. . . . Now, it's called out in our mission and vision for the district, in our strategic plan where we identify specific goals towards equity. (as cited in Boudreau, 2020)

Jackson created an equity office to address fundamental, systemic barriers to success.

Joseph Davis also recognizes that there's an intangible and almost unmeasurable quality to success and growth in racial equity work. Recognizing that many people and communities carry hurt and anger because of racism and injustice, he shares that learning to feel empathy and build connection between people is key.

> We need to teach forgiveness. Forgiveness can't be forgotten, because so many of us have been wronged in so many different ways, and we carry that toxicity with us. We need to learn to forgive people so we can move on, and that allows you to engage and to grow in ways you couldn't before. . . . Those in positions of power need to be ready to take up the call to action and be ready to set an example in this work. It may not be your fault, but it is your fight. (as cited in Boudreau, 2020)

School leaders are like airline pilots. Airline pilots don't hop on an airplane to fly themselves to a destination. Their job is to safely transport passengers to where they want to go. School leaders must put their interests aside while focusing on the interests of students, parents, staff, and community members.

> *School leaders must put their interests aside while focusing on the interests of students, parents, staff, and community members.*

Ethical

In the pursuit of promoting equity at their school, a school leader's ethics play a pivotal role in guiding their actions and decisions. Upholding ethical principles requires the leader to put aside what may be popular or convenient and, instead, prioritize what is right and just for the sake of promoting schoolwide equity. This entails a willingness to take risks, even if it means potentially losing their job or facing backlash from stakeholders who may resist change. By remaining steadfast in their ethical stance, school leaders demonstrate a commitment to challenging systemic inequities and creating a more inclusive and equitable educational environment. They recognize that achieving equity requires making difficult and unpopular decisions, but they are driven by a moral compass that puts the well-being and success of every student at the forefront. Through unwavering dedication to doing what is right, even in the face of adversity, school leaders can advance equity and ensure *all* students have opportunities to thrive.

When a school is interviewing for a new principal, you might hear the phrase, "We are looking for the right fit." School leaders also have to consider if a school and its community is the "right fit" for them. If it's not, there is a higher likelihood of clashing views and disagreements regarding what is in the best interest of the school. This is endemic when school leaders take a job out of financial necessity while knowing that the position may not be a good fit.

Unfortunately, many schools hire principals who will maintain the status quo instead of understand inequity and commit to establishing equitable environments. School leaders who are committed to equitable practices will become increasingly frustrated when working in a district that does not encourage or support them in those endeavors.

Table 6.1 shows the qualities of a school leader who promotes education equity versus a school leader who maintains the status quo, and brings clarity as to why equity-minded leaders are not a good fit in status quo districts.

Table 6.1: Qualities of School Leaders Promoting Equity Versus Maintaining the Status Quo

Qualities	School Leader Actively Promoting Equity	School Leader Maintaining the Status Quo
Vision	Embraces a vision of equity and inclusion for all students	Maintains a traditional or narrow vision of education
Courage	Demonstrates courage to challenge systemic inequities and biases	Avoids confronting uncomfortable issues or taking risks
Empathy	Cultivates a deep understanding of the diverse needs and experiences of students	Lacks awareness or understanding of the unique challenges faced by marginalized students
Collaboration	Actively engages stakeholders to collectively address equity issues and co-create solutions	Works in isolation and resists input or collaboration with others
Decision Making	Makes decisions based on fairness, justice, and the best interests of all students	Makes decisions based on convenience, popularity, or personal bias
Resource Allocation	Prioritizes resources to address the needs of underserved students and reduce inequities	Maintains resource distribution that perpetuates disparities
Professional Development	Invests in ongoing professional development focused on equity and cultural responsiveness	Relies on traditional professional development without a focus on equity
Advocacy	Advocates for policy changes and equitable practices at the local, state, and national levels	Remains silent or indifferent to policy changes that could advance equity
Accountability	Holds themselves and others accountable for achieving equity goals and outcomes	Accepts the status quo and does not prioritize accountability for equitable practices
Resilience	Demonstrates resilience in the face of challenges and setbacks while staying committed to equity	Gives up easily or becomes complacent when faced with obstacles

Note that this table provides a general comparison of qualities and is not meant to represent all possible characteristics of school leaders in either category. It serves as a starting point for understanding the contrasting approaches and mindsets of leaders who actively promote educational equity versus those who maintain the status quo.

In their book *Courage: The Backbone of Leadership*, Gus Lee and Diane Elliott-Lee (2006) offer acts of integrity to process being disheartened and frustrated when a school leader is committed to equity but other stakeholders are unwilling, oppositional, or resistant to equity, and how to navigate this dilemma. They suggest that you honor your conscience when discerning right from wrong. By honoring your conscience, you stay true to yourself. They also stress doing what is right, regardless of the risk to self. This is especially difficult in politically charged environments such as school districts and systems. Many of us have witnessed school decisions that were clearly not in the best interest of students, but more in the interest of adults.

Similar to the business world, personal agendas drive decisions, often at the expense of what is right. Personal agendas and profit-driven decisions can sometimes overshadow what is right, leading to negative consequences in various sectors. In the business world, a prime example of this is when companies prioritize maximizing profits over ethical considerations. For instance, a corporation might knowingly engage in environmentally harmful practices to cut costs and boost their bottom line, disregarding the long-term impact on the planet and local communities.

In health care, a similar scenario can occur when pharmaceutical companies prioritize financial gains over the well-being of patients. One instance of this is the unethical marketing of addictive opioid pain medications by pharmaceutical companies. Despite the known risks and potential for addiction, profit-driven decisions and deceptive sales pitches led to the widespread distribution of these drugs, resulting in a devastating opioid crisis and countless lives affected.

In the field of education, personal agendas and profit motives can manifest in various ways. One example is the push for privatization and for-profit schools, where financial interests take precedence over the quality of education provided to students. In some cases, private entities operating schools may prioritize financial gains and cost-cutting measures at the expense of hiring qualified educators, ensuring equitable resources, and meeting the students' diverse needs, ultimately compromising the quality of education they receive.

Defending what one thinks is right is not always the most advantageous thing to do (Robinson, 2013). Most educators I know are not willing to lose their job, salary, benefits, or career over making a decision they know is right but against what the majority wants to see happen. Unfortunately, this is the position that a lot of school leaders find themselves in when it comes to establishing equity. They want to do what is in the best interest of their students, but also are hesitant to do so when their opinion is unpopular among those who wield power in their district or school community. This is why ethical educational leaders are needed at all levels.

Raymond Pierce (2020) describes the beliefs and actions of an ethical leader working toward social justice as someone who "deeply embraces the critical connection between education and opportunity." Ethical leaders build school cultures governed by fair, clearly articulated expectations rather than cultures driven by personalities or politics. True integrity means not having the luxury of leaving your principles at the door whenever it is convenient.

Leaders with strong integrity measure each decision before implementing it to make sure the decision is an equitable one. Displaying integrity and a commitment to equity as a school leader in education is driven by an unfaltering belief in the dignity and rights of others. If leaders compromise integrity, an insidious sense of unfairness and injustice pervades (Bromley, 2020).

Collaborative

If principals want to create inclusive schools in which the achievement gap between advantaged and disadvantaged groups is shrinking, they need to involve their staff as partners in the improvement effort. This calls for transformational leadership, in which the principal is a facilitator of teacher growth. This type of leadership enhances an organization by raising the values of members, motivating them to go beyond self-interest to embrace organizational goals and redefining their needs to align with organizational preferences (Ross & Berger, 2009).

Many teachers want to see more equity in their schools, but their efforts may be stifled by others on the staff who believe that their school is fine in its current state. Without the principal speaking up and leading equity initiatives, those teachers' voices will fall on deaf ears, with no action taken. Without principals speaking about equity, initiating actions, and setting expectations for the staff to implement, nothing might be done to improve equity.

Creating a collaborative environment within a school can be challenging when some teachers and staff members present conflicting attitudes toward change and equity-driven approaches. Some may resist change, hold onto traditional beliefs and practices, or feel threatened by shifts in the educational landscape. This clash of perspectives can create tension and hinder the creation of a truly collaborative and equitable environment. When faced with this conflict, school leaders must acknowledge and address the underlying concerns and resistance among staff. It is essential to foster open dialogue and provide opportunities for meaningful conversations that allow for differing perspectives to be heard and understood. Building trust and empathy among staff members is crucial, as it can help bridge the gap and promote a culture of collaboration.

It's essential that school leaders are knowledgeable about the students they aspire to serve. Equity focuses on the needs of historically marginalized students, the ones who long have been underserved by educational institutions. According to school equity expert Brian Soika (2020), "Equity work begins with understanding how one's identity will shape interactions with students, families, and the institution in which you work. Your identity and positionality intersect in ways that will play out in the classroom in very subtle manners." Soika (2020) acknowledges that promoting equity can be difficult and that colleagues may feel uncomfortable dealing with topics like race, gender, and access, even when schools and districts have committed to change. They might even admit that an equity problem persists, but don't have the mind or means to address it.

Soika (2020) advises school leaders to identify ways their organization may be impeding growth toward equity. He lists some general institutional obstacles to advancing equity, which include the following. Even though these focus on race, they could apply to all issues of equity:

1. Not knowing how to talk about race
2. A lack of racial equity indicators
3. Failing to set racial equity benchmarks
4. Not having a set of racial equity best practices
5. Lacking procedures to assess the ways in which policies, practices, and initiatives undermine racial equity (Soika, 2020)

These barriers cripple progress toward equity. Leaders need to point them out, discuss them, and eliminate them. Leaders seeking equity should allocate time on meeting agendas and initiate these conversations among staff members.

Other evidence-based strategies leaders can utilize to promote collaboration include the following: providing professional development and training focused on equity, creating structured spaces for collaboration, recognizing and celebrating staff contributions, encouraging collaborative decision making, fostering open dialogue and discussion, and committing to self-reflection to ensure checks and balances are in place.

PROVIDE PROFESSIONAL DEVELOPMENT AND TRAINING FOCUSED ON EQUITY

School leaders can help educate and motivate their staff through professional development focused on equity and cultural responsiveness. Organize workshops or training sessions that focus on equity issues in education, providing research-based information and best practices. These initiatives can help raise awareness, dispel misconceptions, and build a shared understanding of the importance of equity in schools. Provide ongoing training and resources that enhance staff members' understanding of equity issues and equip them with practical strategies for inclusive teaching to help bridge the gap between those embracing change and those resisting change.

CREATE STRUCTURED SPACE FOR COLLABORATION

Creating structured spaces for collaboration, such as PLCs or regular team meetings, can facilitate dialogue, shared decision making, and problem solving around equity-related challenges. By creating structured collaborative spaces and fostering a shared purpose, school leaders can support an environment where all staff members feel valued and empowered to work together toward a more equitable and inclusive school community.

RECOGNIZE AND CELEBRATE STAFF CONTRIBUTIONS

Recognizing and celebrating staff members' contributions and successes in promoting equity can also help build a sense of ownership and motivation. Consider some of the following ways to recognize and celebrate staff successes in promoting equity.

- **Acknowledge staff publicly:** Principals can publicly recognize and acknowledge staff members' contributions to promoting equity during staff meetings, school assemblies, or through schoolwide communication channels. This can include highlighting specific initiatives, projects, or efforts that have had a positive impact on equity within the school community.

- **Organize appreciation events:** Organize appreciation events, such as staff luncheons, breakfasts, or social gatherings to celebrate the collective achievements of the staff in advancing equity. These events provide an opportunity for principals to express gratitude for the dedication and hard work of their staff.

- **Give personalized recognition:** Take the time to write personalized notes of appreciation to individual staff members, recognizing their specific contributions and successes in promoting equity. This personalized approach demonstrates attentiveness and reinforces the importance of their efforts.

- **Bestow awards and certificates:** Create awards or certificates to honor staff members who have shown exceptional commitment and impact in fostering equity. You can present these awards at special ceremonies or events, or even staff meetings, highlighting their achievements and inspiring others to follow their lead.

- **Highlight success stories:** Share staff members' success stories and their impact on promoting equity through school newsletters, social media platforms, or the school website. By showcasing these stories, principals not only recognize individual efforts but also inspire others and foster a collective sense of pride and motivation.

- **Provide opportunities for leadership:** Offer staff members the chance to take on leadership roles within equity-focused committees, task forces, collaborative teams, or special projects or initiatives. Empowering staff members to lead and contribute to equity strengthens their sense of ownership and motivation.

- **Ensure regular feedback and dialogue:** Establish a culture of open communication and ongoing feedback where staff members' contributions and successes in promoting equity are consistently acknowledged and valued. Encourage regular dialogue to ensure that their voices are heard, concerns are addressed, and ideas are shared.

ENCOURAGE COLLABORATIVE DECISION MAKING

Collaborative decision making is another key strategy. Principals can actively involve superintendents and community members in decision-making processes related to equity initiatives. This collaborative approach helps build trust, fosters a sense of ownership, and ensures diverse perspectives are taken into account. By engaging in shared decision making, principals can tap into the expertise and experiences of these stakeholders, creating a more comprehensive and effective approach to promoting equity.

FOSTER OPEN COMMUNICATION AND DIALOGUE

Furthermore, fostering open communication and dialogue is critical. Soika (2020) suggests, "Surround yourself with people who are pursuing equity goals as well. This might be colleagues or even a group of friends. Discuss your interests, objectives, and backgrounds, and look for ways in which you can learn from them." Principals can create platforms for ongoing conversations with superintendents and community members, such as regular meetings or forums. These interactions provide opportunities to address questions, concerns, and misconceptions, allowing for a deeper exploration of equity-related issues.

Engaging in open and respectful dialogue helps build relationships, establish common ground, and promote a culture of collaboration. In my experiences as an educator and principal, relationship building and open communication are essential in collaborative efforts for equity. Trusting relationships, valuing diverse perspectives, and engaging in ongoing dialogue are essential for bridging gaps and promoting equity.

COMMIT TO SELF-REFLECTION

In addition to collaborating with teachers, staff, and superintendents, principals working to maintain ethical leadership and advance equity must also work with themselves. Soika (2020) encourages school leaders to engage in self-reflection to help them build their integrity to higher levels because self-reflection provides a sense of checks and balances. He emphasizes that because equity work requires analysis of institutional structures, school leaders must consider their own role in those structures, continuing to do the work within themselves. In conclusion, Soika (2020) writes:

> Critical self-reflection is an intensive process. As you reflect on your power and privilege, you may find that you implicitly support biased systems that limit opportunities for others. The goal of reflection is not to induce shame, but to increase your awareness. As you become more aware, you can grow into a stronger leader for equity.

Each school leader's charge should be to become a stronger leader for equity. A leader's primary focus should be ethical action for others.

Action Oriented

Principals demonstrate integrity when they put actions behind their words. Principals who support equity communicate their commitment in words and deeds;

they model these ideals for staff through their behavior. Leading by example, or modeling, is associated with authentic and ethical approaches to leadership (Avolio & Gardner, 2005). Equitable school leaders "talk the talk" and, more importantly, "walk the walk." Moving from having conversations about equity to taking actions to establish equity seems to be a quantum leap that many schools have yet to take.

> **Principals demonstrate integrity when they put actions behind their words.**

A gap exists between conversations about equity (talking the talk) and equitable actions (walking the walk). The difference between educators who talk about school equity and educators who actually take action to establish school equity lies in their level of commitment and implementation. Educators who merely talk about equity may engage in discussions, acknowledge the importance of equity, and express support for inclusive practices. However, their efforts often remain at a superficial level, lacking concrete actions to bring about meaningful change.

In contrast, educators who actively work toward establishing school equity go beyond mere discussions and prioritize tangible steps to create an equitable learning environment. They take proactive measures to address systemic inequities, identify and dismantle barriers, and implement inclusive policies and practices. These educators actively seek out professional development opportunities to enhance their understanding of equity issues, collaborate with colleagues to develop equitable curriculum and instructional strategies, and continually reflect on their own biases and privileges.

Educators who prioritize action understand that equity requires intentional and sustained effort. They actively advocate for marginalized students, amplify their voices, and ensure that resources and opportunities are distributed fairly. These educators consistently engage in self-reflection, challenge the status quo, and actively address disparities in student outcomes. Their commitment to action sets them apart, leading to meaningful and lasting change in the pursuit of educational equity.

Paul Fleming is the former rural Blue-Ribbon award-winning school principal and now assistant commissioner for the teachers and leaders division at the Tennessee Department of Education. Fleming (2019) recognizes that integrity and equitable leadership is discussed, but how the action is lacking in many of the rural districts in his area.

My interactions with rural principals demonstrates the importance of viewing equity through two lenses: Improving outcomes for all students is not an exclusively urban problem, and equity needs to be embedded into the DNA of school and district policies and practices if we want to successfully move our collective thinking about equity from an initiative to a necessary and enduring systematic approach for reaching every student. This shift requires us as leaders to grapple with the powerful notion that student outcomes will not improve until adult learning and behaviors change.

Fleming (2019) also writes about the importance of taking action. In his article, he discusses how making a commitment is taking action toward educational equity and goes on to write about the importance of developing an equity action plan for their school where everyone agrees on the meaning of equity and what it looks like in their community. Defining what equity looks like in each person's building is key, and the leader is the determining factor for advancing it. Leading this charge and progressing toward equity is an example of integrity and ethical leadership because it helps establish social justice in education for all.

June Rimmer (2016) emphasizes the importance of role modeling equity when she writes, "To ensure excellence, equity and a quality learning experience for every child in every classroom every day, and to close these gaps, the principal, and other school leaders, working alongside families, must demonstrate equity-centered instructional leadership." School leaders must establish non-negotiable standards of excellence for each student, utilize teachers' beliefs in their ability, and support them as much as possible to do this challenging work. These are the kinds of commitment- and integrity-demonstrating actions required for school leaders to advance equity in their schools. The principal acts as the chassis, which holds all the parts together while keeping the integrity intact.

What It Looks Like in the Real World

Good school leaders are like Spider-Man, and I'm not just talking about their mutual possession of superpowers! I loved reading Spider-Man comic books and watching the cartoon when I was a child. Permeating each new episode was a theme that resonated with me: "To whom much is given, much will be required." All leaders, regardless of how large or small their following, exert power. To exert power over other people carries an ethical responsibility. "The greater the power, the more responsibility a leader has. Therefore, leaders at all levels carry a responsibility for setting the ethical tone and for acting as role models for others" (United Nations Office of Drugs and Crime, 2020).

One might ask, "What is good leadership?" The word *good* has two meanings in this context: technically good, meaning strong skills, and morally good, meaning heart and ethical integrity. The focus on the concept of morally good demonstrates that integrity lies at the heart of leadership (Ciulla, 2014). Leaders have a responsibility to behave ethically. Leaders are held to higher ethical standards. This increases leaders' stress; integrity will be tested when balancing different perspectives of those very same people you lead.

Although they are held to higher standards, school leaders are not perfect. As human beings, we all make mistakes. When principals take ownership of and learn from their inevitable missteps, then forgiveness, encouragement, and better future decision making follow. Mistakes that are combined with dishonesty and deflection breed resentment. I've made a million mistakes throughout my career, and some of them in my principal role. The advice I received from my mentors was to keep my integrity intact and avoid making ethical errors because those are hard to come back from and could kill your career. They also said that whenever you're unsure about a decision, err on the side of the best interests of students.

> **When principals take ownership of and learn from their inevitable missteps, then forgiveness, encouragement, and better future decision making follow.**

Overcoming Conflict

As a principal working in a low-income community in a southern suburb of Chicago, I recognized the urgent need to create a more equitable environment for both staff and students. Understanding the power of collaboration, I embarked on a journey of meeting with staff members over the course of a year to present a compelling case for change. I highlighted the disparities that existed and how they were impacting the academic and social-emotional well-being of our students. My challenge came through several resistant staff members who opposed the notion of change and believed that maintaining the status quo was sufficient. This created a significant conflict and posed a challenge to equity initiatives.

To address this challenge, I engaged in open and honest conversations with these resistant staff members individually, seeking to understand their concerns and perspectives. By actively listening and empathizing, I was able to build a rapport and establish common ground. I emphasized that our goal was not to diminish anyone's contributions or achievements but rather to provide equal opportunities for all students and staff members. Eventually, I was able to shift their mindsets. Even if they didn't help achieve this work, that agreed that they would not hinder or interfere with it. It's not easy to win or convert people who may disagree with your perspectives, but it is possible to work with them and stop them from tugging on the opposite end of the rope.

Facing Moral Dilemmas

In addition, the journey to establish an equitable environment was not without its moral dilemmas. I was faced with situations in which I had to demonstrate ethical leadership and do what I knew was right. One such dilemma arose when a vendor approached me, offering a lucrative deal on educational resources. However, on further investigation, I discovered that the vendor had a questionable track record in terms of ethical business practices. I chose to prioritize the well-being and best interests of our students over financial benefits, and instead sought out alternative vendors who aligned with our commitment to equity and ethical standards.

Another moral dilemma arose when faced with pressure to implement a discipline policy that disproportionately targeted students from marginalized groups. Despite resistance and criticism, I firmly stood my ground and advocated for a restorative justice approach that fostered empathy, understanding, and growth. It was challenging, but I knew in my heart that it was the right path to create a more inclusive and equitable school climate.

Throughout these challenges, I relied on my core values, ethical compass, and collaborative efforts to guide my decisions. By modeling ethical leadership, staying true to convictions, and fostering collaboration among staff, we were able to overcome obstacles and create positive change. The dedication of staff members and the collaboration that took place enabled us to make significant strides toward a more equitable school environment. The impact of these ethical choices proved to be beneficial in the long run.

Integrity has constructive influence on principal performance. According to Melky Malingkas, Johanis Senduk, Suddin Simandjuntak, and Benny Blemy Binilang (2018), "This means that principal performance and equity will increase significantly if principals practice high integrity in their work. It is best to lead with absence of ulterior motives and with the presence of integrity, consistency, honesty, and commitment" (p. 14).

Taking Action to Build Leadership Integrity

Consider taking some of the following action steps to help build your integrity as a leader and establish an equity action plan that promotes and upholds equity in all aspects of school leadership.

ACTION 1:   **Build awareness and understanding.** Conduct regular professional development sessions for school leaders to deepen their understanding of equity, systemic inequities, and the impact on students and staff. Engage in critical self-reflection and explore personal biases and assumptions that may hinder equitable practices. Provide resources, such as articles, books, and videos, to further educate school leaders on equity-focused leadership.

ACTION 2:   **Establish clear equity goals.** Collaborate with staff and stakeholders to develop clear, measurable equity goals that address disparities and ensure opportunities for all students and staff. Embed equity goals in the school's vision, mission, and strategic plans to emphasize their importance and commitment; and regularly assess progress toward equity goals and make necessary adjustments to improve outcomes.

ACTION 3:   **Foster inclusive decision making.** Ensure diverse voices and perspectives are represented in decision-making processes, and establish inclusive committees or task forces that focus on equity-related initiatives. Encourage open dialogue and feedback from staff, students, families, and community members to inform decision making and policy development.

ACTION 4:   **Cultivate collaborative partnerships.** Collaborate with community organizations, local leaders, and advocacy groups to create partnerships that support equity initiatives. Engage in meaningful dialogue with district leaders to align districtwide equity efforts with the school's goals and strategies. Finally, foster strong relationships with families and involve them in decision-making processes to ensure their voices are heard.

ACTION 5:   **Model ethical leadership.** Demonstrate ethical behavior and decision making by prioritizing the well-being and rights of all students and staff.

Uphold high standards of integrity, honesty, and fairness in all interactions and decisions and address and rectify instances of inequity or bias promptly and transparently.

ACTION 6: **Provide support and resources.** Allocate resources, such as time, professional development opportunities, and materials, to support teachers in implementing equitable practices. Offer ongoing coaching and mentoring for staff to enhance their understanding of equity and provide guidance on inclusive instructional strategies. Finally, collaborate with support staff, such as counselors and social workers, to provide resources and interventions that address students' social-emotional needs and promote equity.

ACTION 7: **Monitor and evaluate progress.** Establish data collection systems to monitor equity-related outcomes and progress. Analyze data to identify disparities, trends, and areas requiring improvement. Use data to inform decision making and adjust strategies to ensure continuous improvement toward equity goals.

Conclusion

Leading with integrity and enhancing equity is hard work. School leaders of integrity working to enhance equity don't do the work for awards and accolades; they do the work because they are dedicated to equity and meeting the needs of their students and staff. They are the foundation holding the many different aspects of the school together. When the principal is operating as the integral chassis, other gears turning toward enhanced school equity also will spin smoothly.

Questions for Reflection

Working individually or with a collaborative group, ask yourself the following reflective questions.

1. As a school leader, how do you ensure that all students and staff are treated equitably and without discrimination? How do you communicate this expectation to staff members? How do you address staff members who do not treat all students and staff equitably?

2. As a school leader, how can you maintain your autonomy and impartiality in the face of political pressure when making decisions concerning your school?

3. What can you and your administrative team do to ensure all school policies and procedures are consistent with ethical and legal guidelines?

4. What is the most effective way for school leaders to hold teachers and staff to the highest ethical conduct as it relates to interactions with students and their families and professional responsibilities?

5. Describe a situation in which a school leader faced a moral dilemma and how they made an ethical decision to address it. Do you agree or disagree with these actions?

School Leader Integrity Survey

For each item, circle the response that best describes your integrity as a leader.

1. I am responsible for my own behavior as a school leader.

1	2	3	4	5
Strongly disagree	Disagree	Neutral	Agree	Strongly agree

2. I hold myself accountable for the decisions I make.

1	2	3	4	5
Strongly disagree	Disagree	Neutral	Agree	Strongly agree

3. I model the ethics and integrity I want to see from my staff and students.

1	2	3	4	5
Strongly disagree	Disagree	Neutral	Agree	Strongly agree

4. I follow through on my commitments.

1	2	3	4	5
Strongly disagree	Disagree	Neutral	Agree	Strongly agree

5. I stand up for what I believe in and work to enhance equity at my school, even if I receive resistance from people who are trying to discourage me.

1	2	3	4	5
Strongly disagree	Disagree	Neutral	Agree	Strongly agree

page 1 of 3

6. I advocate for students and do what I say to provide an equitable environment.

1	2	3	4	5
Strongly disagree	Disagree	Neutral	Agree	Strongly agree

7. I carry myself in a way that make others want to follow me.

1	2	3	4	5
Strongly disagree	Disagree	Neutral	Agree	Strongly agree

8. My beliefs dictate my actions.

1	2	3	4	5
Strongly disagree	Disagree	Neutral	Agree	Strongly agree

9. I empower others to do the right thing.

1	2	3	4	5
Strongly disagree	Disagree	Neutral	Agree	Strongly agree

10. I do not let politics shape my decisions.

1	2	3	4	5
Strongly disagree	Disagree	Neutral	Agree	Strongly agree

11. The best interest of my students determines my decisions.

1	2	3	4	5
Strongly disagree	Disagree	Neutral	Agree	Strongly agree

12. I stand up for what I believe and do not fold under pressure.

1	2	3	4	5
Strongly disagree	Disagree	Neutral	Agree	Strongly agree

13. I stay true to my ethics instead of going along with the majority.

1	2	3	4	5
Strongly disagree	Disagree	Neutral	Agree	Strongly agree

Survey Results:

13–18	Low integrity
19–26	Moderately low integrity
27–38	Average integrity
39–51	High integrity
52–65	Very high integrity

CHAPTER 7

REVISING SCHOOL POLICIES AND PROCEDURES

Principals must enforce many district policies and school procedures. Some of these school policies and procedures are inequitable, causing marginalized students to be further disadvantaged. Educational leaders must understand the effects that some school rules, policies, and procedures have on student success and change them when they are detrimental. Just as the technology in cars changes and user manuals are updated to fit the new car model, school policies and procedures must change with the times. Now that you have updated your vision and mission statements (see chapter 4, page 79), you can use them as a guide to update your school policies and procedures to ensure they match your vision and mission statements.

WHETHER IT'S THE ever-increasing number of driver-assist features or internet-connected radios that can stream online music or access live traffic conditions on GPS maps, cars are getting increasingly complicated, and car manufacturers continue to add new features to them year after year. Whenever I get behind the wheel of a different car, I tend to study the dashboard to see if I can figure out how everything works. In most cases, if there is no one around who knows the features of the car, I have to consult the owner's manual to figure it out.

A vehicle owner's manual includes vital information to make you a better driver and car owner, including maintenance and troubleshooting advice (Auto Simple, 2017). Now, just imagine if there was only one user manual for all the many different makes and models of cars. This simply would not work, because each make and model is different. General similarities may exist, but a separate set of instructions is necessary to gain full knowledge of the unique features of each car. If you tried to use the owner's manual that was correct for your make and model but was written for an older version, much of the information would be irrelevant and outdated. To be effective, the owner's manual must be updated every time a new model comes along.

Further, many of the features in new cars are personalized to the owner. While some cars still don't require much setup, many newer models have advanced technological features that require input from the driver, including keyless entry, custom seating positions, and voice recognition, to name a few (Auto Simple, 2017). These features are specific to the individual owner and exist so the car and the owner can be in sync.

Unlike vehicle owner's manuals, many school policies and procedures are not routinely updated, often rendering them out of touch with societal trends. These policies and procedures are sometimes very general in nature, with an intention of fairness. In reality, the one-size-fits-all approach to discipline policies, grading practices, and other school processes and procedures creates inequities.

For schools to be fair in the equitable sense, many policies must be reviewed, updated, and sometimes changed altogether. School districts that adapt with changes in society support inclusive environments for students dealing with issues that may not have been prevalent in years past. School leaders who demonstrate a commitment to putting students in the best possible position to succeed strive to understand students' challenges and derive policies and procedures to promote achievement rather than accelerate failure.

This chapter explores the critical importance of updating school policies and procedures to foster equity and inclusivity within educational institutions. Recognizing the inherent disparities and inequities that exist, this chapter delves into the need for revising disciplinary policies that disproportionately affect students from marginalized groups, implementing restorative practices as an alternative approach, and addressing policies that hinder historically marginalized students from accessing advanced placement classes.

First, this chapter examines the impact of inequitable discipline policies on marginalized students. By shedding light on the disproportionate disciplinary actions faced by certain student groups, including LGBTQ+ students, it emphasizes the urgent need for policy revisions that promote fairness, empathy, and restorative justice. The chapter also explores alternative disciplinary approaches that prioritize student well-being, rehabilitation, and community building.

Second, the chapter discusses the significance of implementing restorative practices as an alternative to traditional punitive measures. By incorporating restorative practices into the school culture, you can foster a sense of accountability, healing, and genuine understanding among all members of the school community. You will learn about the transformative power of restorative practices in resolving conflicts, repairing relationships, and promoting positive behavior.

Last, this chapter addresses policies that hinder historically marginalized students from enrolling in advanced placement classes. It examines the implications of such barriers and their adverse effects on educational opportunities and outcomes.

By engaging in a comprehensive review and update of school policies and procedures, you can foster a more inclusive, supportive, and equitable educational environment for all students. This chapter provides insights, research-based evidence, and practical recommendations to guide educational leaders in making necessary policy changes and embracing practices that empower and uplift all students. Together, we can work toward dismantling systemic barriers and creating a more just and equitable educational experience.

What the Research Says

The importance of establishing and following school policies and procedures is clear. Schools must establish policies and procedures to make sure they run and operate efficiently and effectively. According to PowerDMS (2020), which supports

K–12 schools in being preventive instead of reactive, the purpose of policies and procedures is to:

> Establish expectations, keep students and staff safe, and make sure students receive a good education. The target audience—whether students, parents, or staff—all need to be able to understand the rules in order to follow them, and administrators should regularly review policy handbooks to make sure all policies are up to date.

Many schools recognize the changes that take place in the world and try to keep up with technology and infrastructure. Unfortunately, many schools have fallen behind when it comes to modernizing school policies and procedures, and have held fast to those that are old, outdated, and even inequitable. Policies that stemmed from good intentions when they were adopted can now have negative consequences for students.

> *Many schools have fallen behind when it comes to modernizing school policies and procedures, and have held fast to those that are old, outdated, and even inequitable.*

Change is a constant, and people who fail to adjust also will fail to keep up. It is unfortunate that many schools and districts have not remained current and are having to deal with many issues they have attempted to sweep under the rug. As education systems recognize the need to be current and up to date, they can take advantage and pursue new initiatives that will benefit students. American University (2020b) emphasizes that "the times of greatest challenge can also be the times of greatest opportunity for effecting lasting, positive change." Effective school leaders must be willing to face these challenges head-on.

Practicing Inequitable Discipline

Some policies that need to be reviewed involve school discipline and other inequitable opportunities overall for students from historically marginalized groups. Several common school policies and procedures are in need of change to promote equity and foster an inclusive educational environment. Policies related to disciplinary actions, such as suspensions and expulsions, should be revised to incorporate restorative practices that prioritize rehabilitation, conflict resolution, and the growth of positive relationships. It is also crucial to address policies that prevent historically marginalized students from accessing advanced placement classes, as these policies perpetuate educational inequities and limit opportunities for academic growth and achievement. By reassessing and revising these policies, schools can take significant steps toward promoting fairness, inclusion, and equal opportunities for all students.

One example is the reevaluation of zero-tolerance policies, which often lead to excessively punitive measures and contribute to the school-to-prison pipeline, disproportionately affecting marginalized students. The real failure of zero-tolerance policies has been their exhaustive use with Black, Brown, and other students of color and students with disabilities (U.S. Commission on Civil Rights, 2019).

In the article "Unequal School Discipline Strategies Set the Stage for Lifelong Discrimination," authors Jill Berkowicz and Ann Myers (2018) point out:

> In the United States, where students of color make up 49.6% of the student population, they account for 64.9% of the student population receiving one out-of-school suspension and 71.1% of students with more than one out-of-school suspension. They also account for 71.3% of the school expulsions and 66.6% of school arrests. . . . African American or Black students account for 15.5% of the total population, and yet, in all discipline categories collectively, they represent 30% or more of the students.

Adding to these troubling statistics is the following:

> [One] in 4 boys of color with a disability and 1 in 5 girls of color with a disability (excluding Latino and Asian-American students) receive at least one out-of-school suspension. LGBTQ+ students are also at a disproportionate risk of receiving an out-of-school suspension or expulsion, becoming involved with the juvenile justice system, or becoming homeless. (Berkowicz & Myers, 2018)

Additional research shines a spotlight on the school-to-prison pipeline; students who attend schools with high suspension rates are significantly more likely to be arrested and jailed as adults, especially Black and Hispanic boys. Data have long shown that Black and Hispanic students experience suspension and expulsion at much higher rates than White students, and that as adults, they're also disproportionately represented in the country's prison system (Cameron, 2021).

Students who experience strict school discipline with high suspension rates are more likely to participate in criminal activity in adulthood. In their article "Proving the School-to-Prison Pipeline," Andrew Bacher-Hicks, Stephen Billings, and David Deming (2021) assert:

Young adolescents who are enrolled in schools with high suspension rates are significantly more likely to be arrested and incarcerated as adults. These long-term, negative impacts in adulthood apply across a school's population, and not just to students who are suspended during their school years, and researchers found a direct link to the roles principals play in administering school discipline.

Given the scope and breadth of this problem, it's fair to wonder what actions principals can take to ensure their schools aren't on the wrong side of these grim statistics. Consider that the principals in Bacher-Hicks and colleagues' (2021) study have considerable discretion in how they handle disciplinary action. They have the authority to set parent meetings, after-school interventions, and in-school suspensions, and even the process for short-term, out-of-school suspension is almost completely up to school leaders. After studying the movements of principals across schools, Bacher-Hicks and colleagues (2021) find that "when a principal who has been strict in prior years switches into a new school, suspensions in the new school increase."

Furthermore, a study by Shoshana Jarvis and Jason Okonofua (2020) examines why Black students receive a higher percentage of suspensions in school and finds that some school leaders hold biases toward these students. Black students were more often labeled as "troublemakers," when compared with White students exhibiting the same behavior (Jarvis & Okonofua, 2020). The authors suggest that since principals are the ones making final decisions about punishments (such as suspensions and expulsions), they should be the focus of reducing the school-to-prison pipeline (Jarvis & Okonofua, 2020). This shows that school leadership sets the tone for the prevalence of suspensions—and who is receiving them. Principals can be the driving force behind keeping students in school or suspending them, triggering the school-to-prison pipeline.

The negative impacts from strict disciplinary environments are especially disappointing to parents, students and student advocates, and equity-driven teachers and leaders because historically marginalized and special needs students who benefit enormously from access to a good education are being excluded from school, thereby expanding preexisting gaps in educational attainment and incarceration (Bacher-Hicks et al., 2021).

We know that completing more years of school reduces the incidence of subsequent criminal activity, as does enrolling in a higher-quality school and graduating from high school (Mattos, 2017). Suspension and expulsion cause students to feel rejected and devalued. They may begin to disdain school. Suspensions are proven to lower academic success for students; it is well documented that suspended students miss out on academic learning time while developing resentment that becomes a barrier to classroom engagement (Hammond, 2015).

These students feel that the very people in the school who are supposed to be there to help them do not want them there. Their feelings of rejection grow stronger to a point where they begin hating school. To be fair to administrators and teachers, through their view, they may not dislike the student, but they certainly dislike the behavior that the student exhibits. The problem is that the fastest and only way some know how to get rid of the behavior is by getting rid of the student. As a result, these students may not feel welcomed by the school and end up ditching, becoming chronically truant, or dropping out altogether. Many find themselves making poor choices, becoming further involved with street gangs, entering a life of crime, and ending up dead or in jail at a young age. What a travesty!

Research consistently shows a strong correlation between repeated suspensions and detrimental long-term outcomes for students. Multiple suspensions can contribute to a vicious cycle, leading students toward making poor choices, becoming involved with street gangs, and eventually entering a life of crime. A lack of education resulting from disrupted schooling can significantly compromise job opportunities and lead to low-income circumstances, further perpetuating the cycle of poverty and limited options. A study conducted by Robert Balfanz and Vaughan Byrnes (2012) found that students who were suspended multiple times during their school years were at a significantly higher risk of engaging in criminal activities and facing incarceration in their adult lives. The research also highlights the link between school dropouts and illiteracy with higher rates of imprisonment. According to Sara Wood's 2022 article "Prison Education Programs: What to Know," approximately 68 percent of state prison inmates did not complete high school.

Furthermore, a longitudinal study by Harvard professors Richard Murnane, John Willett, and John Tyler (2000) emphasizes that educational attainment plays a pivotal role in shaping individuals' life outcomes. The study reveals that people with higher levels of education are more likely to secure stable employment, earn higher incomes, and lead law-abiding lives. In contrast, a lack of education significantly increases the likelihood of unemployment, poverty, and involvement in criminal activities. These findings underscore the critical role of education in breaking the cycle of poverty, reducing crime rates, and fostering social mobility. By addressing the root causes of school suspensions, implementing restorative practices, and providing comprehensive support systems, schools can contribute to a more equitable and just society, offering students the opportunity to thrive academically and lead productive lives.

Schools that embrace equitable practices focus on policies that address the root of behavioral problems and address them through interventions (Hannigan, Hannigan, Mattos, & Buffum, 2021). School personnel make it clear to students that they belong, but the behavior doesn't, and proceed to put interventions in place to grow the student and diminish the behavior, and not the other way around.

Some of these interventions might include the following.

1. **Check-in/check-out (CICO):** CICO is a structured program in which students receive daily check-ins with a designated adult to set goals, review behavior expectations, and receive feedback. This intervention helps students stay accountable and provides additional support and encouragement throughout the day.

2. **Behavior contracts:** Behavior contracts are written agreements between the student, teacher, and possibly other stakeholders, outlining specific behavioral goals, rewards, and consequences. These contracts help students understand expectations and provide a clear framework for behavior improvement.

3. **Self-monitoring:** Self-monitoring interventions involve students tracking their own behavior using checklists, charts, or electronic devices. This approach promotes self-awareness and empowers students to take responsibility for their actions. Teachers can provide feedback and support to help students reflect on their behavior and make positive changes.

4. **Social skills training:** Some students may struggle with social interactions, leading to behavior challenges. Social skills training interventions involve explicit teaching of social skills, such as communication, conflict resolution, and empathy. These interventions provide students with the tools they need to navigate social situations more effectively.

5. **Functional communication training (FCT):** FCT focuses on teaching students appropriate communication skills to replace problem behaviors. This intervention helps students identify and express their needs or frustrations in a more constructive manner, reducing the likelihood of engaging in disruptive behaviors.

Since the problem is so massive, there needs to be a sense of urgency when it comes to stopping the inequitable patterns in student discipline. School policies and procedures should be revised with consideration of cultural relativity. For example, policies that require families to conform to antiquated or cultural norms (such as dress codes, hairstyles, or reactions to emotional situations) reinforce past exclusionary systems (Katz-Amey, 2019). When student misbehavior spikes, it's because students do not receive the emotional support they need and sense that they are unwanted in the school community.

Research suggests that student misbehavior can be influenced by various factors, including the lack of emotional support and a sense of belonging in the school community. When students feel disconnected, unsupported, or unwanted, they may exhibit challenging behaviors as a way to express their frustrations or seek attention. Anne Gregory and Rhona S. Weinstein (2008) found that students who felt more connected to their school and had positive relationships with teachers were less likely to engage in disruptive behaviors. They also highlighted the importance of fostering a positive school climate and nurturing relationships to reduce student misbehavior.

Offering Limited Access to Advanced Placement Classes

Another way that poor school policies and procedures marginalize students is by restricting access to honors and advanced placement (AP) classes. AP classes provide high school students with the opportunity to earn college credit while they are still in school, but this is not the only value of these opportunities. Due to the increased rigor and lofty expectations of these courses, AP classes also offer high schoolers enriched opportunities to gain skills and demonstrate competencies in the learning experiences they can expect in colleges, universities, and careers. In their article "Closing Advanced Coursework Equity Gaps for All Students," Roby Chatterji, Neil Campbell, and Abby Quirk (2021) explain further:

> Unfortunately, the opportunity gaps in the advanced coursework system, the inequitable distribution of funding, supports, and pathways for student participation and success have a profound impact on which students are enrolling and succeeding in advanced coursework opportunities. Black, Indigenous, and other non-Black people of color are not enrolled in AP courses at rates comparable to their white and Asian peers and experience less success when they are.

Since Black and Latino students across the United States have unequal access to advanced coursework, they often miss out on essential learning opportunities that can better prepare them for success in college and careers. A report and state-by-state data tool from The Education Trust (2020) examines why these students are shut out and shine a light on the widespread nature of these practices. It follows the trend of the lack of opportunity for marginalized students from elementary school through high school:

> **Elementary school:** Black students represent 16% of overall enrollment in elementary schools, but only 9% of enrollment in gifted and talented programs; Latino students are 28% of students enrolled in elementary schools, but only 18% of those in gifted and talented programs.
>
> **Middle school:** Black and Latino students are not adequately enrolled in eighth-grade algebra. Black students make up 15% of eighth graders, but only 10% of students enrolled in eighth-grade Algebra I. Similarly, Latino students make up 25% of eighth graders and just 18% of eighth graders in the course.
>
> **High school:** Black and Latino students are locked out of Advanced Placement (AP). Black students make up 15% of high schoolers nationwide, but only 9% of students enrolled in at least one AP course. Nearly a quarter of students are Latino, but only 21% of students enrolled in AP courses are Latino. (The Education Trust, 2020)

In the article "Inequities in Advanced Coursework: What's Driving Them and What Leaders Can Do," Kayla Patrick, Allison Socol, and Ivy Morgan (2020) share data from the U.S. Department of Education's 2015–2016 Civil Rights Data Collection and Common Core of Data. Their research identifies two main reasons for the lack of marginalized students enrolled in AP courses: (1) in schools where the predominant groups are Black or Latino, students do not have as many seats in advanced classes as predominantly White students; and (2) racially diverse schools withhold Black and Latino students' access to the seats that are available. The article also points out that fair access doesn't mean sufficient access. "If Black and Latino students had a fair chance to enroll, there would be 157,513 more Black students and 68,102 more Latino students in AP courses" (Patrick, Socol, & Morgan, 2020). Imagine how many more underserved students would be better prepared for college and rigorous coursework at universities if these equitable numbers were realized.

Marginalized students who can succeed in AP classes may not get in due to the perceptions and biases of teachers who hold power in the decision-making process of whether students are allowed to enroll or not. According to Dania Francis, Angela de Oliveira, and Carey Dimmitt (2019), identifying and enrolling students in advanced classes often relies on recommendations from teachers and school counselors. These recommendations can be subject to both conscious and unconscious bias, which can leave some historically marginalized students out in the cold.

The Francis, Oliveira, and Dimmitt (2019) research shows that even in cases where Black female students met the same criteria as other students, school counselors were less likely to recommend them for AP calculus. LGBTQ+ students also have reported that they feel victimized by school policies and procedures.

Lacking Support for LGBTQ+ Students

School policies and procedures pertaining to LGBTQ+ students also need updating to reflect the growing number of students in this group. Research shows that the more students find themselves in environments that feel safe for them to express their identity, the more they report identities other than cisgender or heterosexual. In the article "Big Rise in U.S. Teens Identifying as Gay, Bisexual," author Cara Murez (2021) shares data from surveys that nationwide, significantly more students in the United States are reporting their sexual identity as gay, lesbian, or bisexual:

> Between 2015 and 2019, the percentage of 15- to 17-year-olds who said they identified as 'non-heterosexual' rose from 8.3% to 11.7%, according to nationwide surveys by the U.S. Centers for Disease Control and Prevention. Since 2015, the CDC's Youth Risk Behavior Survey has included questions about respondents' sexual identity and the sex of their intimate contacts. (Murez, 2021)

There are many factors, including but not limited to age, race, location, culture, and perspectives, that make LGBTQ+ students a diverse group, but despite finding accept in many environments, overall and compared with their straight and cisgender peers, LGBTQ+ students are at a higher risk for a variety of adverse experiences and outcomes (Kosciw, Greytak, & Diaz, 2009). Research shows that LGBTQ+ youth experience lower levels of adult support than non-LGBTQ+ youth. This puts them at a significant disadvantage because having adult support is a key factor in both their academic and social-emotional well-being (National Academies of Sciences, Engineering, and Medicine, 2020). Most of the research has been on supports provided by out-of-school adults, but a significant rise in attention has been aimed at adult support in school. Robert Coulter, Shari Schneider, Blair Beadnell, and Lydia O'Donnell (2017) "linked suicidality to lack of adult support out of school but also reported that gay/lesbian, bisexual, and youth questioning their sexual orientation were 5 to 7 percent less likely to have within-school adult support than straight youth."

Research shows that LGBTQ+ youth experience lower levels of adult support than non-LGBTQ+ youth. This puts them at a significant disadvantage because having adult support is a key factor in both their academic and social-emotional well-being.

Sara Day (2013) finds that nonpunitive school policies were associated with less homophobic bullying. Her research also correlates positive and supportive practices with higher levels of school connection among all students and especially LGBTQ+ students. Therefore, schools should review policies related to LGBTQ+ students and determine if and how they are detrimental by reviewing data and having focus-group meetings to find out how these students feel and are affected by school discipline policies and practices. Thomas Hanson, Gary Zhang, Rebeca Cerna, Alexis Stern, and Greg Austin (2019) share the benefits of supportive practices to providing feelings of belonging to LGBTQ+ students, opposite of punitive disciplinary measures and policies. They write:

> Supportive practices serve as a protective factor for students who had experienced homophobic bullying, mitigating its adverse effects. The findings add to previous research demonstrating that punitive practices do not deter bullying or create a safer campus, and that punitive practices reduce student connection.

Despite this concrete evidence, many schools continue to exacerbate feelings of nonbelonging and rejection through rules that harm the psyche and self-esteem of LGBTQ+ students. The research on LGBTQ+ youths' lack of adult support argues for prioritizing developmental supports at school (Hanson et al., 2019).

Helping students feel valued and welcomed is critical for them to be successful in school and later years. However, many do not feel supported in their school environments. GLSEN (2022) finds that they "disproportionately report being subjected to unsafe school climates, and thereby are denied equal access to educational opportunity and the opportunity for healthy social and emotional development" (p. 1). To ensure a supportive environment for *all* students, it is essential to implement specific policies and procedures that support LGBTQ+ students, affirming their identities and creating safe and healthy learning environments to advance equity and respect for all students (GLSEN, 2022).

> *Helping students feel valued and welcomed is critical for them to be successful in school and later years.*

What It Looks Like in the Real World

Clearly, there is a need for updates in school policies to enhance equity relating to school discipline, enrolling historically marginalized students in advanced classes, and supporting LGBTQ+ students. Schools need to respond in ways that are both current and sustainable. Reflecting on my time as a high school dean of students and as an assistant principal, I recall witnessing how poorly written, outdated policies negatively affect students. Some were flat-out detrimental, inspiring me to study innovative and alternative practices. Serving on the district's handbook committee provided the perfect opportunity to review policies and procedures and suggest needed changes. When there is follow-through, such reviews greatly benefit students and school communities. Unfortunately, some districts persist in operating with outdated policies and procedures that exacerbate the inequities endured by students. The following sections examine the impact of these as well as alternatives in the form of restorative justice practices and equitable access to AP classes.

Revising Harmful Discipline Policies

Research supports the connection between harsh discipline and negative outcomes. As a dean of students, I saw students' reactions when zero-tolerance policies resulted in harsh measures. It was common for students to receive ten-day suspensions for involvement in a fight or for being under the influence of any controlled substance or alcohol. The administration was more concerned with doling out the punishment rather than finding out *why*, for example, the student was using drugs and what personal or emotional problems had that caused them to cope in this manner. One of the school policies also stated that insubordination, or failing to show school identification when asked, warranted an automatic three-day suspension.

The problem with these exclusionary practices is that it makes students feel further rejected. An African proverb says, "When a child does not feel embraced by the village, they will burn it down to feel its warmth." Are students at your school acting out to get attention that they feel is lacking? Or are they exacting revenge because they feel rejected? To de-escalate these feelings of students who I suspended, I stressed the consequences of such behavior to them. While I didn't want to see them continue any negative, unhealthy coping methods and behaviors, I also didn't want to see them suspended, leading to a higher incidence of disconnection and academic failure. I wanted students to learn how to self-correct, how to make the choices that not only would serve them well outside of school but would also keep them in school. I knew that when I had no choice in meting out the lengthy suspensions connected to zero-tolerance policies, the consequence may be the student's academic failure.

> **An African proverb says, "When a child does not feel embraced by the village, they will burn it down to feel its warmth."**

Such punishments can snowball. Students may suffer academically and financially as well. Consider attendance policies that state students will be dropped from class if they accrue five unexcused absences or five unexcused tardies. Making up these classes in summer school can cost a lot of money. That means the student or their family would have to pay to make up a class if they failed both semesters because of being late or absent more than five times. Many families cannot afford to pay for their child to attend summer school.

Meanwhile, embattled teachers are asking, "What are we going to do to get students to behave?" Good question. We have to have school discipline. But for it to be truly effective—and by that, I mean both behavior modifying *and* academically supportive—we need to reshape how it looks. When I use the term *discipline*, I am defining it as "to train or develop by instruction and exercise, especially in self-control" (Merriam-Webster, n.d.b) and not the definition that states "to punish or penalize for the sake of enforcing obedience and perfecting moral character" (Merriam-Webster, n.d.b). The first definition means *to teach*, and the second definition means *to punish*. Schools must find innovative ways to teach rather than continually veer down the dead-end punishment path.

Thankfully, restorative practices and alternatives to zero-tolerance and punitive consequences are being implemented in some schools. Research suggests that implementing well-designed restorative discipline programs in schools that serve a high number of diverse and historically marginalized students has the potential to reduce the disproportionate suspensions, expulsions, and dropout rates of Black and Latino students (Davison, Penner, & Penner, 2021). Viable restorative justice programs are deeply entrenched into the school culture. The main objective of implementing restorative justice is establishing a respectful, tolerant, and supportive environment among students and staff (Morgan, 2021).

Implementing Restorative Justice Practices

When I became principal in 2016, I had the opportunity to work with the school district to implement restorative justice practices at my school. We focused on staff having caring attitudes and teaching empathy to teachers, students, and their families. We worked on harm prevention as well as on how to smooth things out amicably after harm had been done. We reduced out-of-school suspensions by 55 percent and saw school climate surveys top the 80 percent favorable mark compared to less than 35 percent favorable in previous years.

Following are some of the actions I took as principal to reduce suspensions and ensure my staff and I were implementing culturally responsive practices at my school. Consider implementing some of these practices in your own school.

1. **Implement restorative practices:** Use restorative approaches to address disciplinary issues by focusing on repairing harm, fostering empathy, and promoting dialogue and understanding among students.

2. **Provide social-emotional support:** Develop comprehensive social-emotional learning programs that equip students with skills like self-awareness, self-management, and relationship building, which can help prevent misbehavior and promote a positive school climate.

3. **Foster positive teacher-student relationships:** Encourage teachers to build strong, supportive relationships with students by getting to know them individually, showing empathy, and providing mentorship and guidance.

4. **Promote cultural responsiveness:** Ensure that the curriculum and teaching practices reflect and respect students' diverse cultural backgrounds and experiences. Create an inclusive environment that values and celebrates diversity.

5. **Offer professional development:** Provide ongoing training and support for teachers and staff on effective behavior management

strategies, restorative practices, cultural competency, and trauma-informed approaches.

6. **Encourage student voice and involvement:** Establish mechanisms for student input and involvement in decision-making processes, such as student advisory boards or leadership opportunities, to foster a sense of ownership and belonging within the school community.

7. **Implement proactive interventions:** Identify and address potential challenges or triggers that may lead to misbehavior by implementing proactive interventions, such as early intervention programs, counseling services, and academic support.

8. **Engage families and the community:** Foster strong partnerships with families and your community to support students' holistic development. Involve parents or guardians in school activities, provide resources and workshops, and communicate regularly about students' progress.

9. **Create a positive school climate:** Develop a positive and inclusive school culture by promoting respect, kindness, and cooperation among students, staff, and stakeholders. Implement initiatives like anti-bullying campaigns, peer-mentoring programs, and positive behavior reinforcement.

10. **Monitor and analyze data:** Regularly collect and analyze discipline data to identify patterns and trends. Use this information to inform decision making, adjust strategies, and target interventions where they are most needed.

It's important to note that each school community is unique, so principals should adapt these strategies to suit their specific context and needs. Additionally, consulting with experts in the field of education, such as Solution Tree Associates, and collaborating with other principals and educators can provide additional insights and support in implementing these strategies effectively.

Implementing restorative justice practices in schools instead of zero-tolerance and exclusionary discipline makes an enormous difference in curtailing the high rates at which Black and Hispanic students are disciplined. Hani Morgan (2021) states, "When six elementary and middle schools in Texas piloted restorative discipline programs to address high suspension rates, they experienced a 70% reduction in in-school suspensions and a 77% reduction in out-of-school suspensions." Although researchers are in the early stages of rigorous studies on restorative justice programs, existing studies predict that when these programs are implemented, positive outcomes are likely. School leaders can extinguish the school pipeline-to-prison problem that has ballooned out of control as a result of harsh punitive discipline and zero-tolerance policies (Morgan, 2021).

For schools looking to implement restorative justice practices, the Schott Foundation for Public Education (2014) offers a guide titled *Restorative Practices: Fostering Healthy Relationships and Promoting Positive Discipline in Schools—A Guide for Educators*. The guide illustrates how one might effectively embed restorative practices into their entire school culture. It clearly spells out what restorative practices are, explains why they are a promising approach for fostering healthy relationships in educational settings, and demonstrates how they are beneficial processes for learners, teachers, and school communities.

The Schott Foundation's (2014) guide shares four Ps that schools must consider when incorporating restorative justice:

1. **Person:** The way each individual (teacher, principal, counselor, support staff) interacts with others in the school community and how that interaction impacts relationships.
2. **Place:** The environmental conditions and factors that affect how individuals interact with one another.
3. **Practice:** Opportunities for educators to prevent conflict, resolve challenges, and create chances for relationship growth.
4. **Plan:** A school community's plan for making restorative practices a regular part of school culture.

These four Ps can be applied at all school levels. Practitioners can start envisioning how each of the four Ps currently supports restorative justice practices in their school.

This guide is beneficial for schools because it provides eight easy action steps for schools to adopt restorative justice practices. The eight steps include the following (Schott Foundation for Public Schools, 2014).

1. Talk with other teachers and administrators in your school or district about different types of restorative practices. Do they understand the benefits of restorative practices?

2. Put together a team of students, parents, teachers, and community members to evaluate the school or district's approach to discipline, school climate, and restorative practices.

3. Set aside time in the school day to practice restorative techniques including restorative circles, peace circles, and conflict-resolution skills.

4. Gather input from various community stakeholders, including parents and students.

5. Ensure district policies are aligned with a restorative philosophy.

6. Analyze data throughout the process to find out what's working and what's not working.

7. Provide ongoing training and professional development.

8. Allocate funding for restorative practices at the school and district level.

These steps provide clarity on how to implement restorative justice practices and were the ones I followed during my tenure as a K–8 school principal. You can use restorative practices to improve school culture, build trusting relationships with students and staff, reduce discipline disparities, involve learners and families, grow students' social-emotional well-being, and hold students accountable in a supportive manner. This leads to higher attendance rates, improved student behavior, and increased graduation rates (McMorris, Beckman, Shea, & Eggert, 2013). All these factors significantly enhance equity in schools and help school leaders think differently about traditional school discipline policies.

Opening Access to Advanced Placement Classes

This chapter also addresses historically marginalized students' access to honors and AP classes. There are many ways you can increase equity in your school by making these classes more accessible. Consider the following suggestions to provide a more equitable school environment.

- **Eliminate prerequisites for honors and AP classes:** These entry barriers are a major challenge for many Black and Brown students. If schools instead evaluate students by their potential and use honors and AP as opportunities to identify those who can make that educational leap, more students will be able to take these classes and stretch their academic muscles.

- **Talk with students individually about taking advanced courses (Joseph, 2021):** Interview students. Coach them. Tell them, "I believe in your ability to do this work, and you might even surprise yourself."

- **Offer students support and convince them that they will succeed:** Rather than counseling students to avoid such classes, supporting the bias that they can't handle the challenge, do the opposite. Schools need encouragement warriors willing to encourage students and provide the resources needed for them to gain confidence and succeed with more challenging coursework.

> *Interview students. Coach them. Tell them, "I believe in your ability to do this work, and you might even surprise yourself."*

Schools also need to develop specific supports to enable marginalized students to succeed in advanced coursework. Following is a list of seven equity-based actions schools can take to help all students succeed in AP courses.

1. **Provide access to all students:** Provide equal access to AP courses for all students, regardless of their background or previous academic performance. If possible, offer a diverse range of AP courses to accommodate students' interests and talents, avoiding tracking or limited options based on stereotypes. Ensure that information about AP courses, benefits, and application processes are easily accessible to all students and their families. Proactively reach out to traditionally marginalized students and encourage them to consider AP courses.

2. **Offer preparatory programs:** Establish pre-AP programs or summer bridge programs to introduce students to the expectations and rigor of AP courses. Offer preparatory workshops or tutorials that focus on study skills, time management, and effective note-taking strategies. Provide resources, such as textbooks, online study materials, and practice exams, to familiarize students with the AP curriculum.

3. **Offer professional development for teachers:** Conduct professional development sessions for AP teachers to promote cultural competency and sensitivity. Train teachers on differentiated instruction techniques to accommodate diverse learning styles and support students who may need additional assistance. Encourage the use of inclusive teaching

practices that value and incorporate diverse perspectives in the classroom.

4. **Provide mentorship and support:** Assign mentors or academic advisors to marginalized students, who can provide guidance, support, and encouragement throughout their AP journey. Create peer mentorship programs where students who have successfully completed AP courses can support and mentor their peers. Offer tutoring services or study groups led by experienced AP students or teachers.

5. **Supply financial assistance:** Ensure that financial barriers, such as AP exam fees, are not a hindrance for marginalized students. Provide scholarships or fee waivers to alleviate these costs. Seek external funding or partnerships to support students who may require additional resources, such as textbooks or technology.

6. **Celebrate achievements:** Recognize and celebrate the achievements of marginalized students in AP courses through awards, ceremonies, or announcements. Showcase success stories and accomplishments of students from diverse backgrounds to inspire and motivate others.

7. **Ensure ongoing evaluation and improvement:** Regularly assess the effectiveness of support programs and initiatives for marginalized students in AP courses. Collect feedback from students, parents, and teachers to identify areas of improvement and make necessary adjustments. Continuously evaluate data on student performance, participation, and representation to track progress and address any disparities.

By implementing these strategies, schools can create an inclusive and supportive environment that enables all students to excel in AP courses and prepare for their future academic endeavors.

Clearly, the goal is not simply getting historically marginalized students into AP classes; it is also to provide the support needed for success once they are enrolled (Roegman & Hatch, 2016). For school leaders to be effective in maintaining and sustaining equity and achievement in AP courses for all students, they must establish and execute plans for both access *and* success. The previous list is robust, but most certainly doable. There is also a shorter three-step process to accomplish maintaining and sustaining equity and achievement in AP courses for *all* students. According to Rachel Roegman and Thomas Hatch (2016), districts that have successfully increased AP opportunities for students implemented three strategies:

1. Structural changes in offerings;
2. Policy changes in requirements and reporting; and
3. Educational or professional development strategies to increase the quality of teaching and advising.

For school leaders to be effective in maintaining and sustaining equity and achievement in AP courses for all students, they must establish and execute plans for both access *and* success.

If school districts were to apply these equity-based frameworks, they could eliminate barriers to access. The following sections examine each of these in more detail.

STRUCTURAL CHANGES IN OFFERINGS

The first strategy is implementing structural changes that allow a higher number of AP course options—more AP offerings accompanying expectations for students to enroll in these classes. It is crucial to provide equal access to AP courses for all students, regardless of their background or previous academic performance. This ensures that every student has an equal opportunity to enroll in rigorous courses and benefit from the valuable learning experiences they offer.

Additionally, schools should offer a diverse range of AP courses that cater to students' various interests and talents, avoiding tracking or limiting options based on stereotypes. By providing a wide selection of AP courses, schools can create an inclusive environment that values the diverse aspirations and abilities of all students.

Furthermore, it is important to ensure that information about AP courses, their benefits, and the application processes is easily accessible to all students and their families. This includes transparent communication, clear guidelines, and readily available resources that facilitate informed decision making and encourage traditionally marginalized students to explore and pursue AP opportunities. Students can meet high expectations when teachers and staff communicate upfront with positive messages that they believe in students' ability to achieve and that they will be supported.

POLICY CHANGES IN REQUIREMENTS AND REPORTING

The second strategy is implementing policy changes in requirements and reporting. One effective strategy is to review and revise the prerequisites for AP courses to ensure inclusivity and avoid reliance solely on traditional academic criteria. This can be achieved by considering alternative pathways or multiple entry points that allow students to demonstrate their readiness for AP courses through diverse measures such as portfolios, projects, or teacher recommendations.

By providing flexibility in prerequisites, schools can recognize and accommodate the potential and motivation of students who may not meet initial criteria but have the capability to succeed in AP courses. Additionally, eliminating GPA or test score barriers is crucial to ensure equitable access. Schools can remove or reduce strict GPA or test score requirements that may disproportionately disadvantage historically marginalized students. Instead, you could adopt a holistic assessment approach, taking into account factors such as students' motivation, work ethic, recommendations, and other qualitative aspects alongside their academic performance. You might implement alternative assessment methods, like interviews or essays, to gain a more comprehensive understanding of students' abilities and potential. These changes help level the playing field for historically marginalized students to participate and succeed in AP courses.

STRATEGIES TO INCREASE THE QUALITY OF TEACHING AND ADVISING

The third strategy is providing professional development and training to strengthen the quality of teaching and advising. One essential aspect of this training is cultural competency, in which teachers participate in professional development sessions that enhance their understanding of the unique needs and experiences of historically marginalized students. These sessions help foster an inclusive classroom environment that respects and values students' diverse backgrounds, while also addressing biases, stereotypes, and cultural misconceptions that may impact teaching practices. By equipping teachers with cultural competency skills, schools promote equitable treatment and create a more supportive learning environment.

Another important element of professional training is implementing differentiated instruction techniques. Training can help teachers learn strategies that cater to diverse learning styles, abilities, and backgrounds. Teachers learn to adapt their teaching methods to meet the needs of historically marginalized students, providing targeted support and accommodations when necessary. The training emphasizes personalized learning experiences, in which teachers consider students' individual strengths and challenges to ensure their success in AP courses.

Equity-focused pedagogy is another crucial aspect of professional training. Schools can provide training to teachers on equity-focused approaches that aim to close achievement gaps and ensure all students have equal opportunities to succeed in AP courses. Teachers gain knowledge and resources to address systemic barriers and create an inclusive learning environment. They are encouraged to incorporate diverse perspectives and culturally relevant materials into their curriculum to enhance student engagement and connection.

Professional training also focuses on providing social-emotional support to historically marginalized students. Teachers and advisors can develop skills in creating a safe and supportive space where students feel comfortable expressing their emotions and discussing their concerns. These training sessions equip educators with strategies such as active listening, empathy, and understanding, fostering positive relationships and trust between teachers and students.

Finally, schools can provide professional development opportunities to enhance teachers' and advisors' knowledge of college and career guidance specifically tailored to historically marginalized students. They can learn how to identify scholarship and financial aid opportunities, assist with college applications, and help students navigate the college admission process. This training ensures that staff have the resources and skills to support historically marginalized students in pursuing higher education.

By providing professional training in these areas, schools empower teachers and advisors with the necessary skills and knowledge to effectively support historically marginalized students in AP courses. This comprehensive training creates an inclusive and supportive learning environment that promotes students' academic success and overall well-being.

Taking Action to Revise School Policies and Procedures to Promote Equity

Schools can take action to promote equity by revising their policies and procedures. This includes reviewing and revising school discipline policies to ensure fairness and reduce any potential biases. Consider taking some of the following action steps to revise your school policies and procedures to advance equity.

ACTION 1: **Obtain feedback from students to determine if they feel school is "fair." Listen to their concerns and take any warranted action to ensure students are being treated fairly.**

   a. Conduct regular student surveys to gauge students' perceptions of fairness and solicit their feedback on school policies, procedures, and interactions with teachers and staff.

b. Encourage student representation by establishing a student council or government where students can voice their concerns, propose changes, and collaborate with school administrators on addressing fairness issues.

c. Implement anonymous reporting systems that allow students to confidentially report incidents of unfair treatment, bias, or discrimination.

d. Organize open forums or town hall meetings where students can openly express their views, share concerns, and engage in constructive discussions with school leaders and staff.

ACTION 2: **Promote equity in access to AP classes by implementing some of the following strategies.**

a. Establish specific goals and targets for increasing the enrollment of historically marginalized students in AP courses. This demonstrates a commitment to creating a more inclusive and diverse AP program.

b. Actively reach out to marginalized students and their families, providing information about the benefits of AP courses and dispelling any misconceptions or barriers that may exist.

c. Conduct a thorough assessment to identify the barriers and challenges that prevent marginalized students from enrolling in AP courses. This may include factors such as limited access to information, lack of support or encouragement, or cultural and social perceptions.

d. Offer academic support programs and resources to help marginalized students prepare for and succeed in AP courses. This may include tutoring, study groups, or additional coursework to fill any knowledge gaps.

ACTION 3: **Make sure your school is a safe place for *all*, including LGBTQ+ students.** Following are some actions you can take to ensure your school is a safe and welcoming place for LGBTQ+ students.

a. Continue to learn and educate teachers and staff through professional development and workshops about inclusion and culturally responsive practices.

b. Post a "safe space" sticker or a pride flag to show your willingness to support LGBTQ+ students. Over 50 percent of the LGBTQ+ students stated they feel more comfortable talking with educators and counselors who hang pride flags in their rooms or offices (Kosciw, Greytak, Zongrone, Clark, & Truong, 2018).

c. Respect students' personal pronouns. More than 42 percent of transgender students stated their schools prevented them from using their preferred name or pronouns, and it was a major source of stress (Kosciw et al., 2018).

d. Place some LGBTQ+-inclusive books in your library and classrooms. Books about LGBTQ+ historical figures, like Alan Turing, or written by LGBTQ+ authors and poets, like Audre Lorde, also promote inclusivity. Without proper role models and historical figures, LGBTQ+ students have a harder time envisioning their futures (Yoon, 2020).

Conclusion

This chapter reviewed the connections between overly harsh discipline and academic failure, and how that can lead to even worse outcomes beyond school, as in the school-to-prison pipeline. It also discussed how to provide access for marginalized students to AP courses and pave the way for their success. Finally, it explored the changes needed to school policies and practices with regard to supporting LGBTQ+ students, including validating their identities, providing safe and healthy learning environments, and promoting equity and respect for *all* students (GLSEN, 2022).

Consistently reviewing school policies and updating them with new ones that reflect current pressing issues in education, and that promote equity and equitable practices, demonstrates school leaders' commitment to support and serve all students. Keeping the school's "owner's manual" up to date is how leaders can be the driving force for enhancing equity in their school.

Questions for Reflection

Working individually or with a collaborative group, ask yourself the following reflective questions.

1. What support services and resources are available to Black and Brown and other historically marginalized students in your school?

2. Are school leaders and teachers managing the praise-to-punishment ratio in your school? Are historically marginalized students reprimanded more and praised less in your classrooms? If so, why?

3. How do school leaders address inequitable discipline practices that disproportionately impact historically marginalized students?

4. What conscious or unconscious biases affect enrollment decisions for advanced courses in your school? What vital learning opportunities may historically marginalized students be missing that can set them up for success in college and careers? What policies exists at your school that prevent certain groups of students from enrolling in AP courses?

5. How do school leaders ensure that LGBTQ+ students feel safe and supported in your school environment, and to what extent do school policies and practices promote inclusivity and respect for LGBTQ+ students?

School Policies and Procedures Survey

For each item, circle the response that best describes the way you approach school policies and procedures.

1. I ensure that revised policies and procedures are responsive to the unique needs of historically marginalized students.

1	2	3	4	5
Strongly disagree	Disagree	Neutral	Agree	Strongly agree

2. I incorporate the perspectives and experiences of LGBTQ+ students when revising school policies and procedures.

1	2	3	4	5
Strongly disagree	Disagree	Neutral	Agree	Strongly agree

3. I address policies and procedures that may have a disproportionate impact on students living in poverty.

1	2	3	4	5
Strongly disagree	Disagree	Neutral	Agree	Strongly agree

4. I often evaluate the effectiveness of revised policies and procedures in promoting equity within the school community.

1	2	3	4	5
Strongly disagree	Disagree	Neutral	Agree	Strongly agree

5. School policies and procedures support the academic success of Black and Brown and other historically marginalized students.

1	2	3	4	5
Strongly disagree	Disagree	Neutral	Agree	Strongly agree

page 1 of 3

6. I address policies and procedures that may disproportionately impact students with disabilities.

1	2	3	4	5
Strongly disagree	Disagree	Neutral	Agree	Strongly agree

7. I ensure that revised policies and procedures are sensitive to the needs of students who have experienced trauma.

1	2	3	4	5
Strongly disagree	Disagree	Neutral	Agree	Strongly agree

8. I ensure that revised policies and procedures align with the values and mission of the school community.

1	2	3	4	5
Strongly disagree	Disagree	Neutral	Agree	Strongly agree

9. I address any concerns about the financial impact of revising school policies and procedures with the appropriate stakeholders.

1	2	3	4	5
Strongly disagree	Disagree	Neutral	Agree	Strongly agree

10. I ensure that revised policies and procedures are sustainable and adaptable to changes in the school community.

1	2	3	4	5
Strongly disagree	Disagree	Neutral	Agree	Strongly agree

page 2 of 3

11. My school has a team in place to ensure that historically marginalized students have access to AP classes.

1	2	3	4	5
Strongly disagree	Disagree	Neutral	Agree	Strongly agree

12. My school provides access and support to students in AP classes to ensure success.

1	2	3	4	5
Strongly disagree	Disagree	Neutral	Agree	Strongly agree

Survey Results:

12–18	School policies and procedures need a severe overhaul.
19–24	School policies and procedures are outdated.
25–36	School policies and procedures need improvement.
37–46	School policies and procedures are somewhat supportive of historically marginalized students and LGBTQ+ students.
47–60	School policies and procedures provide bridges and take into consideration ways to support all students and especially historically marginalized, low-income, and LGBTQ+ students.

Note: The results of this survey serve as a reflection tool and conversation starter regarding the alignment of school policies and procedures with the principles of equity and inclusivity. It is important to note that the scores obtained in this survey provide an initial assessment of your approach to various aspects of policy development and implementation. These scores should not be considered definitive or comprehensive evaluations of your school's policies and practices. Its purpose is to prompt self-reflection and encourage discussion among school personnel to identify areas where policies may need to be updated or revised to better support historically marginalized students, including LGBTQ+ students and students of color. It is recommended that schools engage in ongoing evaluation and continuous improvement efforts to create a more equitable and inclusive environment that addresses the unique needs of all students.

CHAPTER 8

MANAGING EFFECTIVE COMMUNICATION

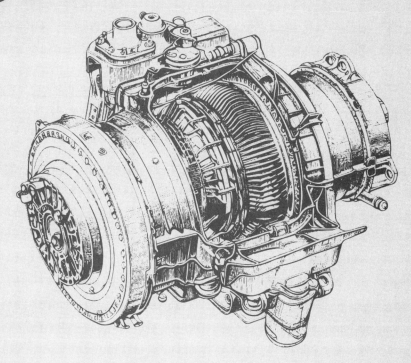

Excellent leaders manage communications effectively. Without effective communication skills, a principal's efforts to positively influence student outcomes will fall short. In fact, the clarity of written and verbal expressions is as important to a principal as a transmission is to a car. A smoothly running, well-maintained transmission sends kinetic energy from the car's engine to the wheels; a school leader who communicates clearly and concisely drives the message home, moving the staff further along the equitable education path.

A CAR TRANSMISSION IS one of a vehicle's most important components; it's part of the heart of a car. This vital part of a vehicle is designed to either manually or automatically shift a car into the correct gear and keep it running smoothly, whether it's slowing down or speeding up. "The transmission is what moves the power from the engine to the wheels. When healthy and working properly, your car's transmission should shift gears automatically, giving you the pace and performance you need on the road" (Zafar, 2021). When a car's transmission is not properly maintained, a drop in fuel economy and eventual engine failure may follow (Synchrony Car Care, 2023).

Just as the transmission of a car is vital to the vehicle's performance, communication and messaging are vital to a school leader's performance. A smoothly running transmission does not struggle to accelerate or slow down. A skilled communicator in the principal's seat keeps teachers, students, staff, and the community informed and on pace with what is going on at the school. Throughout this book, I've emphasized the importance of collaborating with specific stakeholders to accomplish goals on the road to leading with equity. Even when principals do this effectively, it's easy to lose track of the numerous other stakeholders schoolwide and even community-wide who are affected by the decisions of narrower groups. Even the most excellent school-improvement efforts will sputter and fail if these decisions are not effectively communicated with staff, students, and stakeholders. Conversely, school administrators who communicate clearly, with a style that engages and informs, are more likely to succeed in achieving their goals.

In the diverse educational landscape, effective communication plays a pivotal role in fostering equitable school engagement. As the primary leaders of their schools, principals have a critical responsibility to ensure that communication reaches all stakeholders in an inclusive and equitable manner. This chapter explores the strategies and practices that school leaders can employ to facilitate effective and equitable communication with families, utilizing various modes of communication, promoting equitable access to information, and fostering open lines of communication with staff members.

This chapter also examines the various modes of communication that principals can employ to reach diverse stakeholders effectively. From traditional methods such as newsletters, parent-teacher conferences, and phone calls to digital platforms like email, social media, and school websites, principals need to adopt a multifaceted approach that accommodates the preferences and accessibility needs of all stakeholders. It provides insights, best practices, and practical guidance to help principals navigate the complexities of managing effective and equitable school communication.

What the Research Says

Reviewing your communications strategy is time well spent, especially considering the many different forms of communication now available and the different preferences people have. Many problems, in and out of school, trace directly to the effectiveness of communication.

> **Many problems, in and out of school, trace directly to the effectiveness of communication.**

School leaders also must consider the community they serve, including what barriers may exist for students' families. How do you overcome these barriers? Almost every day, school leaders learn something new about the importance of communication, the modes of which evolve as the school introduces new tools, revises old approaches, and learns new lessons (Hopkins, 2017). Ultimately, if done well, good communication makes administrators more effective, stakeholders more satisfied, and students more successful.

Communication is effective when the person delivering the message makes it clear for the intended audience and it is understood by the audience in the manner the message was intended. Dan Mager (2017) describes it like this: "Communication is the transmission of information from a source to an audience. Effective communication requires that the audience understand the message in its intended form." Too often, people underestimate how often their audience misconstrues their message or does not understand it. Mager (2017) writes that "the process of communication is complex. Many factors determine whether a particular communication mode will succeed. Internal factors affect [people] participating in the communication process, and interactional factors affect how information is sent and received." Adding to this complexity are external factors like the physical environment, modes of transmission, and various cultural factors.

From students and teachers to administrators and staff to the families of those who are working or learning in the school and the community at large, schools have many stakeholders. Each group has high expectations and competing demands, and fulfilling those expectations depends on excellent communication skills, both verbal and nonverbal (Glaze, 2014). "Education is continually changing, and effective communication builds the positive school culture required to implement change" (Hollingworth, Olsen, Asikin-Garmager, & Winn, 2017).

In education, we have more communication tools at our disposal than ever before, including cell phones, email, social media, district websites, word of mouth, mail, apps, and more. Certainly, there is no shortage of means for disseminating information about what is happening in your school. But this means that educators must learn how to use all these new media to effectively communicate with stakeholders. To support these efforts, district office and school-based administrators need to stay on the cutting edge of new technologies in communication, even going beyond just being aware of them but actually experimenting with them and becoming competent and comfortable utilizing and harnessing their power.

The power of rumors, word of mouth, and the media is a force to be reckoned with and is the reason schools need to promote positive accomplishments and activities. Whenever I turn on the nightly news, the "bad news" stories are the ones that play first, get the most attention, and are sensationalized. Common phrases about the news include, "If it bleeds, it leads" and "Good news travels, but bad news travels faster!" Schools' reputations can suffer when news comes out that fails to tell the entire story and when the media magnifies the negative aspects of what happens.

School leaders can give context to stories and communicate messages that calms the public's concerns when they utilize communication outlets that reach their constituents swiftly. That's why it is critical to build a communications infrastructure and to be prepared to handle issues that arise. As leaders, we must also approach communication through an equity lens. Are we reaching every group and every family that is a part of our school community? How are we effectively communicating important initiatives and vital details about school operations to staff?

Communicating With Families

School communication breakdowns can lead to inequitable outcomes, particularly when barriers such as language and technology come into play. Language barriers can create difficulties for students and their families who are not fluent in the dominant language used in the school. Inadequate translation services or a lack of multilingual staff can hinder effective communication and lead to misunderstandings or exclusion of important information. Technology barriers further exacerbate inequities, as not all students have equal access to digital tools and internet connectivity. Online communication platforms, virtual meetings, and email updates may exclude those without reliable internet access or appropriate devices, widening the digital divide. This can impede parents' and guardians' ability to engage with teachers, stay informed about their children's progress, or participate in school activities.

Cultural barriers and differing communication norms also can contribute to communication breakdowns. Some families may have different expectations about their involvement in their children's education or have limited experience navigating the school system, making it challenging to effectively engage in communication. This can lead to missed opportunities for support, limited access to resources, and decreased parent-teacher collaboration. Socioeconomic factors also can play a role. Families facing financial constraints may struggle to afford necessary communication tools, such as smartphones or internet subscriptions, making it difficult to stay connected with the school. This further perpetuates disparities and hampers the ability of marginalized students and their families to fully engage in the educational process.

Overall, addressing these communication breakdowns requires a multifaceted approach that includes providing language support, bridging the digital divide, fostering cultural understanding, and implementing inclusive strategies that consider the diverse needs and circumstances of students and families.

Equitable communication with families means schools and districts exhaust all efforts and mediums to reach as many families as possible with the information they need from the school. According to Catherine Jacques and Alma Villeagas (2018):

> Equitable school communication focuses on meaningful engagement activities and systems between schools and families that do not pigeonhole any parent groups as deficient. This includes specific practices or approaches that reflect the values of a general group of families, as well as systems that foster tailored supports, flexible engagement options, and coordination between families and schools. (p. 1)

This is especially true for minority, immigrant, and refugee families, and schools must accommodate these groups to promote equitable communication and engagement. Effectively communicating with immigrant and refugee families has never been more important, but many districts are finding it increasingly difficult to connect with these groups.

MODES OF COMMUNICATION

Choosing appropriate home-to-school communication methods for migrant and immigrant students, students living in poverty, busy parents, and other historically marginalized groups promotes equity by ensuring accessible and inclusive channels that address language barriers, digital disparities, and cultural differences, thereby enabling meaningful engagement, involvement, and equitable support for these students and their families. As the use of technology grows, administrators, teachers, parents, and students are becoming more adept at utilizing new forms of communication. Leveraging different platforms enables school leaders to expand their reach and connect with different families and community members that may have been unintentionally left out of the loop.

More than at any time in the history of education, it is more convenient to engage families and students through SMS messaging, email blasts, or social media updates. There are a variety of ways for principals, teachers, and families to connect. Many texting and other apps are available for educators that can make communications faster, easier, and more secure (Remind, 2022). This is especially beneficial in any crisis communications. The time that elapses between an incident and notification is key in affecting the audience's response. And it is crucial to deliver the facts as they are known first from the school or district itself, rather than risk secondhand information or inaccurate rumors to gain the leading edge.

Educational leaders are increasingly using social media to share news and information with their constituents and members of their school communities. Posting on social media sites takes less time than drafting letters, creating memorandums, printing flyers, and mailing them or sending them home with students. These are effective communication practices, but they take considerably more time and resources to distribute compared to making a post on social media. According to Remind (2022):

> Twitter is best used for sharing news, tips, and emergency information that not only teachers and students but also the public should know. Instagram is best used to build up the reputation of the school, while Facebook is an ideal way to reach out to parents, publicize the school event calendar, and invite guests.

School leaders who are comfortable using social media should go beyond posting messages and images and use an even more personal approach to communicating important information. Principals can incorporate a personal touch in their communication by sending handwritten notes or personalized emails to students and their families, addressing them by name and acknowledging their unique strengths and achievements. Additionally, schools can schedule regular one-on-one meetings with families to listen to their concerns, provide individualized support, and build trusting relationships.

Video messaging is another way of providing a more personal touch that is increasingly popular with principals and school leaders. It's easy to record a selfie video right from your phone and text it or email it out to parents or teachers. It makes the message more personal, engaging, and authentic. To truly take advantage of video messaging to connect with families whose primary language is different from English, the speaker can load the video message to YouTube so parents can then click the option that allows them to hear the message in their preferred language.

You can also provide information to families in multiple formats and languages, such as written materials, audio recordings, and visual presentations. Making sure these resources are readily available in school offices, on the school website, and through digital platforms ensures easy access for all families. Principals may rely on assistance from their tech department or from their communication directors for digital inclusion by recognizing the digital divide and working to bridge it. Providing resources such as loaner devices, internet access, and digital literacy training for families who lack the necessary tools are great ways to provide support.

Offer alternative methods of communication for families with limited online access, such as phone calls or in-person meetings. Parent-teacher collaboration also establishes regular channels for communication between parents and teachers. Encouraging two-way dialogue through parent-teacher conferences, progress reports, or online platforms facilitate ongoing communication and parent involvement.

EQUITABLE ACCESS TO COMMUNICATION

When parents make a connection with a staff member who establishes trust, puts them at ease, and takes a special interest in their child, this often leads to equitable family engagement. The staff member might invite the parent to contact them in multiple ways, but most importantly, in the form that works best for the family to stay in touch. Families also want to feel that they are welcome and valued at the school. Schools accomplish this when staff members are being receptive, open, honest, caring, and flexible about communication and parent-teacher partnership efforts to support students' success (LaRocque, 2013).

> *When parents make a connection with a staff member who establishes trust, puts them at ease, and takes a special interest in their child, this often leads to equitable family engagement.*

The manner in which school staff communicates with families and the experiences families encounter significantly influence how they receive the communication. For example, when teachers personally call parents to discuss their child's progress and address concerns, it fosters positive relationships and enhances communication. On the other hand, if important information is only shared through complex online platforms without additional support, it may lead to communication breakdowns, especially for families with limited digital literacy or access to technology.

Marci McFadden (2021) emphasizes that school is one commitment out of many for busy families. Communication with the school can easily get buried among every-day obligations. If the school sends uncoordinated messages too often, families might experience message fatigue and stop paying attention. To keep families engaged, schools must be intentional and strategic while using a variety of messaging to make sure that the information does not fall on deaf ears and blind eyes. Schools must initiate, engage, and sustain communication. To do this effectively, schools can take some of the following actions.

- Provide regular updates about student progress, upcoming events, and important deadlines to help families stay informed and involved.

- Organize workshops, parent education sessions, or webinars on relevant topics to empower families with knowledge and skills to support their children's education.

- Create a user-friendly and multilingual school website to serve as a centralized hub for information, resources, and announcements.

- Encourage face-to-face interactions through parent-teacher conferences, open houses, or community events to build strong relationships and trust between families and school staff.

By adopting these approaches, schools can create a comprehensive and supportive communication ecosystem that caters to the diverse needs and preferences of families.

SENSITIVITY TO CULTURAL DIFFERENCES

Promoting equity in family engagement also entails being aware of and sensitive to cultural differences and overcoming difficulties and barriers to effective communication. School leaders experience greater levels of successful communication when forecasting and embracing cultural values different from their own. "This requires self-awareness of one's own culture and values and understanding how various factors influence interpersonal dynamics and experiences" (Olsen, Bhattacharya, & Scharf, 2006). Equitable family engagement means families from all different cultures and backgrounds are positively involved in their children's education; engagement is equitable, inclusive, accessible, and culturally competent. Even though the field of research on general family engagement is expansive, there is still a need among schools and districts about how to engage all families equitably (McFadden, 2021).

Communicating With Staff

Communicating with staff in the manner they prefer is not always easy. It may require extra effort to be truly equitable. But such effort is worth it. As the saying goes, "You only get out what you put in." Since you want the maximum effort from your staff, you must put in maximum effort to communicate with them effectively. This applies to information regarding tasks, initiatives, due dates, professional responsibilities, districtwide updates, and any other message that an administrator must convey.

> *Since you want the maximum effort from your staff, you must put in maximum effort to communicate with them effectively.*

Research shows that being clear and concise is a best practice when principals are communicating with staff. According to Megan Doyle (2021), good verbal communication means saying just enough. Not too much and not too little. Quality over quantity takes precedence in communicating with staff, as getting your message across with fewer words is better received and easier understood. Whether communicating in a memorandum, an email, or a one-on-one conversation, or speaking to the entire staff at once, be concise and make your point so you don't lose your audience. In the article "Top 10 Communication Skills," Irrfan Sk Md (2015) writes that to speak effectively, you should "say what you want to say clearly and directly, whether you're speaking to someone in person, on the phone, or via email. If you ramble on, your listener will tune you out."

Overly verbose messaging from principals is muddled messaging, and the result may be misunderstanding among your staff. In conversation, principals should be aware of their body language and the recipient's. Nonverbal cues will tell you how a person is really feeling and whether they are tuned in. A principal's body language—eye contact, hand gestures, tone of voice—all affect the message the principal is trying to convey: "Through a friendly tone, a personal question, or simply a smile, you will encourage your co-workers to engage in open and honest communication with you" (Doyle, 2021). This is also the case when using written communication. Written communication doesn't leave the receiver the luxury to ask for clarification or read the body language of the transmitter. So, principals must write with this in mind to ensure the staff are not offended and to leave little chance that the wrong message is received.

Principals should take every opportunity to personalize emails to teachers and staff. A short "Good morning, I hope you are having a great week" at the start of an email can personalize a message and make the recipient feel more appreciated. State the topic of a memorandum or email and include only information about that topic in the email or document. Staff can become confused about the importance of issues if the writer tries to make too many points in written communication.

Folwell Dunbar (2016) puts it like this: "When it comes to written documents, less is not more, and more is not necessarily better. It needs to be systematic, intentional, and transparent." Teachers need more time and want to save time whenever possible. So, when there is a need to issue memorandums to my staff or letters home to parents, I employ the same adage as when I have to get a workout in and I'm short on time: "Half as long, twice as strong!"

Finally, learn the communication style and mode preferences of staff members, and you will be a step ahead. Staff members need to feel heard and valued to welcome change. Change without consultation is like expecting a transmission to perform well without oil. Effective communication from principals to staff primes motivation and builds staff culture, while poor communication creates dissatisfaction (Tyler, 2016). When implementing new programs or initiatives, teachers' voices disappear without established relationships and effective communication (Safir, 2017).

What It Looks Like in the Real World

In this section, I share my personal experiences, including mistakes and triumphs I have had as a principal, in an effort to help other school leaders gain strategies to promote equitable communication within their own schools. Effective communication is vital for fostering strong connections between families, staff, and the broader school community. By implementing these strategies, school leaders can ensure that communication with families is inclusive, responsive, and takes into account the diverse needs and backgrounds of students and their families.

Equitable communication among principals and their staff is crucial for building a positive and collaborative school culture. I will share how I implemented proactive steps as school principal to improve overall equitable communication, creating an environment where students' and parents' voices were heard, valued, and actively included in the school's communication.

Communicating Equitably With Families

At the school where I worked as principal, 57.3 percent of my students were Hispanic, and 37.4 percent were Black. English learners (ELs) accounted for 38 percent, and 99 percent were from low-income families (Illinois School Report Card, 2020–2021). Many of my Hispanic students' parents did not speak English and preferred to communicate in Spanish. Most of my students' parents worked and were very busy. But this did not mean that they were not engaged because most families were very active and hands-on in their children's education. My staff needed to communicate effectively *and* efficiently, with user-friendly messaging that met parents where they lived.

I became aware of the importance of equitable communication early, during my first year of being a principal. During my first open house, families filled the gym as they waited for the program to start. They were excited to visit their children's classrooms and meet their teachers. But before that portion of the program started, we wanted to provide them with general information about the school, including policies, procedures, curriculum, and expectations. I also wanted to introduce myself as the new principal, along with my teachers and staff. I eagerly grabbed the microphone and began speaking.

I felt very comfortable speaking at programs like this, and I understood the effectiveness of using humor to connect with the audience. I walked out in front of about five hundred people, introduced myself as the new principal, and told a joke, fully expecting a big laugh from the entire crowd. However, only about a third of the audience responded. They laughed hysterically, while two-thirds of the audience just stared back at me, puzzled. The problem was not that they didn't understand the joke, but that they did not understand English! I knew then that I was in trouble.

As I scanned the audience, feeling embarrassed and unsure how to move forward because I did not speak Spanish, I felt a tap on the back of my shoulder. My reading interventionist whispered in my ear, "Dr. Parker, I will interpret." As she took the microphone and repeated in Spanish everything that I had said in English, the previously silent two-thirds of the gym erupted in laughter. Her interpreting skills saved the day.

Later that evening, she teased me. "Dr. Parker, your joke is lame," she said. "I used one of my own jokes that I know Mexican people can relate to!" She then told me that I had to buy her lunch for the rest of the week.

You would think that I had learned my lesson then, but it took one more incident for it to stick. A few days after our open house, a parent came in to see me. She had a concern to discuss, and I quickly learned that she did not speak English. My bilingual secretary was out for lunch, and my hero reading interventionist was in a group meeting. Both my emerging English learners' mathematics and reading teachers also were busy instructing their classes. So, I asked my other secretary to please hunt down another bilingual staff member to interpret for the parent. The secretary looked at me, paused, and said, "Dr. Parker, you are the one who needs an interpreter, not the parent," she said. "Spanish is the dominant language spoken around here."

That was it. I was the one who was disadvantaged because of my lack of Spanish proficiency. I recognized how that could be viewed as, frankly, culturally insensitive. That day I vowed to start learning Spanish so I could communicate more effectively with EL students, their parents, and members of my school community. I have since learned *un poquito de español*, but trust me, I still have a long way to go. The moral of the story is that a school community should not be left in a communications quagmire based on the primary language of school leadership. Instead, great school leaders will "flush their transmissions," adjusting communications as necessary for educational equity.

After that, we began issuing surveys at the beginning of each school year, asking parents how they preferred to receive information from the school. A high percentage responded that they preferred to communicate through texts and letters sent home. We sent letters to parents with English on one side and Spanish on the other.

> **Great school leaders will "flush their transmissions," adjusting communications as necessary for educational equity.**

Fortunately for me, one of my two secretaries was bilingual, quickly translating any memo I gave her. But if you lack this luxury, you can use translation tools such as Google Translate (n.d.) to translate your document:

1. In your browser, go to Google Translate (https://translate.google.com).
2. At the top, click Documents.
3. Choose the languages to translate to and from.
4. Click Browse Your Computer.
5. Select the file you want to translate.
6. Click Translate and wait for the document to finish translating.

We established a goal of communicating information about upcoming events at least one month in advance and provided reminders throughout the month leading up to the event. In addition to sending flyers home, we used a messenger app that reached parents at the phone numbers we had on file. Voice and text messages in English and Spanish can be sent through this system. We also sent our regular email blasts in English and Spanish. Teachers became comfortable using parent communication apps like Class Dojo (www.classdojo.com) and Remind (www.remind.com). Non-Spanish-speaking staff collaborated with my secretary and other bilingual staff when they needed assistance in communicating with parents on the phone. This is another advantage of having a diverse staff, as discussed in chapter 5 (page 101).

Communicating Equitably With Staff

Not only did I practice equity with family communications, I also practiced equity when communicating with teachers and staff. Fortunately, my school had a diverse staff who also had communication preferences, ranging from written documents and memorandums, emails, texts, phone calls, large-group staff meetings, small-group collaborative meetings, and one-on-one conversations in classrooms and the principal's office, to name a few. Great communication starts with respect and positive relationships, as stated in chapter 2 (page 37). Because I had strong relationships with staff members, I knew their individual communication preferences.

Principals and administrators who do their utmost to ensure they get to know staff professionally and personally have greater success in establishing trust. In his book *The 3 Ships: Relationships, Leadership and Partnerships*, Randy L. Russell (2020) writes, "Trust and communication are building blocks for any great relationship. Trust and communication contribute to strong relationships with family, friends, and colleagues. When we are in 'sync' with one another, the relationship positively impacts all of those involved" (p. 19).

> **Principals and administrators who do their utmost to ensure they get to know staff professionally and personally have greater success in establishing trust.**

During any interactions with staff, I always asked them how they were doing and how things were going in both their personal and professional lives. This is great practice before individual meetings, collaborative team meetings, staff meetings, and even before pre-observation and post-observation meetings. Asking someone if they are OK, how they are feeling, and how their day is going are great icebreakers that lead to productive conversations. But sometimes, in the daily rush of things, these pleasantries may go by the wayside. What a mistake, as an abrupt start to a meeting sets a cold tone that is not conducive to a sincere exchange.

In the beginning, as they were still getting to know me, most of my staff would just respond, "I'm fine," when I asked how they were doing. I learned from working with both children and adults that F.I.N.E. is an acronym for "feelings inside not expressed." Effective leaders have great discernment and can sense when things aren't really fine, but they may not be able to get to the root of the problem unless they use their interpersonal skills and spend the time necessary to help staff members open up. Often, I'd look them in the eye and say, "That's good. Feel free to see me when you are comfortable discussing what's really going on." Again, this is far more readily accomplished in scenarios featuring mutual respect, trust, and open lines of communication. As time passes and positive relationships develop, conversations naturally flow more freely.

With the passage of time, staff members engaged with me as often as I engaged with them. Meaningful personal and professional conversations became the norm, whether in my office or in their classroom. Comfort and sharing levels grew to the point where I kept tissue boxes at the ready in my office. I normally had them on hand for parents and students who might be in my office during a time of crisis or for the occasionally emotionally raw parent-teacher conference. Staff members, too, can be emotionally vulnerable when sharing what's really going on in their lives, and sometimes, they need a tissue as well.

It should go without saying, but professionalism must be maintained even as principal-teacher relationships grow and communication channels widen. It is a myth that a leader cannot be personal and professional at the same time. Principals should convey professionalism steadily through body language as well as in all verbal and written communications. A mentor once told me, "If it's not in writing, it wasn't said." Heed this advice. Ensure that formal communication is put in memorandum form and placed in staff mailboxes as well as in their email inboxes.

Take the time at staff meetings to do personal and emotional check-ins before getting to the formal portion of the agenda. At the beginning of each school year, inform staff that meetings are more than just a one-way information street. There are opportunities for relationship building, celebrating each other's professional accomplishments and personal milestones, collaborating, and personal and professional growth. When sharing information, expectations, professional responsibilities, and upcoming events, remind them that you encourage open dialogue. Make time for and encourage staff to ask questions during staff meetings. This is a great chance for them to gain clarification and share their thoughts, feelings, and responses. Establishing an atmosphere of trust and reserving time during staff meetings for this dialogue to occur leads to optimal and equitable communication.

These practices also will lead to better relationships, which are essential because strong leaders have strong relationships, and strong relationships correlate with effective communication skills. According to Tracey Salamondra (2021), veteran high school social studies and mathematics educator, "Excellence in education stems from high-quality stakeholder relationships, and communication is the key to building these relationships. Trust is essential to build strong relationships among stakeholders" (p. 25). For school leaders to gain the trust of those they serve, they must be open, honest, and willing to share their concerns and listen to the concerns of their learning community. No one likes being told that they are on a "need-to-know basis." This makes people feel less valued and unimportant, or worse, that their feelings don't matter.

Salamondra (2021) continues that "clarity of intent increases transparency, and active listening supports people to process feedback and implement changes for growth. These essential characteristics build the strong stakeholder relationships necessary for productive schools focused on improvement" (p. 25). This is vital for school leaders to consider while transmitting information and enhancing equity by creating partnerships with staff and other stakeholders.

Taking Action to Improve Equitable Communication

It is crucial for schools to ensure equitable communication with students, families, and the community—it promotes meaningful engagement and involvement, fostering a sense of belonging and empowerment. Equitable communication ensures that information, resources, and opportunities are accessible to all, addressing disparities and promoting fair educational outcomes for every student. Consider taking some of the following action steps to improve equitable communication with families, staff, and other stakeholders.

ACTION 1:   **Make the first contact.** Have teachers reach out to parents when they know which students will be in their classes for the year. An email or text provides parents and teachers an opportunity to meet one another. Parents gain peace of mind knowing they can communicate with their child's teacher (Gonsalo, 2021). Principals should also send a letter to parents in advance of the upcoming school year that contains information about the school's processes and procedures and how parents can get in touch with you. The letter should be provided in the different languages spoken in students' homes.

ACTION 2:   **Use instant chat applications.** Schools with a desire to improve parent engagement and strengthen their communication use school communication software with an instant chat feature. This enables parents and teachers to send direct messages and discuss school-related issues privately. Teachers can use these features to engage parents and keep them updated about their children's education (Gonsalo, 2021).

ACTION 3:   **Plan school events and awards.** School administrations can plan events, so parents, teachers, and students can connect. This provides opportunities for principals to create positive energy and enjoyable times for students and parents (Gonsalo, 2021).

ACTION 4:   **Have an interpreter ready.** When holding family conferences, have an interpreter available to translate for families. Also, have translators available at school events like family reading and mathematics night or open house. This demonstrates that you are sensitive to students' families' needs and are happy to accommodate them.

Conclusion

Just as a failing car transmission may whine, grind, or slip out of gear, poor communication can bring your school's progress to a clanking halt. Maintenance is key in either situation. It's my experience-based hope and belief that by implementing the suggestions in this chapter, you will enjoy deep and meaningful communication with school staff and stakeholders, students, and families as you continue to be the driving force for equity at your school.

Questions for Reflection

Working individually or with a collaborative group, ask yourself the following reflective questions.

1. What are the most important topics you, as a school leader, should communicate to parents, students, and community members?

2. How can you ensure that you are communicating in a way that is accessible to all members of the school community, including those with disabilities?

3. Describe a situation in which transparency may not be the most effective approach when communicating with parents, students, and community members.

4. What kind of feedback should you seek from parents, students, and community members when making decisions that impact the school?

5. What are your strengths and weaknesses in seeking input from staff, and what perceptions may exist about how well you listen to staff and consider their suggestions and feedback?

6. What should you consider when attempting to communicate important information to parents, students, and community members who do not speak the same language?

School Communication Survey

For each item, circle the response that best describes the communication approach at your school.

1. I understand the importance of communication, and I communicate very often.

1	2	3	4	5
Strongly disagree	Disagree	Neutral	Agree	Strongly agree

2. My school reviews its communications strategies and ideas and utilizes new technology.

1	2	3	4	5
Strongly disagree	Disagree	Neutral	Agree	Strongly agree

3. I consider the barriers that might exist in communication with students' parents and the community I serve.

1	2	3	4	5
Strongly disagree	Disagree	Neutral	Agree	Strongly agree

4. The school's communication strategies contribute to increasing student achievement.

1	2	3	4	5
Strongly disagree	Disagree	Neutral	Agree	Strongly agree

5. My school's communication strategies are equitable, and family engagement includes acknowledging and navigating cultural differences through communication and sensitivity.

1	2	3	4	5
Strongly disagree	Disagree	Neutral	Agree	Strongly agree

6. I leverage different platforms of communication to expand my reach and connect with families and community members that may have been unintentionally left out of the loop.

1	2	3	4	5
Strongly disagree	Disagree	Neutral	Agree	Strongly agree

7. My staff and I engage families and students through SMS messaging, email blasts, and social media updates several times per month.

1	2	3	4	5
Strongly disagree	Disagree	Neutral	Agree	Strongly agree

8. I try to ensure stakeholders get the facts from me first rather than through secondhand means or rumors.

1	2	3	4	5
Strongly disagree	Disagree	Neutral	Agree	Strongly agree

9. My staff feel heard and valued, and I communicate with them effectively to build a strong school culture.

1	2	3	4	5
Strongly disagree	Disagree	Neutral	Agree	Strongly agree

10. I take every opportunity to personalize emails to teachers and staff to strengthen relationships.

1	2	3	4	5
Strongly disagree	Disagree	Neutral	Agree	Strongly agree

11. My emails and memorandums to staff are systematic, intentional, and transparent.

1	2	3	4	5
Strongly disagree	Disagree	Neutral	Agree	Strongly agree

12. I send communications in the language that accommodates students' families in both written and spoken form.

1	2	3	4	5
Strongly disagree	Disagree	Neutral	Agree	Strongly agree

13. I am accessible and have systems in place that allow for two-way communication.

1	2	3	4	5
Strongly disagree	Disagree	Neutral	Agree	Strongly agree

14. Communication is a skill I use not only to provide information but also to build stronger relationships.

1	2	3	4	5
Strongly disagree	Disagree	Neutral	Agree	Strongly agree

Survey Results:

14–25	Assess what is not working and prioritize adopting an effective communication plan.
26–37	Work with staff to derive an effective communication plan.
38–49	Good, but you should consider different communication strategies you might employ.
50–61	Keep up the good work communicating with the school community.
62–70	You do an excellent job of communicating with the school community.

CHAPTER 9

IMPLEMENTING CULTURALLY RESPONSIVE PRACTICES

Responsive cars react quickly to driver inputs; the driver and the car connect. In education, responsive teachers readily adjust instructional methods based on how their students best absorb course material. They are adept at reading behavioral cues and body language. Culturally responsive educators meld students' cultures, languages, and life experiences with the subjects and topics covered in the classroom. Like a responsive car that readily adapts to its terrain, culturally responsive educators and school leaders form the connections that help students access rigorous curriculum and develop higher-level academic skills. After all, the classroom is where the "rubber meets the road."

WHEN MY FATHER retired, he decided to buy a new car as a retirement gift for himself. He asked me and my younger brother to accompany him to several dealerships for test drives. Together, we test drove several Cadillac CT4s and CT5s. My father liked the feel of the Cadillacs and their luxury options, but he still wanted to check out the Lucerne. So off we went to the Buick dealership to test drive the Lucerne.

"This is the one!" my dad exclaimed within thirty seconds of pulling off the lot.

"What makes you so sure?" I asked him.

"I feel one with this car," he said. "It's like the car knows what I'm thinking." To my dad, the Lucerne knew whether he wanted to speed up or slow down, or even whether he wanted to maneuver in traffic. "Before we made that last turn, it was going into the turn as I was thinking about it," he said. "This car is so responsive!"

Responsive cars react quickly and seamlessly to a driver's inputs. My dad was a keen driver and found delight in the Buick Lucerne because of its responsiveness and handling. And so, he bought it.

Similarly, effective school leaders must be responsive to the school culture and the students and staff they serve. And they must ensure teachers promote equity through culturally responsive teaching. *Culturally responsive teaching* is an educational approach that recognizes the diverse cultural backgrounds, experiences, and perspectives of students. Culturally responsive teaching entails using students' customs, characteristics, experience, and perspectives as tools for better classroom instruction. The term was coined by researcher Geneva Gay in 2000, who wrote that "when academic knowledge and skills are situated within the lived experiences and frames of reference for students, they are more personally meaningful, have higher interest appeal, and are learned more easily and thoroughly" (as cited in Will & Najarro, 2022). It involves adapting instructional strategies, curriculum, and classroom environments to reflect students' cultural identities and creating inclusive learning spaces.

It is important for school leaders to promote culturally responsive teaching because it supports positive academic and social-emotional outcomes for all students. By acknowledging and valuing students' cultural identities, school leaders foster a sense of belonging, build stronger relationships, and promote equity in education. Culturally responsive teaching also enhances student engagement, motivation, and academic achievement by connecting curriculum content to students' lived experiences, promoting cultural competency, and empowering students to express themselves authentically (Will & Najarro, 2022).

Principals play a crucial role in promoting culturally responsive teaching within their schools. By doing so, they create an inclusive and supportive educational environment that benefits all students, especially those from diverse backgrounds. Principals should emphasize the importance of culturally responsive teaching to their staff by highlighting the positive impact it has on student engagement, achievement, and overall well-being. They can share research, case studies, and success stories that demonstrate the effectiveness of this approach. Additionally, principals can provide professional development opportunities and resources to help teachers deepen their understanding of cultural diversity, develop their cultural competency, and enhance their instructional practices.

To encourage teachers to engage in culturally responsive teaching practices, principals need to foster a supportive and collaborative school culture. They can encourage open dialogue and promote ongoing discussions about culturally responsive practices, encouraging teachers to share their experiences, challenges, and successes. Principals should also establish a feedback system that allows teachers to receive constructive input and support as they implement culturally responsive strategies. By modeling culturally responsive practices themselves, principals can lead by example and show teachers the importance of embracing and honoring cultural diversity in the classroom. Ultimately, principals should provide the necessary resources, time, and support for teachers to develop and implement culturally responsive teaching practices, ensuring that all students have equal opportunities to succeed and thrive academically and socially.

Good teachers are like cars in the sense that their responsiveness to learners' needs will go a long way toward students' ultimate success or failure. Students have more positive feelings about learning when they feel connected—both to their instructor and to the course material. Teachers are better at being responsive to learners when they know about students' lives, in and out of school. As the student population continues to diversify, teachers must be culturally responsive to increase their effectiveness on student growth.

> *Good teachers are like cars in the sense that their responsiveness to learners' needs will go a long way toward students' ultimate success or failure.*

According to Understood Education Team (2022), *culturally responsive teaching* is "a research-based approach to teaching that connects students' cultures, languages, and life experiences with what they learn in school. These connections help students access rigorous curriculum and develop higher-level academic skills." This form of equitable instruction gives each student what they need to grow academically by relating academic content to students' cultures and experiences, helping them better grasp the material and its relevance to their lives.

This chapter explores the topic of culturally responsive teaching, examining its significance and practical implications within the classroom as it relates to education equity. It examines how culturally responsive teaching fosters strong relationships between teachers and students, and emphasizes the importance of teachers critically examining their own beliefs and biases to create an inclusive learning environment. It also discusses the benefits of including diverse texts in the curriculum, promoting representation and offering students a broader perspective of the world. Lastly, this chapter explores the role of high expectations in culturally responsive teaching, stressing the importance of educators setting challenging goals for *all* students to support their ongoing academic success.

What the Research Says

This section explores the intricacies of practicing culturally responsive practices, illuminating the profound impact it has on dismantling systemic inequities and nurturing students' identities and aspirations. It examines the impact of teacher-student relationships and teacher beliefs and biases, recognizing their influence on classroom dynamics and the potential barriers they create. By engaging in reflective practices, educators can confront and transcend their biases, thus fostering inclusive spaces where all students thrive. Additionally, it explores the significance of incorporating diverse texts and classroom materials, ensuring representation and amplification of voices that have historically been marginalized. Finally, it unpacks the profound impact of expectations, both high and low, on students' academic and social trajectories, and the imperative role educators play in fostering a growth mindset and equitable opportunities.

Building Positive Relationships With Students

In my book *Building Bridges* (Parker, 2019), I talk about the importance of building relationships with students and the positive impact it has on student learning.

Teachers who connect with their students can use what they learn about them to make content relevant. Sara Rimm-Kaufman and Lia Sandilos (2015) explain it this way:

> Students who have close, positive, and supportive relationships with their teachers will attain higher levels of achievement than those with more conflict-riddled relationships. Positive teacher-student relationships draw students into the process of learning and promote their desire to achieve, assuming that the content and material of the class is engaging, age-appropriate and well matched to the student's skills.

Effective teachers who have positive, supportive relationships with students should have more success in connecting their lessons to students' culture and interests. Principals can play a pivotal role in supporting teachers in building positive relationships with students by taking some of the following actions.

- Provide professional development opportunities focused on cultural competency, awareness, and strategies for building relationships with diverse student populations. This may include workshops, guest speakers, or training sessions led by experts in the field.

- Facilitate collaboration among teachers, creating spaces for sharing best practices and experiences related to culturally responsive teaching. This can involve regular collaborative meetings and team-building activities dedicated to exploring effective strategies for building positive relationships with students from diverse cultural backgrounds.

- Allocate resources and support systems to help teachers incorporate culturally responsive practices into their instruction. This could involve providing access to diverse and inclusive instructional materials, culturally relevant resources, and technology tools that facilitate differentiated instruction.

- Advocate for a curriculum that reflects the diversity of the student body, ensuring that students see themselves represented in the learning materials.

- Foster a supportive and inclusive school climate where teachers feel empowered to take risks and experiment with new approaches to building relationships. Encourage teachers to reflect on their own beliefs and biases, provide constructive feedback, and engage in ongoing professional growth in culturally responsive teaching.

Practicing Culturally Responsive Teaching

Gloria Ladson-Billings (2014) states that culturally responsive teaching is an approach that empowers students intellectually, socially, emotionally, and politically by using cultural referents to grow knowledge, skills, and attitudes; therefore, connecting content to students' culture and interests makes content more engaging. Geneva Gay (2010) describes culturally responsive teaching as using diverse students' cultural knowledge, prior experiences, frames of reference, and learning styles to make lessons more relevant and effective for learners. Students engage with academic content if it piques their interests, it is authentic to what they experience in real life, and they can perceive it from their own perspective. Culturally responsive teaching is not meant to replace traditional best practices in instruction, but it will amplify comprehension and retention.

High-quality instruction should be appropriate to students' educational levels. It should also offer opportunities for students to think, analyze, and use feedback to effectively guide their thinking and extend prior knowledge (Rimm-Kaufman & Sandilos, 2015). Culturally responsive teaching uses best practices and strategies that support a constructivist view of knowledge, teaching, and learning. The constructivist view assists students in accruing knowledge, building on their personal and cultural strengths, and examines the curriculum from multiple perspectives, which creates an inclusive classroom environment (Krasnoff, 2016). In this sense, culturally responsive teaching does exactly what traditional best practices and evidence-based research tells us to do—scaffold and build on students' prior knowledge.

The most effective teachers adjust their teaching to their students' learning styles—this is just one example of equity in education. Some students are auditory learners, who process information aloud and ask questions. Some are visual learners who access learning through pictures, illustrations, and graphics. Tactile learners act out concepts to make sense of them, and use models, experiments, games, and real-world experiences to gather information. Teachers can also adapt their teaching style to meet students' learning styles, providing the support students need to learn (Western Governors University, 2021). They may not be labeled as culturally responsive teaching methods, but they are methods that benefit *all* learners, making them equitable teaching practices.

The Venn diagram in figure 9.1 shows how many strategies associated as best practices of teaching are also the same as culturally responsive teaching.

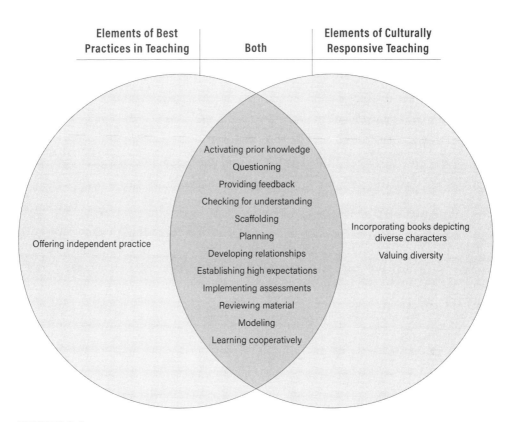

FIGURE 9.1: Best practices for teaching versus culturally responsive teaching.

Culturally responsive teaching is proactive; it is designed to prevent students from falling behind, slipping below grade level, and experiencing deficits in instruction. Too often, educators take reactive measures like implementing response to intervention (RTI), multitiered system of supports (MTSS), and individualized education programs (IEPs), and place students in special education programs at the expense of maintaining all students' access to core grade- and course-level instruction.

As RTI experts Austin Buffum, Mike Mattos, and Janet Malone (2018) emphasize, students at higher intervention levels should still *never* lose access to this instruction. It's as if administrators and teachers are eating soup with a fork instead of a spoon. By receiving interventions at the expense of access to core grade- and course-level instruction, students are *more* likely to slip through the cracks (Buffum et al., 2018). It's time to proactively close the achievement gap by using equitable teaching practices, culturally responsive teaching practices, and targeting both core instruction and necessary interventions in ways that accelerate student learning (Kramer & Schuhl, 2023).

Teaching in a way that students learn and presenting them with material in a format they are familiar with promotes learning by leveraging their prior knowledge, experiences, and cultural backgrounds. When teachers align their instructional methods and materials to students' existing knowledge and cultural contexts, it enhances engagement and comprehension. It allows students to access the content through channels that are comfortable and familiar to them. This personalized approach caters to diverse learning styles and ensures that all students have equitable opportunities to learn and succeed. The Western Governors University (2021) writes:

> Equity in education is seen when students from different races and ethnic groups can see examples of people of their race and community around them in the classroom. History lessons, story problems, and books that are inclusive and show all different types of people are key to helping students of different races feel that equity in the classroom. Equity in education aims to provide equal opportunity to all students to develop valuable skills and knowledge that help them live a full life and contribute to society.

Note that some researchers suggest that culturally responsive teaching is politically divisive. Wen-Chia Chang and Kara Mitchell Viesca (2022) explain that culturally responsive teaching assumes the understanding that teaching itself is inherently complex and never detached from sociopolitical issues. It is both practical and political. Culturally responsive teachers do not tell students what to think; they simply encourage academic success as well as cultural competence while building students' capacity to think critically about issues and injustices that affect their lives and communities.

Studies also have noted that both White teachers and teachers of color require preservice preparation to work with diverse student populations, even though they might possess varied levels of commitment to serving diverse student populations equitably and confronting racism and other forms of institutional oppression (Picower, 2009; Sleeter, 2008).

Considering Teacher Beliefs and Biases

Teachers who hold cultural biases, whether conscious or unconscious, and do not believe in every student's ability to succeed will not work at their full capacity to help marginalized students reach their full potential. Teachers' beliefs about their students often dictate their actions as teachers. If a teacher truly believes their students can achieve at high levels, they invest more time, energy, and effort in planning, instructional delivery, and a positive attitude. On the flip side, if a teacher does not believe that their students can achieve at high levels, they tell themselves, "What's the use?

Why put all this effort into the lesson if these students can't learn it?" If students sense that their teacher does not believe in them, they may fall victim to a negative pattern of thinking that says, "If my teacher doesn't care, then why should I? If they don't believe I can learn, then maybe I can't."

In *Culturally Responsive Teaching: A Guide to Evidence-Based Practices for Teaching All Students Equitably*, Basha Krasnoff (2016) advises teachers who truly pursue educational equity that, in order to build a genuine community of learners, "[they] must believe in the intellectual potential of all students and unequivocally accept responsibility to assist its realization without ignoring, demeaning, or neglecting students' ethnic and cultural identities" (p. 9). Diverse students need a base of cultural validation and strength to experience academic success. Students can learn about their cultural heritages and positive ethnic identity along with mathematics, science, reading, critical thinking, activism, and the positive contributions made by members of their community (Krassnoff, 2016). As students learn and make connections, they also gain a sense of pride for their own culture and understand the importance of diversity and inclusion by appreciating the accomplishments and contributions from cultures other than their own.

Culturally responsive teachers believe that regardless of cultural or linguistic background, ability, or disability, each student has the potential to learn. Many students stop trying because of a history of failure. Perhaps they had teachers who did not believe in them or who failed to push them to try harder. Krasnoff (2016) writes that students who are "disenchanted by low-level or irrelevant curriculum work just hard enough to get by. Teachers have a responsibility to continually motivate all students by reminding them that they are capable and by providing them with a challenging and meaningful curriculum" (p. 20).

Many marginalized students lack hope. They don't believe that they can live a good life and foresee no version of success within their reach. Culturally responsive teachers understand the environments in which their students live and understand the toll of personal, family, and community issues they might face. They are in tune with students' emotions and know well the signs of depression and fatigue. Upon noticing the related attitudes or behaviors, these teachers encourage students to shift their thinking by providing positive affirmations, expressing belief in them, and reinforcing the importance of students finding that same belief in themselves. To be effective, teachers must be aware of the challenges posed by poverty, racism, food insecurity, and language barriers, and recognize how to frame such circumstances as being no fault of the students themselves.

Students who believe in their futures and trust that there are no limits to what they can be or accomplish are much further along the road to their loftiest dream destination. It's fitting symbolism for a chief tenet of culturally responsive teaching, which is to continually challenge students to strive for excellence—and to believe they are capable of achieving it.

Including Diverse Texts and Classroom Materials

Encouraging students to learn about their own and others' cultures is part of culturally responsive teaching. There are many ways to provide this support for marginalized students. You can begin by offering diverse texts and learning materials in the classroom. Rudine Sims Bishop (2015), known as the mother of multicultural literature, published an essay about the significance of giving young students books that reflect the diverse society and multicultural world they live in. She coined the phrase "windows, mirrors, and sliding glass doors." The phrase is used to explain how children see themselves in books they read and how books also serve as windows that give readers a look into the lives and experiences of others (Potter, 2019).

When readers can walk into a story (as if through a sliding glass door), they become part of the author's world, fully immersed in another's experience. "Approaching children's stories through the lens of windows, mirrors, and sliding glass doors prioritizes diversity, honors many cultures, and promotes empathy" (Strobbe, 2021). Literature is a powerful tool in helping students develop empathy and compassion. As Bishop (2015) explains, "When there are enough books available that can act as both mirrors and windows for all our children, they will see we can celebrate both our differences and our similarities" (p. 2).

In *There's More to the Story*, Gwendolyn Cartledge, Amanda L. Yurick, and Alana Oif Telesman (2022) write, "Students who come from diverse backgrounds need to find books that represent themselves and others as commonplace in their environment, not the exception" (p. 3). They continue, "Children who read books that reflect people who look like them with shared language and experiences are undoubtedly empowered, resulting from self-affirmations and connections with others" (p. 26). Supporting this concept, clinical psychologist Beverly Daniel Tatum (2017) emphasizes that the use of diverse children's books and other media can help children develop a critical consciousness regarding racism, sexism, and classism, even from the earliest ages.

Having more culturally rich texts is more inclusive, making coursework more meaningful to diverse student populations. In my school, teachers decided on content materials and readings to use in the classroom to reflect the diversity of students in the school. Meanwhile, I maintained a strong relationship with a book salesperson who brought in culturally rich texts, which I purchased based on teacher recommendations. They used diverse novel sets to teach reading and social studies, and my librarian consulted with the book salesperson to get her bookcases filled with culturally diverse texts that students enjoyed reading.

Understanding the Impact of High and Low Expectations

Culturally responsive teachers understand the importance of acknowledging how their students feel. They counsel students to keep a positive mindset and remind them that continually working and striving toward improvement will lead to a better life. They let students know that they are there to support them and equip them with the academic and social-emotional skills they need to build students' self-esteem and determination.

> **Culturally responsive teachers understand the importance of acknowledging how their students feel.**

UCLA professor Tyrone Howard (2020) asserts that all educators must have high expectations for every student, accompanied by a set of positive attitudes about them. His work is inspired by Zaretta Hammond (2015) and the research discussed in her book *Culturally Responsive Teaching and the Brain*. She defines a "warm demander" in a similar fashion to what many of us understand as "tough love." In this context, her explanation of warm demanders are teachers who understand what students have going on in their personal lives and are supportive and warm toward them. However, they do not let the students off the hook when it comes to working hard academically and behaviorally to meet high expectations and standards. Teachers must offer concrete guidance and support so students can meet high standards, usually in the form of corrective feedback, opportunities for information processing, and culturally relevant meaning making.

In his article "Can Teachers Be Warm Demanders During the Pandemic?," Chris Kubic (2021) warns that "educators must ensure they can meet the warm component before being a demander and need to reconsider what exactly they're demanding." Being a warm demander is part of a strategy that starts with teachers making an agreement with students and establishing themselves as an ally. *This is critical.* Without the agreement, teachers can't be warm demanders. They are just demanders. In the absence of a teacher-student relationship and context to establish the warmth, in Hammond's words, "I haven't earned the right to demand" (Kubic, 2021). Without the relationship, barriers exist, and the student is too far from the teacher to feel their warmth. Demanding without the warmth may cause the student to further disengage.

Teachers can be businesslike, organized, and even have effective classroom management, but without warmth, this teacher lacks the essential element to push students to their highest potential. According to Kubic (2021), "This has a chilling effect on our ability to live up to the warm part of a warm demander. Additionally, our ability to be wise demanders is in question." The concept of a warm demander is predicated on knowing what a student can do on their own and what they can do with support. Most students demonstrate perseverance, effort, respect, and a willingness to please their teacher by meeting academic goals after teachers establish warm and caring relationships with them.

Learning about students' interests, likes, dislikes, family members, and aspirations are all ways to build relationships. But some students come from a mental and emotional place that is sadly void of aspirations. In these instances, the warm, demanding teacher points out the students' positive qualities, helping them to feel valued, competent, and good about themselves. They do not allow students to continue to have low expectations for themselves. As I noted in *Building Bridges* (Parker, 2019), "To be effective, teachers must achieve awareness of the typical challenges children who suffer from trauma, loss, and attachment difficulties face" (p. 42).

The harm in having low expectations is that it hinders learning and negatively affect students' attitudes and motivation. This results in negative self-fulfilling prophecies that students already fear. Krasnoff (2016) states, "If they are to eliminate persistent disparities in student achievement, educators must consciously and consistently demonstrate the same specific, observable, and measurable behaviors and practices to all students, regardless of the students' current academic performance" (p. 4). However, when teachers demonstrate confidence in students, the students become more confident in their learning, which leads to higher achievement. Effective teachers use psychology and teaching strategies that boosts students' confidence.

Culturally responsive teachers will work on building students' confidence, which leads to building students' competence. To put it simply, especially when working with historically marginalized students, in order to build their academic achievement, teachers must first build their self-esteem. Culturally responsive teaching embodies this philosophy.

> **Culturally responsive teachers will work on building students' confidence, which leads to building students' competence.**

This corresponds with what was stated previously in this chapter: Many of the teaching practices, including ways to build students' self-esteem and motivation, are considered traditional best practices as well as culturally responsive practices. This means getting students motivated to learn, but also allowing them to shed enough stress to turn their attention to learning.

According to Hammond (2015), culturally responsive teaching is not a single, specific strategy that teachers can pick up and implement tomorrow. It involves promoting social-emotional learning, building teacher-student relationships, and motivating students. It's a framework and approach for how to teach and make changes in instruction that increase students' cognition. Culturally responsive teaching and pedagogy recognizes and appreciates diversity and inclusion by seeking ways to encourage student engagement. Maintaining a welcoming, positive, inclusive classroom where everyone feels they belong will surely enhance equity in schools.

What It Looks Like in the Real World

Many classrooms brim with students from different nationalities, cultures, beliefs, and mindsets. No wonder the spotlight is shifting toward recognizing, celebrating, and including students who may otherwise feel disconnected. When I became principal, I spoke to my staff about the importance of culturally responsive teaching and how crucial it was for teachers to build relationships with their students. After making sincere connections, teachers can put the knowledge they've gained about their students to use making content relevant. I followed six steps to lead this effort in the school.

1. Helping teachers learn relationship-building strategies
2. Facilitating culturally responsive lessons

3. Conducting bias checks

4. Engaging students' families and the community

5. Showing respect for students' cultures

6. Reinforcing confidence and belief in students

The following sections explore each of these steps in more detail.

Helping Teachers Learn Relationship-Building Strategies

During the first step, I concentrated on helping teachers learn strategies to build relationships with their students. I stressed how they must go beyond viewing it as a duty to learn the behaviors, backgrounds, and challenges our students face. It should be an educator's desire to do these things so they are better equipped to address them. I modeled icebreakers and get-to-know-you activities with my staff to help them facilitate these activities in their classrooms with students. Encouraging teachers to prioritize building relationships with students relieves some of the pressure of other tasks. They become more confident in taking time to execute this step when they are given the time and space to do so. My staff worked with me to build a special bell schedule used during the first two weeks of school to allow more time for students to get to know their teachers as well as each other.

We then built an extra forty minutes into first-period homeroom classes each Monday to sustain this relationship building throughout the year. This provided time for Monday morning meetings and student check-ins. The committee collaborated with me to shave about five minutes off every other period on Mondays to make this possible. We selected Mondays because research shows that students' traumatic experiences may spike over the weekend, and students bring that stress into the classroom first thing on Monday mornings. Maura McInerney and Amy McKlindon (2020) write:

> By understanding and responding to trauma, school administrators, teachers, and staff can help reduce its negative impact, support critical learning, and create a more positive school environment. By being sensitive to students' past and current experiences with trauma, educators can break the cycle of trauma, prevent re-traumatization, and engage a child in learning and finding success in school.

When students trust their teachers, they might share personal experiences that have deeply affected them. Having this information assists staff to better meet students' needs. In addition to breaking the ice at the beginning of each year and at Monday morning meetings, it also is essential to engage in regular check-ins with students on an ongoing basis. Sometimes during the school year, we learn that students' situations have changed. As is the case at most every school, there were students at my school who faced homelessness and had to cope with parents divorcing or remarrying, or their own life-changing circumstances (health, bullying, and so on). The more the staff learned, the better able we were to empathize and assist.

> **When students trust their teachers, they might share personal experiences that have deeply affected them. Having this information assists staff to better meet students' needs.**

Facilitating Culturally Responsive Lessons

The second step involved reviewing the curriculum and mindfully revisiting how to facilitate lessons that were culturally responsive, a critical need in our changing times. The team reviewed curriculum to ensure it didn't contain hidden forms of oppression or bias, with teachers becoming increasingly aware of how class activities offered the potential for either positive or negative impacts. As the instructional leader in the building, I was active in teacher cooperative meetings and team meetings. My assistant principals and I facilitated conversations, discussions, and professional development activities for the staff to work toward meaningful changes to incorporate culturally responsive lessons.

Let's consider the impact of these practices at a more personal level, using the example of an eighth-grade student (I'll call him DJ to protect his identity) who was the biggest student in the entire school. DJ had some emotional problems and was easily angered. His temper and his size made him a little intimidating for some of his classmates and teachers. DJ was being raised by foster parents who were hands-on and partnered with the school to keep track of his progress. They also kept DJ involved in sports. He was a standout offensive tackle on his youth football team, and I had been to several of his games during the fall to watch him play. He absolutely loved playing and watching football and learning more about the sport. DJ also had an IEP and had a difficult time understanding mathematics concepts.

One day during mathematics class, the teacher was reviewing integers. Although most of the class had demonstrated that they understood the concept of moving along the number line and adding and subtracting integers, DJ did not grasp the concept. He did not raise his hand to answer any of the teacher's questions as she checked for understanding. One of DJ's classmates, Sam (pseudonym), who had earned the reputation as the class comedian, cracked a couple of jokes about DJ not being able to respond to any of the teacher's questions. At the end of the lesson, the teacher passed out candy as a treat for students.

"I hope this is diet candy, so DJ won't gain any more weight!" Sam yelled. The class erupted in laughter, but DJ was hotter than a french fry cooking in sputtering grease. He stood up and threatened Sam, ready to fight. The teacher redirected him, but he was still very aggressive and threatening toward Sam. Security went to the class and escorted DJ to my office.

When DJ came into my office, I told him that everything was going to be all right, take a seat, practice deep breathing, and count to ten forward and backward in his head. I also gave him a bottle of water, because drinking water is a scientifically proven method to help students calm down in highly charged emotional situations (Schwartz, 2020). It does this by flushing cortisol (a stress hormone) from the system, along with other toxins. Water also reduces anxiety and improves depression. It promotes optimal functioning in the brain and body while at the same time boosting serotonin levels (Leamey, 2023). These trauma-informed actions helped DJ regulate his emotions and get in the right mental state to be able to learn.

After DJ calmed down, I asked him to tell me what happened in class. He gave me an accurate summary based on the discipline referral from his teacher. I then drew a sketch of the football field, numbering the yards from zero to fifty. I explained integers to DJ by showing how you count up on a football field from zero to fifty until you get to your own side of the fifty-yard line, and then you count down as you advance to your own end zone. I asked him to draw a marker and add or subtract numbers as he moved the marker up and down the field diagram. He did this, and I praised him every time he got it right. He told me that he now understood the concept; no one had ever explained it to him like that before.

I then asked DJ what position he played in football, and in that position, what his job was on the field. He responded that he played offensive tackle, and his job was to protect the quarterback during a passing play and block for the rusher during a running play. I said, "Excellent! Now what happens if you jump offsides or get a penalty for unnecessary roughness?"

DJ responded that they have to move backward and lose yards. I then asked him why that was problematic based on the goal of the offense.

"Because the goal of the offense is to score touchdowns and get into the end zone," he said, "and you can't do that if you are always getting penalized!" I gave him a big high five.

"You got it, li'l bro!" I told him. "Now check this out. Football is a lot like integers and a lot like life as well. Our goal for you is to graduate this year and go on to be successful in high school and college, and maybe even play in the NFL someday. But each time you lose your temper or get a discipline infraction in class, it's like a penalty, and it sets you back, keeping you further from your goal. Since you want to make it to graduation, which is like the end zone, you have to be positive and manage your emotions. On the field, you can be as assertive as a lion, but within the walls of this school, you need to be as gentle as a lamb."

"Got you, Dr. Parker!" DJ replied. Going forward, he improved at managing his behavior and did not get into any fights for the remainder of the school year. DJ successfully graduated eighth grade, and at the time of this writing, he was enjoying success as a high school student and football player.

This is an example of culturally responsive teaching and best practices of connecting content to students' prior knowledge and interests. After the incident, I used this example and modeled it for my staff at our next staff meeting, emphasizing how they could apply this form of differentiation to their own instructional practices. I remain confident that imploring and empowering teachers to draw connections to their students' cultures is the only way forward. It reinforces learning and helps students to make the connection between content and their personal life experiences (Restorative Practice Working Group, 2014).

Conducting Bias Checks

The third strategy I used with staff was to conduct bias checks. In educational settings, teacher bias (whether conscious or unconscious) is all too real, as demonstrated in a study by Seth Gershenson and Nicole Papageorge (2018). Their study suggests that teacher expectations not only project student outcomes but also influence outcomes by becoming self-fulfilling prophecies. Their research found that "the nature of White teachers' expectations places Black and other students of color at a disadvantage, citing that when projecting the likelihood of college completion, White teachers are less optimistic when the student in question is Black" (Gershenson & Papageorge, 2018). They concluded that expectation-leveling policies placing Black and other students of color on an equal footing with White students could narrow achievement gaps. (See chapter 7, page 151, to learn more about the achievement gap.)

Their study is just an example of how implicit bias exists in many forms. The Restorative Practice Working Group (2014) writes that these biases might stem from:

> Inherent world views that were indoctrinated in many of us during childhood. If a student perceives that their teacher is being unfair or that grading practices are not consistent from one student to another, the student will lose trust in the teacher. Being unaware of our biases may influence pedagogical decisions.

Implicit biases potentially contribute to flawed thinking.

Implicit biases potentially contribute to flawed thinking. Encouraging my staff to be more aware of the notion that all people have biases helped us rethink decisions and thinking processes that led to decisions we made about students. Valuing different perspectives mitigates the chances of perpetuating inequality. Teachers and school leaders can conduct occasional bias checks using some of the following approaches.

- **Reflective practices:** Engaging in regular self-reflection and introspection is essential. Teachers can consciously examine their thoughts, attitudes, and assumptions to identify any biases they may hold. Reflective practices can include journaling, participating in critical dialogues or collaborative teams, and seeking feedback from colleagues or mentors.

- **Seeking multiple perspectives:** Teachers should actively seek out and incorporate diverse perspectives in their teaching materials, resources, and classroom discussions. By intentionally exposing students to different viewpoints, cultures, and experiences, teachers can challenge their own biases and promote inclusivity and understanding. It's important to consider a variety of perspectives when planning lessons and choosing instructional materials.

- **Collaborative decision making:** Collaborative decision making with colleagues and students can help mitigate biases. Teachers might involve others in curriculum development, lesson planning, and assessment design to ensure diverse input and perspectives.

Encouraging open dialogue, respecting student voice, and valuing different ideas helps create an inclusive and equitable learning environment.

Engaging Students' Families

The fourth step in this process was to involve students' parents and the community. Engaging families in what students experience in school makes the school more culturally responsive. When parents and communities are involved, students are more likely to have better attendance, do their homework, achieve more academically, increase social skills, and have higher self-esteem (Singhal & Gulati, 2020). Tried-and-true methods of involving parents include inviting them to volunteer, keeping them abreast through effective communication, having them serve on committees, including their suggestions when making decisions, and hosting ongoing family events at the school.

Principals can host a variety of family events at school, including multicultural nights where families can share and celebrate their diverse cultural backgrounds, parent education workshops that provide resources and information on navigating the educational system, and family engagement sessions that focus on building strong school-home partnerships. By organizing these events, principals create opportunities for parents from all backgrounds to actively participate in their children's education.

Educators often make the mistake of only communicating with parents when there is a discipline issue, but who wants to hear only negative information about their child? This causes parents to do the opposite of becoming involved and leads to them avoiding contact with the school. However, the power of positive phone calls, texts, emails, and notes sent home reporting good news about students has a positive influence on parents' willingness to be more involved at their child's school. "Open and honest communication with families can lead to greater trust and develops a nurturing relationship which allows teachers to ask questions and learn more about their students and their backgrounds" (Singhal & Gulati, 2020). This gives teachers a distinct advantage of learning more about how they can support their students. This leads to the fifth and most important step.

Showing Respect for Students' Cultures

The fifth step is committing to ongoing reinforcement of and respect for students' cultures. School leaders and teachers must validate their students' cultures and make content relevant to what students experience on a daily basis. Principals can implement several practical ideas, such as the following.

- Host cultural celebrations and events that highlight and honor students' diverse backgrounds. This can include organizing cultural festivals, heritage months, or assemblies where students can share their traditions, music, dances, and cuisines.

- Display diverse artwork, flags, and artifacts from different cultures throughout the school building.

- Encourage teachers to incorporate culturally diverse literature, resources, and examples into the curriculum to provide students with a well-rounded and inclusive educational experience.

- Create opportunities for cross-cultural interactions and dialogue. This can be done through activities such as cultural exchange programs, buddy systems, or peer-mentoring initiatives that foster connections and understanding among students from various cultural backgrounds.

- Establish advisory committees or student councils that represent the diverse voices within the student body, ensuring decisions are made with a comprehensive understanding of students' needs and perspectives.

Overall, by embracing and celebrating students' cultures, principals demonstrate their commitment to equity and inclusivity.

When I deliver professional development to schools, the best compliments I get are when teachers tell me that I was engaging and say they can take what I taught them and apply it the very next day. *They prefer learning practical skills that they can see themselves implementing successfully.* This is also true for students. "By valuing each student's culture, we contribute to their self-concept, which in turn influences their academic success" (Singhal & Gulati, 2020). This includes everything from interactions to instructional choices. Students show up to class with beliefs and characteristics that make them unique. Along with these are experiences that shape their identity and their perceptions of how you view them.

> **Students show up to class with beliefs and characteristics that make them unique. Along with these are experiences that shape their self-identity and their perceptions of how you view them.**

Reinforcing Confidence and Belief in Students

The sixth and final step is finding ways to reinforce confidence and belief in students. As the building leader and driving force at my school, I contributed to my students' self-concept daily by delivering an inspirational message over the intercom. As soon as we finished reciting the Pledge of Allegiance and our school pledge, I gave my entire student body some words of affirmation.

"Excellent morning, scholars!" I might say. "It's already a great day because all of you are great students. You all are brilliant, special, talented, and capable of learning and mastering what your teachers are going to present to you today. Be kind to one another and do your best, and you can accomplish anything."

When students are transitioning in the hall, that's a great time to follow up on a morning affirmation. I'd use that time to tell individual students how much I cared about them and believed in them. I'd be generous with high fives, fist bumps, or pats on the back followed up with a positive word geared toward a specific student.

I'm sure that I am not the only building leader who makes this part of their daily practices. I do it to get the ears, hearts, and minds of my students in a place where they are ready to learn and behave appropriately in school. Students feel more confident in themselves when they know their principal and teachers believe in them.

> *Students feel more confident in themselves when they know their principal and teachers believe in them.*

While the principal is responsible for creating an environment conducive to success for both teachers and students, teachers are responsible for providing all students with opportunities to learn to their highest potential. Culturally responsive teachers accomplish this not only by teaching each student how to learn, but also by instilling in them a desire for lifelong learning. Krasnoff (2016) writes that students can apply what they learn to acquire greater self-awareness, attitudes, and skills that make them responsible, contributing citizens. "A culturally responsive teacher creates a supportive, responsive, and enriched learning environment that allows every student to comfortably examine their attitudes and share their ideas" (Krasnoff, 2016).

Taking Action to Implement Culturally Responsive Practices

Implementing culturally responsive practices is crucial for promoting equitable and inclusive education. Consider taking some of the following action steps to help implement culturally responsive practices at your school.

ACTION 1: **Provide targeted support to students to increase equity in the classroom.** Positive Action is an educational company that publishes an online blog titled *A Practical Guide to Equity in Education.* The blog provides practical recommendations and strategies for implementing equitable practices. For example, imagine giving a mathematics assessment, and every student has a writing utensil, notebook, and calculator. You can consider these students as equal, correct? Yes, they may be equal, but they are far from equitable. According to Positive Action (2021), the following are some ideas for solving this challenge through targeted support:

1. Help EL students (English learners) understand instructions in an unfamiliar language.
2. Provide text-to-speech technology for visually impaired students.
3. Set aside a quiet space for students with attention-deficit hyperactivity disorder (ADHD) to complete assignments.
4. Allow students who may have test anxiety to do a grounding activity before the test.

When you cater to these physical abilities, language skills, and other needs, your challenged students can compete with their peers at the same level.

ACTION 2: **Implement easy changes in the classroom to promote equity.** Minor changes in the classroom can have a major impact on you and your students. Equity is a continual process that should exist in classroom expectations and procedures. Check out these four easy ways you can achieve equity in the classroom (Positive Action, 2021).

1. Welcome students as they enter the classroom, using their names and asking for the correct spelling and pronunciation.

2. Elicit various perspectives and viewpoints when asking questions, such as, "That's one good idea! Does anyone else have an idea to add?" This way, you can validate all perspectives in the classroom.

3. Use different kinds of body language, gestures, and expressions to demonstrate to students that you value their questions and opinions. For example, nod your head, smile, lean in toward them, and gesture in positive ways.

4. Confirm students' prior knowledge before you begin the lesson so you can develop more inclusive instruction. To elicit this information, you can use some of the following tools.

    a. Word walls

    b. K-W-L charts

    c. Anticipation guides

    d. Brainstorming

    e. Webs and other graphic organizers

Conclusion

School principals play a pivotal role in ensuring their schools embrace cultural responsiveness to foster inclusive and equitable learning environments. By prioritizing building positive relationships among students and staff and facilitating culturally responsive pedagogy and practices, principals create a sense of belonging and promote positive interactions that honor and embrace diverse cultural backgrounds.

Principals also must encourage regular bias checks to promote self-reflection, challenge assumptions, and address implicit biases that may hinder equitable practices. Through their leadership, principals have the power to drive the transformation toward culturally responsive schools, where every student feels valued, empowered, and equipped to succeed in an increasingly diverse world. Like a car that seemingly senses its driver's next move, equity-driven school leaders help their schools incorporate culturally responsive teaching into a driving force for equity.

Questions for Reflection

Working individually or with a collaborative group, ask yourself the following reflective questions.

1. How are the teachers in your school building positive relationships with students? How are they using the knowledge they gain about students to make connections to academic content?

2. What are you doing to actively promote and support professional development opportunities for teachers that focus on cultural competency and culturally responsive practices?

3. How can you consistently review and evaluate the curriculum, instructional materials, and assessments to ensure they are culturally relevant, inclusive, and representative of the diverse backgrounds and experiences of your students?

4. What are you doing to foster a collaborative and inclusive school culture that encourages dialogue, respect, and understanding among students, staff, and families from different cultural backgrounds?

5. What can you and your staff do to help students gain a sense of pride in their own culture and understand the importance of diversity and inclusion by appreciating the accomplishments and contributions from cultures different from their own?

Culturally Responsive Practices Survey

For each item, circle the response that best describes the culturally responsive practices at your school.

1. I ensure that the school's curriculum reflects the cultural diversity of the students.

1	2	3	4	5
Strongly disagree	Disagree	Neutral	Agree	Strongly agree

2. I am knowledgeable about the cultural backgrounds of the students in my school.

1	2	3	4	5
Strongly disagree	Disagree	Neutral	Agree	Strongly agree

3. I make a conscious effort to increase cultural awareness among teachers and staff.

1	2	3	4	5
Strongly disagree	Disagree	Neutral	Agree	Strongly agree

4. I support teachers in incorporating culturally responsive teaching practices into their classroom instruction.

1	2	3	4	5
Strongly disagree	Disagree	Neutral	Agree	Strongly agree

5. I provide resources that teachers need to effectively incorporate culturally responsive practices into the curriculum.

1	2	3	4	5
Strongly disagree	Disagree	Neutral	Agree	Strongly agree

6. I invite parents and families to play a role in promoting culturally responsive teaching and practices.

1	2	3	4	5
Strongly disagree	Disagree	Neutral	Agree	Strongly agree

7. My team ensures that culturally responsive teaching is consistently implemented across all classrooms.

1	2	3	4	5
Strongly disagree	Disagree	Neutral	Agree	Strongly agree

8. I often assess the effectiveness of culturally responsive teaching in improving equity.

1	2	3	4	5
Strongly disagree	Disagree	Neutral	Agree	Strongly agree

9. I promote cultural sensitivity and awareness among students.

1	2	3	4	5
Strongly disagree	Disagree	Neutral	Agree	Strongly agree

10. I make an effort and have a plan to recruit and retain teachers and staff from diverse backgrounds.

1	2	3	4	5
Strongly disagree	Disagree	Neutral	Agree	Strongly agree

page 2 of 3

11. I encourage teachers to incorporate the perspectives and experiences of diverse cultures in their instruction.

1	2	3	4	5
Strongly disagree	Disagree	Neutral	Agree	Strongly agree

12. I collaborate with community organizations to promote culturally responsive teaching and equity in education.

1	2	3	4	5
Strongly disagree	Disagree	Neutral	Agree	Strongly agree

Survey Results:

12–18	I am ineffective at incorporating culturally responsive practices in my school.
19–24	I need improvement in incorporating culturally responsive practices in my school.
25–36	I am emerging as a leader who incorporates culturally responsive practices in my school.
37–46	I am effectively incorporating culturally responsive practices in my school.
47–60	I am highly effective at incorporating culturally responsive practices in my school.

CHAPTER 10

CHARGING YOUR BATTERY THROUGH SELF-CARE

Burnout has become an epidemic among leaders in education at all school levels. A school leader's professional world is filled with overwhelming responsibilities, information overload, and emotional anxiety. It's no surprise that burnout has long been cited as the reason so many educators leave the profession. It's a level of fatigue that can be compared to a drained car battery. Without a powered-up battery, the vehicle is at a standstill. The battery provides power to everything from the motor that starts the engine to the air conditioning that keeps occupants comfortable. Great school leaders help teachers and staff to recharge their batteries through self-care to combat feelings of exhaustion and despair. They also must be cognizant of their own physical and mental wellness and ensure their own batteries are not depleting.

*T*RADITIONALLY, A CAR battery had a limited role in starting the car, but in a growing world of electronic cars, it has even more significance. If the battery is drained or disconnected, your car will not start, and you're not going anywhere. It needs to stay charged to keep the car going. Similarly, we as a society are placing increased awareness of and value on keeping our own batteries charged.

One evening after a hard day's work and hosting a junior high boys' basketball game, I did my final walkthrough of the school. I went into my office to straighten out some papers and shut down my computer. I put on my coat and grabbed my laptop to take home and headed to my car. I turned the key and . . . *nothing*. I was so frustrated. To make matters worse, the temperature outside was freezing on this late January night in Chicago. It was so cold that I thought the frigid temperatures were the reason why the car wouldn't start. I needed someone to give me a jump so I could start my car and get home. The only staff member left in the building was the janitor, but his wife had dropped him off at work, so he could not help. I went back to my office and called AAA. Forty-five minutes later, the serviceman arrived and jumped my car. He gave me some advice as he finished his task.

"Some people just push their cars to the limit and ignore warning signs that their battery is going out," he said. "They take for granted that their battery is always good, but you have to constantly check it to make sure it's in good shape. Especially in weather like this."

How many of us push so hard and ignore signs that we need to charge our battery, and then discover, after exhausting ineffective solutions, that we may need professional help? Educators and school leaders are under an extreme amount of stress and pressure and need to make self-care a priority, especially in this climate.

> *How many of us push so hard and ignore signs that we need to charge our battery, and then discover, after exhausting ineffective solutions, that we may need professional help?*

The quest for school equity can be demanding, emotionally taxing, and filled with numerous stressors and challenges. Recognizing the importance of self-care and supporting staff well-being becomes paramount for principals in preventing burnout and ensuring sustainable progress. This chapter examines strategies and practices that principals can employ to safeguard their own well-being while also supporting their staff in preventing burnout. By adopting healthy coping methods, fostering a culture of self-care, and promoting a healthy personal and professional balance, principals can cultivate a resilient and thriving community within their schools.

What the Research Says

There is a familiar saying that you can't pour from an empty cup. Leaders cannot be the driving force if they are not healthy mentally, physically, and emotionally. The COVID-19 pandemic was extraordinarily difficult due to its effect on education and life in general. But the truth is that educators have extremely challenging jobs, even under more "normal" circumstances, and have been under extreme stress and pressure for years. With long hours and a heavy workload, it's easy for school leaders and teachers to fall prey to burnout. Without proper support, they may become overworked, allotting too little significance or time to their own mental and physical health needs.

Coping With Stress and Burnout

Burnout, which *Psychology Today* describes as "a state of chronic stress that leads to physical and emotional exhaustion, cynicism, detachment, and feelings of ineffectiveness and lack of accomplishment" (Tapp, 2017), is one of those road hazards in life that high achievers should be aware of. Sadly, often because of their "I can do everything" attitude, they rarely see it coming. Because high achievers are passionate about their work, they put in extremely long hours, shoulder heavy workloads, and take on enormous pressure while trying to surpass expectations, which causes them to be at susceptibly higher risk of burnout (Carter, 2013).

Principals and teachers work excessively long hours and wear it as a badge of honor, not realizing the toll it takes on them physically and emotionally. They are so used to working long hours that it has become normal to work twelve- to fourteen-hour days. This leads to neglecting important things in life that should be priorities, such as family, friends, health, and relationships. These should all be priorities, yet some people continually push them further down the to-do list because "work comes first." They slip into unhealthy habits that need correcting. Near the beginning of the COVID-19 pandemic, educators used downtime to try to get in shape or focus on these areas of their life that they had neglected.

After this brief period, they were thrust into the vortex of learning how to accommodate the "new normal." Meeting the special social-emotional needs of students, staff, and communities that were arising in connection with the COVID-19 pandemic became the number-one priority. This created even more stress and anxiety because the change was neither gradual nor optional. Educators had to pivot before the word *pivot* ever vaulted into position as one of 2020's top buzzwords. Change is often uncomfortable and is accompanied with anxiety and fear. Research indicates that a fear of change is one of the single most limiting aspects of progress. Neuroscience research also teaches us that uncertainty registers in our brain much like an error does. We need to "correct" it before we can feel comfortable again, so we'd rather avoid it if we can (Bovey & Hede, 2001).

People also fear change because they are afraid that they might lose something associated with that change (Mautz, 2022). Principals and teachers especially feared the effects of COVID-19 because they worried about their own personal health, as well as teaching and safety protocol changes the pandemic necessitated. Educators were not alone in their fears; the general public suffered an elevated level of stress and battled depression at higher rates than before. The general population suffered from mental health issues as a result of the pandemic (Centers for Disease Control, 2020). The Yale Center for Emotional Intelligence teamed up with the Collaborative for Academic, Social, and Emotional Learning (CASEL) to launch a survey to discover how teachers were fairing emotionally during the pandemic. "The five most-mentioned feelings among all teachers were: anxious, fearful, worried, overwhelmed, and sad. Anxiety, by far, was the most frequently mentioned emotion" (Brackett & Cipriano, 2020).

I'm sure we all can relate to these feelings. Principals and teachers alike found themselves spending more time in front of the computer late into the night figuring out how to do remote learning, planning instruction, and thinking about what else they could be doing better to educate students. Principals were trying to support teachers and monitor their activities online, while running staff meetings on Zoom and other platforms and implementing new initiatives and mandates coming from the district office. Accompanied by this was the shared concern among teachers and administrators of what was happening in their students' home lives and whether their students were OK.

Exposure to others' trauma can lead to vicarious trauma and compassion fatigue. Principals and teachers alike work with students who have experienced trauma and must constantly monitor their own feelings and emotions. *The level of stress may be compounded for principals as they are responsible for both students and staff.*

Principals are expected to maintain equanimity in stressful situations. Yet, a 2021 survey states, "52% reported that working to address mental health-related issues of students was the most or one of the most emotionally exhausting parts of their job" (DeMatthews, Reyes, Carrola, Edwards, & James, 2021). Principals pour out immeasurable emotions when supporting students who are victims of physical and emotional abuse, neglect, and trauma. Many principals also are charged to work with students and families who are dealing with homelessness, anxiety associated with immigration, deportation, and poverty. Many principals are also concerned about the violence that take place in some students' neighborhoods. All these factors have a negative effect on students' well-being and development (DeMatthews et al., 2021). These realities can cause principals' stress levels to spike and sometimes get out of control.

These studies on principal stress levels do not stand alone. According to Julia Mahfouz (2018), "Numerous studies document principals' stress related to heavy workloads and long hours, erratic and unpredictable problems, and lack of control and autonomy." In a review of literature focused on principals' experiences, Izhar Oplatka (2017) identifies five career experiences that lead to high stress levels.

1. A sense of shock or surprise as novice principals gain a full understanding of what it means to be a principal;
2. An overemphasis on technical aspects of the principalship at the expense of instruction, which can result in frustration and limited professional fulfillment;
3. Confusion, frustration, and exhaustion while dealing with multiple tasks and unexpected negative events;
4. Feelings of enthusiasm for their job contrasting with high levels of stress, loneliness, professional insecurity, and fears of failure and losing their legitimacy; and
5. A sense of uncertainty, which can bolster suspicion toward staff.

There is no shortage of factors that contribute to principals' high stress levels. Despite this reality, principals must have enough physical, mental, and emotional strength to support their students and staff.

Staff members look to the principal to fix any problems that may exist in the school, ranging from lack of resources to student discipline, and any issues related to the physical building. Principals working in low-income communities and principals working in affluent communities share some of the same problems. But as we continue to focus on equity, you might notice that principals serving in low-income communities also deal with the kind of problems that those in affluent communities do not, such as old, increasingly dilapidated buildings that are not warm and inviting. They may not feature adequate heat and air conditioning. Nor do their school systems have sufficient resources for enhancing instruction. They also must constantly worry about gangs, unsafe neighborhoods, poverty, and other aspects that come with being in underserved communities. Their counterparts leading in affluent communities have relatively few comparable experiences. This, too, creates a heightened level of stress and discomfort.

> *Principals working in low-income communities and principals working in affluent communities share some of the same problems.*

If principals are not able to effectively cope with stress, irritation, disappointment, exasperation, and mental exhaustion, they may find themselves unsuccessful in this role. While life's problems are wide ranging, how people deal with them unveils their resilience and also strongly affects the level of stress that they will experience. School leaders must be resilient to cope with stress.

Embracing Healthy Coping Methods for Stress

To be effective leaders, principals need to invoke healthy coping methods and keep an optimistic attitude. Administrators are hired to perform the duties according to their job description, as well as some tasks that fall outside of it. They are expected to be problem solvers; they must be emotionally stable, even during highly intense, stressful moments and emotionally charged crisis situations. Over time, this can take a toll on health. Teachers and school administrators also have personal lives. Relationships, families, and personal issues all can add to the pressures of daily school life.

Principals can combat these negative effects by being aware of their stress triggers, utilizing grounding activities, and consistently participating in activities that are considered healthy coping methods. In a study by David DeMatthews, Pedro Reyes, Paul Carrola, Wesley Edwards, and Lebon James (2021), principals reported multiple ways for coping with burnout: "The most common coping behaviors were: (1) spending time with family/children; (2) talking/networking with other principals; (3) exercising; (4) meditating; and (5) attending church, praying, engaging in spirituality."

These are effective coping strategies to maintain mental health and reduce stress. Others who need more intense support often seek counseling: "Studies indicate that providing access to counseling services and encouraging creativity and innovation in educational practices are effective strategies to combat burnout and compassion fatigue" (Barr, 2022).

School leaders need supports like these for their staff as well, and they should make it a priority to address the effects of loss, grief, and trauma educators might be experiencing. McInerney and McKlindon (2020) also identify self-care activities that help principals relieve stress, including physical exercise, creative outlets, and adequate rest. They advise that by taking care of yourself first, you will be in a better position to help others while also avoiding burnout.

> **To be effective leaders, principals need to invoke healthy coping methods and keep an optimistic attitude.**

What It Looks Like in the Real World

Ignoring the signs of burnout can have severe consequences. Burnout affects physical and mental health, leading to chronic stress, fatigue, and increased vulnerability to illnesses. It also can contribute to the development or worsening of mental health conditions. Ignoring burnout can result in decreased productivity, difficulty concentrating, and strained professional relationships. Over time, burnout can lead to a loss of passion for work, disengagement, and negative long-term consequences for personal and professional life. Recognizing and addressing burnout is crucial for preserving health, improving performance, and promoting a balanced and fulfilling life (DeMatthews et al., 2021).

Heeding Signs of Burnout

I am well aware of just how devastating burnout can be and how stress and pressure can literally kill people. I remember reading a news story about an Australian principal, Trish Antulov, who died at her desk at age sixty-five (Hiatt, 2018). Since she typically worked long hours and went into the buildings to work on Saturdays and

Sundays, her husband did not become too concerned when she did not come home one Sunday evening—until several phone calls he placed to her went unanswered.

About 10 p.m., he went to the school where she worked and found her deceased. She had died at her desk! Mr. Antulov said that his wife did not believe she had the time to look after herself properly, and the long hours she worked had contributed to her high stress levels. He shared that she was under too much pressure in her job as a principal (Hiatt, 2018).

According to the annual Principal Health and Wellbeing Survey (Riley, 2018), unrealistic workloads were identified as the biggest source of stress that takes a toll on school leaders. Many principals just work too many hours to exercise and do other things they need to do to maintain their health. Hiatt (2018) notes the following:

> On average, 53% of principals worked more than 56 hours per week, and 27% were working upwards of 61 to 65 hours per week. Like many other professions, being a school leader is not a job that you can switch off from easily. Principals are juggling priorities including curriculum, student behavior, facilities, the needs of their staff, and expectations from parents.

> *Many principals just work too many hours to exercise and do other things they need to do to maintain their health.*

In addition to this stress, principals feel the crunch of teacher shortages and are running buildings without enough certified teachers to fill every classroom. Walker (2022) shares that "pre-existing staff shortages have deepened during the pandemic. Eighty-six percent of members say they have seen more educators leaving the profession or retiring early since the start of the pandemic in 2020." The media coined the phrase *The Great Resignation* in response to the number of teachers and principals leaving their positions because they are totally burned out. Walker (2022) continues:

> Exhausted and exasperated, principals, classroom teachers, and other school staff are under an unprecedented level of strain, made worse by recent dire staff shortages that have plagued school systems across the country. According to the U.S. Bureau of Labor Statistics (BLS), there were approximately 10.6 million educators working in public education in January 2020; today there are just 10 million, a net loss of around 600,000.

Schools will struggle at the rate that teachers are resigning, and principals will struggle physically and mentally to deal with the reality of this situation, which causes their stress levels to rise.

When I was an athletic director, I heard about a colleague who also was an athletic director. He was working out in the school's fitness center and suffered a heart attack. As you know, school athletic directors also work many long, late, and weekend hours to keep up with the demands of the job. Fortunately for me, I learned about this before a health scare of my own. I was suffering from diverticulitis, and the doctor informed me that, in my case, he did not believe this was a hereditary condition. Far more likely, he said, it was an acute condition brought on by stress. After taking me through a battery of questions, he concluded that the stress was brought about by the pressures, demands, and long hours on the job. I had to have emergency surgery to correct the problem. I also had to use the Family Medical Leave Act; it took me six months to fully recover.

During the 2020–2021 school year, I witnessed a staff member succumb to stress she was facing both on the job and at home. She had a forty-five-minute commute from home to work. She would arrive at work at 7:30 a.m. but would sit in her car before coming into the building and signing in at 8:00 a.m. One day, my assistant was reviewing the time sheets and noticed that this teacher had not signed in yet. I asked if she had called in because she was not on my absence report for the day. My secretary said that she'd seen the teacher in her car when she arrived at 7:35 a.m. We went to her car in the parking lot and found her slumped over the steering wheel. We immediately dialed 911. An ambulance arrived and took her to the hospital. Her spouse met us at the hospital and spoke to the emergency room doctor. He informed us that she had a panic attack and had suffered a nervous breakdown.

This incident, along with recent studies and reports about teacher burnout being on the rise, prompted me to pay more attention to my battery and make a commitment to monitor my staff's well-being and emotional health more closely. As schools consider ways to address the mental health needs of students, they must also do the same for staff. My doctor advised, "Work on yourself, or somebody else will."

> **As schools consider ways to address the mental health needs of students, they must also do the same for staff.**

Offering Supportive Strategies for Self-Care

As my experiences with the effects of burnout on teachers increased, I intentionally did more individual and small-group check-ins with my staff. I also incorporated self-care activities in staff meetings and school-improvement activities. These activities weren't necessarily life changing, but they did spark an awareness of the importance of self-care. In some cases, it was the catalyst for staff members to incorporate healthier activities into their out-of-school routines. Our exercises included walking, Zumba, yoga, meditating, discussion, self-reflection, coloring, deep breathing, and other low-impact, grounding activities.

Based on the positive response and appreciation I received from my staff on supporting them with their mental and emotional health during the COVID-19 pandemic, I built a popular workshop in which staff could participate in person or online, *Burning Up Instead of Burning Out: Improving Educator Mental and Emotional Health*. In this workshop, I share how I got sick as a result of burnout and stress and almost died as a result. I then take participants on my journey of how I made transformational life changes that led to great improvements in my physical, mental, emotional, spiritual, and financial health. Through self-reflection and discussion, and exploring topics such as educator mental health, physical health, intellectual growth, and fear management, I help participants realize how they can optimize their own professional and personal lives.

It requires patience to encourage school leaders and teachers to improve their emotional health and participate in social-emotional learning (SEL) activities. It demands vulnerability, which is challenging. Some will embrace this journey immediately, but it takes more time to see prominent improvements in staff culture. Over time, skepticism decreases, and people become more open to the idea. Events that cause dysregulation force us to stop and think and self-reflect before continuing our daily lives. We must set aside time to process emotions and forge collegial support networks we can implement during challenging times.

According to Barr (2022), "Crisis experiences show us that schools can do so much more to create networks of care for teachers and staff in ways that pay dividends to the entire community." Administrators can lessen the stress for their teachers by giving them a voice in the decision-making process, being transparent, and adjusting policies and procedures. Administrators can use these practices to support fatigued teachers and concentrate on well-being. School leaders also can utilize tools to support themselves and be the driving force behind their own physical and emotional health.

School leaders also can utilize tools to support themselves and be the driving force behind their own physical and emotional health.

Fellow educational leader and friend, William D. Parker, who graciously wrote the foreword for this book, emphasizes the importance of exercising in his book *Pause. Breathe. Flourish.* (Parker, 2020). Parker (2020) writes, "Why is exercise so important? It's great for your cardiovascular health. Just like your car needs an oil change, your body needs air flowing to every one of its cells" (p. 4).

Reading his book was a timely reminder of the importance of self-care and how educational leaders can incorporate healthy practices into their daily lives. It reminded me to begin spending more time exercising, meditating, reading, and praying. I also gave myself a monthly budget to pay for things to enhance my health, including massages, vitamins, supplements, gym memberships, and healthy foods. I decided to adopt the "actions speak louder than words" motto and set aside time to do what's necessary to improve my physical and emotional health. My methods may not be yours, but no matter how you choose to practice self-care, it's important to make it a priority to ensure you have a healthy work-life balance.

Taking Action to Improve Self-Care

Practicing self-care is of paramount importance for educators, particularly principals, as it directly impacts their well-being and effectiveness in their roles. It helps educators maintain their physical and mental health, serves as a preventive measure against burnout, and models healthy behavior for students and staff. Consider taking some of the following action steps to improve your level of self-care.

ACTION 1:   **Check to see if you have any of the following physical or emotional signs of burnout, and think about how long you may have had them.** Physical signs of burnout include the following:

     a. Feeling tired and drained

     b. Low immunity, frequent bouts of illness

     c. Headaches and body aches

     d. Inconsistent appetite

     e. Irregular sleeping habits (Smith, Segal, & Robinson, 2022)

Emotional signs of burnout include the following:

    a. Feelings that you cannot meet expectations

    b. Lack of creativity and feeling stuck in life

    c. Feelings of loneliness

    d. Lack of purpose and motivation

    e. Negative attitude and sad outlook on life

    f. Difficult to find satisfaction and feelings of undervalued (Smith et al., 2022)

If educators and principals are experiencing signs of burnout, it is crucial for them to take proactive steps to address their well-being. They can seek support from trusted colleagues, mentors, or mental health professionals to discuss their feelings and concerns. They also can participate in self-care activities such as hobbies, mindfulness, exercising, and maintaining a healthy work-life balance. Both principals and teachers need to advocate for their own needs and communicate with supervisors or school leadership about their situation to explore potential solutions or accommodations.

ACTION 2: **Go see a doctor.** There are several good reasons to see a doctor. Annual checkups are important to make sure your body systems are all in good working order and you are free from disease. Have your bloodwork done, get an annual physical, and ask what exams you should receive based on your age range (for example, colonoscopy, stress test, mammogram, vision). This way, you will catch any concerns proactively and be aware if any actions need to be taken to prevent any illness from progressing.

Another good reason to schedule a doctor visit is to get clearance for exercise and any other supplements, vitamins, or health aids you may be considering to kick-start your exercise regimen and give you a boost during your daily routines or workouts.

ACTION 3: **Take time to rest or participate in either a fun or relaxing activity.** We all may be short on time and have numerous responsibilities, which leaves little time for leisure activities. But think about it this way: there are twenty-four hours in a day and 168 hours in a week. If you took one hour for yourself each day, that would equate to seven hours each week. So, seven hours to yourself out of 168 hours is not a lot of time. You deserve it, and it is an absolute must to get or stay healthy physically, mentally, and spiritually.

ACTION 4: **Identify barriers that prevent you from exercising.** A lot of people want to exercise but place other responsibilities as a priority. For example, it was hard for me to get to the gym and work out because I had to watch my daughters (they were at an age where they needed adult supervision). To overcome this barrier, I paid my next door neighbor's daughter to come over and babysit while I worked out. I also joined a gym that offers childcare. If you're thinking that you can't afford to do that, flip the script in your mind by placing your health as a priority and telling yourself that you can't afford *not* to do it.

For people who don't want or can't afford to join a gym, there are numerous alternative ways to exercise. One option is outdoor activities such as running, jogging, or brisk walking in a nearby park or neighborhood. These cardiovascular exercises can be tailored to individual fitness levels and offer the added benefit of fresh air and natural scenery. Additionally, engaging in bodyweight exercises at home, such as push-ups, squats, lunges, and planks, provides a convenient and effective way to build strength and improve muscle tone without any equipment.

For those who enjoy group activities, joining a sports team or participating in recreational activities like cycling, swimming, tennis, or hiking can provide a social and enjoyable way to stay active. Online workout videos, fitness apps, and virtual fitness classes are also readily available and offer a wide range of exercise routines that can be done from the comfort of home. The key is finding activities that align with personal interests, preferences, and fitness goals, making it easier to maintain a consistent exercise routine.

ACTION 5: **When setting exercise, nutritional, or mental health goals, also set systems.** Goals are great, but having systems to help you achieve those goals increases your chance to achieve them. If your goal is to be in bed every night by 10:00 p.m. to get adequate rest of eight hours of sleep, set an alarm on your phone for 9:00 p.m. as a reminder to wrap up whatever activity you're doing so you can be in bed by 10:00 p.m. If your goal is to eat healthier, create a system to where healthy snacks are accessible, or prep meals or pack a lunch that is healthy to avoid eating fast food when you are short on time and desperately need to eat.

ACTION 6:   **Get an accountability partner.** It's always a good idea to have a per-son in your corner who wants to help you win by motivating you and holding you accountable to your goals. You also can be an account-ability partner for someone else. When holding others accountable, it's almost impossible to be hypocritical—you must do what you say you're going to do. For example, when I was writing my dissertation, one of my classmates was my dissertation partner. We made a pact to write an average of five chapters per week. In my heart of hearts, I could not call him and say, "Hey make sure you get those chapters written," if I hadn't finished or gotten started on my own. An accountability partner helps you because you have someone to go through the process with and check on them while they are checking on you!

ACTION 7:   **Tell yourself that you are a priority and you deserve it.** This is simple, but it is also psychologically the most challenging thing to do. Maybe you have gone all this time putting others first or telling yourself you must put others first and using that as an excuse not to care for yourself. Set boundaries and show others that you care for them; one way you can be strong for them is by being strong yourself. You are worth it!

ACTION 8:   **Make a list of all the people in your life who love and care about you so you can reach out to them for support, as needed.** Burnout can make problems appear impossible to overcome. But there is always hope. Remember that your loved ones need you in their life and want to see you succeed. Stop hesitating to reach out to them because you think they don't have time or don't care. They will be happy that you reached out to confide in them and will take the time to listen. They also may encourage you to "remember your why" and rekindle your passion to keep your flame going, but also to take time for yourself to charge your battery so you can continue to be the driving force at your school.

Conclusion

This chapter shed some light on the critical topic of coping with burnout and stress. By exploring effective coping strategies and promoting healthy methods of managing stress, educators can safeguard their well-being and sustain their com-mitment to equitable practices. Recognizing the signs of burnout, practicing self-care, and seeking support are essential steps in maintaining resilience and preventing long-term negative consequences. By prioritizing their own well-being, educators can create a positive ripple effect within their schools, fostering a supportive culture that promotes both personal and professional growth. As leaders, principals play a crucial role in championing self-care practices and modeling healthy coping methods, thereby ensuring the sustainability of equity work and cultivating an environment where everyone thrives.

To be the driving force, school leaders must charge their batteries and understand that self-care is just that. We must take care of ourselves so we can perform at an optimal level and maintain the energy required to continue to work to enhance equity in our schools.

Questions for Reflection

Working individually or with a collaborative group, ask yourself the following reflective questions.

1. Burnout has become an epidemic among educational leaders at all grade levels. What are your stress triggers, and what actions can you take to reduce them?

2. Are you working too many long hours and missing time with your loved ones? What are some tasks you can delegate to others on your staff? Do you have unrealistic expectations of yourself, or do others have unrealistic expectations of you? Do you tend to reach for perfection or strive for excellence? What can you do to have a healthy work-life balance?

3. How are you prioritizing your self-care and well-being as a school leader? Are you setting aside dedicated time for activities that recharge your batteries and replenish your energy? How can you ensure that self-care remains a consistent practice in your daily routine?

4. How are you supporting and promoting a culture of self-care and well-being among teachers? What strategies and resources are you providing to empower teachers to prevent burnout and prioritize their own self-care? How can you strengthen communication and collaboration to foster a supportive environment where teachers feel valued and supported in their well-being?

5. How are you monitoring and addressing signs of burnout among teachers? Are you actively seeking feedback and creating opportunities for open dialogue about workload, stressors, and emotional well-being? How can you proactively identify and address potential sources of burnout to ensure the well-being and longevity of your teaching staff?

Self-Care Survey

For each item, circle the response that best describes your level of self-care.

1. I eat healthy regularly and balance what I eat for nutrition and what I eat for pleasure.

1	2	3	4	5
Strongly disagree	Disagree	Neutral	Agree	Strongly agree

2. I get some form of exercise for at least thirty minutes each day.

1	2	3	4	5
Strongly disagree	Disagree	Neutral	Agree	Strongly agree

3. I regularly dance, swim, walk, run, play sports, or do some other physical activity or hobby that I enjoy.

1	2	3	4	5
Strongly disagree	Disagree	Neutral	Agree	Strongly agree

4. I take time to be romantic with my partner on a consistent basis.

1	2	3	4	5
Strongly disagree	Disagree	Neutral	Agree	Strongly agree

5. I get enough sleep and feel well rested every morning.

1	2	3	4	5
Strongly disagree	Disagree	Neutral	Agree	Strongly agree

page 1 of 3

6. I make time for self-reflection.

1	2	3	4	5
Strongly disagree	Disagree	Neutral	Agree	Strongly agree

7. I read literature that is unrelated to school or work.

1	2	3	4	5
Strongly disagree	Disagree	Neutral	Agree	Strongly agree

8. I talk to someone I trust about issues in my life.

1	2	3	4	5
Strongly disagree	Disagree	Neutral	Agree	Strongly agree

9. I sometimes say "no" to taking on extra responsibilities.

1	2	3	4	5
Strongly disagree	Disagree	Neutral	Agree	Strongly agree

10. I spend time with others whose company I enjoy.

1	2	3	4	5
Strongly disagree	Disagree	Neutral	Agree	Strongly agree

11. I give myself positive affirmations, praise myself, and love myself.

1	2	3	4	5
Strongly disagree	Disagree	Neutral	Agree	Strongly agree

12. I seek out and enjoy comforting activities, objects, people, relationships, and places.

1	2	3	4	5
Strongly disagree	Disagree	Neutral	Agree	Strongly agree

page 2 of 3

13. I spend time in nature and find spiritual or community connections.

1	2	3	4	5
Strongly disagree	Disagree	Neutral	Agree	Strongly agree

14. I identify projects or tasks that are exciting and rewarding, or support causes I care for.

1	2	3	4	5
Strongly disagree	Disagree	Neutral	Agree	Strongly agree

15. I strive for balance among school, family, relationships, play, and rest.

1	2	3	4	5
Strongly disagree	Disagree	Neutral	Agree	Strongly agree

Survey Results:

15–18	Get professional help to make self-care a priority. You are worth it.
19–32	Seek assistance and consider getting professional help to create a self-care plan.
33–49	You may be going through the motions. Consider adding healthy activities.
50–59	You have healthy self-care strategies. Keep those positive habits going!
60–75	Self-care is a priority for you. Keep living your best life!

Epilogue

It is time to render the term *disadvantaged student* obsolete. This dream is within our grasp as educators and leaders, but it will take devotion, understanding, innovative approaches, and in some cases, the abandonment of archaic, unfortunately entrenched methods of leading a school and failed efforts of advancing school equity. To achieve equity, we must infuse the opportunities presented to students with the support and resources required to turn the education system into a level playing field. Success and achievement should be accessible, regardless of income, race, identity, ability, or ethnic makeup; whether a student is first-generation or legacy; or whether a student is academically gifted or grappling with disabilities.

The challenge is how to actualize this dream. Historically marginalized students require additional resources to catch up with their peers and, once there, maintain that equitable footing. They require educational leaders who understand their unique challenges and who are willing to devise programming and structures that dissolve barriers—all while supporting and encouraging the academically gifted as well. Principals are in the key position to be the driving force propelling each student toward success.

By becoming more aware of issues that affect subsets of students—variables like poverty, ethnicity, gender, LGBTQ+, and more—principals can create action plans to circumvent associated educational pitfalls. We may not be able to single-handedly overcome all the challenges that arrive at our doors. But the more we understand how learning capabilities are affected by our students' unique backgrounds, the better we can adopt effective, equity-enhancing solutions. School leaders who understand how systems operate and impact their students can create better opportunities for students who attend their schools (Western Governors University, 2021).

To overcome systemic barriers that inhibit equity, school leaders must be confident in who they are in their role as leaders. It requires integrity and courage to speak out about inequities and assert the power of one's position to make needed changes. Such confidence develops over time. It grows along with experience and competence. It is energized by the support of both those who hire us and those who report to us.

To stay committed to promoting equity, however, we must never confuse those for whom we work with those we serve. We may work for the school district, but we serve teachers, staff, students, and the community. Keep this in the forefront, and be better able to do what's right, even when what's right is not what's popular.

> **To overcome systemic barriers that inhibit equity, school leaders must be confident in who they are in their role as leaders.**

One of my mentors—my principal when I was an assistant principal—faced adversity for doing what was right by students rather than what was popular. Days before the school board was set to vote on her job status, she made a statement that resonated with me. "They don't determine my fate," she said. "I took this job with my hand up, not with my hand out." She meant that she wanted this job to have a positive impact; she took the job to help others, not herself. Within days of the board's decision to terminate, another school district was calling her in for an interview to become the new principal at their school. Her integrity was intact, she said, adding that she would more likely lose sleep over not doing what was right and equitable for her students than she would over any job loss.

The COVID-19 pandemic highlighted existing socioeconomic inequalities in our education system and has prompted important conversations about equity in schools. According to the National Center for Education Statistics (2021b), "Between fall 2009 and fall 2018, the majority of public-school students in America shifted from white to nonwhite, and as of 2018, 12.6 million children were in families living in poverty." There's really no such thing as a typical student. Maria Kampen (2022) states, "If education doesn't actively work to break down existing barriers, it ends up reinforcing the inequalities that were there all along." When equity in the school is a priority, all students benefit. Principals must make this part of their school vision and mission statements and work every day to promote it.

What is the vision for your school as it relates to equity? Does serving your students, staff, and community feel more like a job or more like a mission? A job is ordinary, but a mission is extraordinary. A job is rewarded with pay, but a mission is rewarded with a feeling of accomplishment. A job asks, "Are you qualified for this?" A mission tells you, "You are made for this!" A job requires work. A mission requires inspired action! What actions are you taking to fulfill your vision and mission to promote equity for each student you serve? Each school leader will have a unique vision and mission statement for their school. The answers to these questions will help you formulate yours, and your purposeful desire to achieve them will help you to be the driving force in doing so. In the absence of this passion, educational leaders must choose between their calling and their comfort.

> **What actions are you taking to fulfill your vision and mission to promote equity for each student you serve?**

When you have passion for equity, your actions speak louder than words, and your message will be loud and clear to staff, students, and parents. Part of building relationships with students is building relationships with students' parents. Parent support is one of the most important factors for students' success in school, so leaders must promote positive school-home relationships. As noted previously, equitable communication is key to engaging parents to support their children in school (Davis, 2022).

Just as vehicles require a multitude of parts to operate efficiently and in sync for top performance, schools require various groups of people and programs to operate efficiently and in sync to propel students forward. A car body encloses and protects most of the critical parts of a vehicle, including its engine, without which there is no forward motion. School leaders are the engines of their institutions. Facilitating and overseeing all the moving parts in a school while advancing equity can seem daunting, overwhelming, and stressful. We know that stress and long work hours can damage mental and physical health, so the best leaders adopt healthy lifestyle habits that, like the well-maintained body of a car, protect against corrosive effects.

> **Part of building relationships with students is building relationships with students' parents.**

Principals also are responsible, in large part, for the mental health and well-being of their staff. They serve as sounding boards and problem solvers for teachers, who carry the emotional weight of things going on in their personal lives along with challenges they have on the job. To make matters worse, as noted previously, many teachers suffer from secondary trauma as the result of the pain, stress, and trauma of their students (Tate Sullivan, 2022). Just as many teachers also play the role of counselor for their students, principals find themselves counseling their teachers and encouraging them to stay strong.

Therefore, to be effective leaders, principals must attend to their physical and mental health and make it a priority. The better you care for your car, the further it will take you, and the better you take care of your mind and body, the further you will be able to go to support and guide others. The need to promote health and wellness among principals is just as urgent as the need to promote equity in schools, for without the first, the second has no chance. I urge you to improve your work-life balance. Stay healthy so you can continue to do the important work of promoting equity in your school. Easier said than done? Of course. But try this: Keep a daily time budget for one week—in other words, write down start and finish times for each daily task for one week, or even one day. I assure you, you will find certain tasks that can be accomplished much more efficiently, or ditched altogether, to make room for a daily walk, yoga, meditation, exercise, or any number of healthy activities. Not only will you find you feel better physically, but you likely will gain clarity and increased peace of mind as well.

As I've studied equity and promoted it in schools, I have come to learn that it is a complex and critical issue to help all students thrive. I also have learned that there is no simple solution or easy answer, but every school leader can work to take the wheel to drive equity each day in their school. Leaders who are focused on promoting equity are critical to the success and forward momentum of each student. Understanding and focusing on equity is crucial to making the life of each student better.

> *There is no simple solution or easy answer, but every school leader can work to take the wheel to drive equity each day in their school.*

In closing, I charge you to take the wheel and be the driving force to ensure equity in every classroom at your school!

References and Resources

Abrams, A. (2018). *Yes, impostor syndrome is real. Here's how to deal with it.* Accessed at https://time.com/5312483/how-to-deal-with-impostor-syndrome on November 28, 2021.

Academics Learning & Teaching. (2022). *Star assessments.* Accessed at https://mn0190 9691.schoolwires.net/Page/6501 on November 5, 2022.

Ackerman, C. A. (2018). *What is self-efficacy theory?* Accessed at https://positivepsychology .com/self-efficacy on April 26, 2023.

Acquisitions International. (2020). *5 effective leadership styles in education.* Accessed at www.acquisition-international.com/5-effective-leadership-styles-in-education on June 12, 2022.

Allen, K., & Kern, P. (2018). *School vision and mission statements should not be dismissed as empty words.* Accessed at https://theconversation.com/school-vision-and-mission -statements-should-not-be-dismissed-as-empty-words-97375 on January 26, 2022.

American University. (2020a). *5 effective principal leadership styles.* Accessed at https:// soeonline.american.edu/blog/principal-leadership-styles on June 1, 2022.

American University. (2020b). *7 education policy issues that need to be solved in 2020.* Accessed at https://soeonline.american.edu/blog/education-policy-issues-in-2020 on April 8, 2022.

American University School of Education. (2019). *Six highly effective educational leadership styles.* Accessed at https://soeonline.american.edu/blog/education-leadership-styles on June 10, 2022.

Anderson, M. (2017). Transformational leadership in education: A review of existing literature. *International Social Science Review, 93*(1), 1–13.

Arar, K., & Saiti, A. (2022). Ethical leadership, ethical dilemmas, and decision making among school administrators. *Equity and Education and Society, 1*(1), 1–16.

Auto Simple. (2017). *The owner's manual is your best friend.* Accessed at www.autosimple .com/blog/vehicle-owners-manual on April 6, 2022.

Avolio, B. J., & Gardner, W. L. (2005). Authentic leadership development: Getting to the root of positive forms of leadership. *The Leadership Quarterly, 16*(3), 315–338.

Bacher-Hicks, A., Billings, S. B., & Deming, D. J. (2021). Proving the school-to-prison pipeline. *Education Next, 21*(4). Accessed at www.educationnext.org/proving-school -to-prison-pipeline-stricter-middle-schools-raise-risk-of-adult-arrests on April 8, 2022.

Baldwin, J. (1966). A report from occupied territory. *The Nation.* Accessed at www. thenation.com/article/culture/report-occupied-territory on August 24, 2023.

Balfanz, R., & Byrnes, V. (2012). The importance of being in school: A report on absenteeism in the nation's public schools. *The Education Digest, 78*(2), 4–9.

Bandura, A. (Ed.). (1995). *Self-efficacy in changing societies.* New York: Cambridge University Press.

Barr, K. (2022). *Supporting educators to rise stronger after a traumatic event.* Accessed at www.ascd.org/el/articles/supporting-educators-to-rise-stronger-after-a-traumatic-event on May 30, 2022.

Bass, B., & Riggio, R. (2005). *Transformational leadership* (2nd ed.). London: Psychology Press.

Berkowicz, J., & Myers, A. (2018). *Unequal school discipline strategies set the stage for lifelong discrimination.* Accessed at www.edweek.org/leadership/opinion-unequal-school -discipline-strategies-set-the-stage-for-lifelong-discrimination/2018/04 on April 8, 2022.

Bertrand, L. A., Stader, D., & Copeland, S. (2018). Supporting new school leaders through mentoring. *School Leadership Review, 13*(2), 82–94.

Bishop, R. S. (2015). *Windows, mirrors, and sliding glass doors.* Accessed at https:// scenicregional.org/wp-content/uploads/2017/08/Mirrors-Windows-and-Sliding -Glass-Doors.pdf on May 30, 2023.

Blazar, D. (2021). *Teachers of color, culturally responsive teaching, and student outcomes: Experimental evidence from the random assignment of teachers to classes.* Accessed at https://edworkingpapers.com/sites/default/files/ai21-501.pdf on May 31, 2023.

Boudreau, E. (2020). *Future of education: Leading for equity.* Accessed at www.gse.harvard .edu/news/20/09/future-education-leading-equity on September 23, 2022.

Bovey, W. H., & Hede, A. (2001). Resistance to organizational change: The role of cognitive and affective processes. *Leadership & Organization Development Journal, 22*(8), 372–382.

Brackett, M., & Cipriano, C. (2020). *Teachers are anxious and overwhelmed. They need SEL now more than ever.* Accessed at www.edsurge.com/news/2020-04-07-teachers -are-anxious-and-overwhelmed-they-need-sel-now-more-than-ever on May 30, 2022.

Bromley, M. (2020). *COVID-19: Why we need ethical leadership more than ever—and what it looks like*. Accessed at www.headteacher-update.com/best-practice-article /covid-19-why-we-need-ethical-school-leadership-more-than-ever-and-what-it-looks -like-1/232071 on March 16, 2022.

Brown, B. (2018). *Dare to lead: Brave work. Tough conversations. Whole hearts*. New York: Random House.

Bryk, A. S., Sebring, P. B., Allensworth, E., Luppescu, S., & Easton, J. (2010). *Organizing schools for improvement: Lessons from Chicago*. Chicago: University of Chicago Press.

Buffum, A., Mattos, M., & Malone, J. (2018). *Taking action: A handbook for RTI at Work*. Bloomington, IN: Solution Tree Press.

Byrne, R. (2010). *The secret*. New York: Simon & Schuster.

Cameron, L. (2021). *Study confirms school-to-prison pipeline*. Accessed at www.usnews.com /news/education-news/articles/2021-07-27/study-confirms-school-to-prison-pipeline on April 8, 2022.

Cantor, P., Osher, D., Berg, J., Icon Steyer, L., & Rose, T. (2018). Malleability, plasticity, and individuality: How children learn and develop in context. *Applied Developmental Science, 23*, 307–337.

Carter, S. (2013). *The telltale signs of burnout . . . Do you have them?* Accessed www .psychologytoday.com/us/blog/high-octane-women/201311/the-tell-tale-signs-of -burnout-do-you-have-them on May 30, 2022.

Cartledge, G., Yurick, A. L., & Oif Telesman, A. (2022). *There's more to the story: Using literature to teach diversity and social-emotional skills in the elementary classroom*. Bloomington, IN: Solution Tree Press.

Center for School Change. (2022). *Vision and mission*. Accessed at https://centerfor schoolchange.org/publications/minnesota-charter-school-handbook/vision-and -mission on January 23, 2022.

Centers for Disease Control. (2020). *Mental health, substance use, and suicidal ideation during the COVID-19 pandemic—United States, June 24–30, 2020*. Accessed at www.cdc.gov/mmwr/volumes/69/wr/mm6932a1.htm on May 30, 2023.

Chang, W. C., & Viesca, K. M. (2022). Preparing teachers for culturally responsive/ relevant pedagogy (CRP): A critical review of research. *Teachers College Record, 24*(2). https://doi.org/10.1177/01614681221086676

Chatterji, R., Campbell, N., & Quirk, A. (2021). *Closing advanced coursework equity gaps for all students*. Accessed at www.americanprogress.org/article/closing-advanced -coursework-equity-gaps-students on April 10, 2022.

Cherng, H. S. (2017). If they think I can: Teacher bias and youth of color expectations and achievement. *Social Science Research, 66*, 170–186.

Chua, J. (2019). *Power or responsiveness: Which one matters more?* Accessed at www.torque .com.sg/features/power-responsiveness-matters-more on May 20, 2019.

Ciulla, J. B. (Ed.). (2014). *Ethics, the heart of leadership* (3rd ed.). Santa Barbara, CA: Praeger.

Clash, C. (2020). *Unfinished learning, or unfinished teaching? A mindset shift.* Accessed at www.achievementnetwork.org/anetblog/unfinished-learning-or-unfinished-teaching on January 26, 2022.

College and Career Alliance and Support Network. (2022). *Developing vision and mission statements in a multiple pathways school.* Accessed at https://casn.berkeley.edu/wp -content/uploads/resource_files/School-Wide_Mission_Process.pdf on November 7, 2022.

Cooperative Children's Book Center, University of Wisconsin-Madison. (2018). *CCBC diversity statistics.* Accessed at https://ccbc.education.wisc.edu/literature-resources /ccbc-diversity-statistics on May 29, 2022.

Coulter, R. W. S., Schneider, S. K., Beadnell, B., & O'Donnell, L. (2017). Associations of outside- and within-school adult support on suicidality: Moderating effects of sexual orientation. *American Journal of Orthopsychiatry, 87*(6), 671–679.

Cozolino, L. (2017). *The neuroscience of psychotherapy: Healing the social brain* (3rd ed.). New York: Norton.

Crippen, C., & Willows, J. (2019). Connecting teacher leadership and servant leadership: A synergistic partnership. *Journal of Leadership Education, 18*(2). Accessed at https:// journalofleadershiped.org/jole_articles/connecting-teacher-leadership-and-servant -leadership-a-synergistic-partnership on May 28, 2023.

Curry, J. R., & Csaszar, I. E. (2021). *Mitigating teacher stress and burnout for the pandemic.* Accessed at https://afrotc.lsu.edu/chse/education/bestpractices/2021/december.php on January 7, 2021.

Dao, F. (2008). *Without confidence, there is no leadership.* Accessed at www.inc.com /resources/leadership/articles/20080301/dao.html on December 1, 2021.

Darling-Hammond, L., Hyler, M. E., & Gardner, M. (2017). *Effective teacher professional development.* Palo Alto, CA: Learning Policy Institute.

Davis, R. (2022). *Equitable, inclusive, parent communication is key is helping students thrive.* Accessed at https://edsource.org/2022/equitable-inclusive-parent-communication-is -key-to-helping-students-thrive/670489 on May 30, 2022.

Davis, S. (2018). *LeBron James reportedly spends $1.5 million per year to take care of his body; here's where it goes.* Accessed at www.businessinsider.com/how-lebron-james-spends -money-body-care-2018-7 on February 3, 2023.

Davison, M., Penner, A. M., & Penner, E. K. (2022). Restorative for all? Racial disproportionality and school discipline under restorative justice. *American Educational Research Journal, 59*(4), 687–718. https://doi.org/10.3102/00028312211062613

Day, S. (2013). "Terms of engagement" not "hard to reach parents." *Educational Psychology in Practice, 29*(1), 36–53.

The Decision Lab. (2023). *Impostor syndrome.* Accessed at https://thedecisionlab.com/reference-guide/organizational-behavior/impostor-syndrome on May 17, 2023.

Defensive Driving. (2020). *Defensive driving tip #12: Look down the road!* Accessed at http://2passdd.com/taylor/defensive-driving-tip-12-look-down-the-road on January 16, 2022.

DeMatthews, D., Reyes, P., Carrola, P., Edwards, W., & James, L. (2021). Novice principal burnout: Exploring secondary trauma, working conditions, and coping strategies in an urban district. *Leadership and Policy in Schools, 22*(1), 1–17. https://doi.org/10.1080/15700763.2021.1917624

Dinham, S. (2007). *Authoritative leadership, action learning, and student accomplishment.* Accessed at https://research.acer.edu.au/cgi/viewcontent.cgi?article=1001&context=research_conference_2007 on January 23, 2023.

Dowd, M. (2018). *Duties and responsibilities of school principals.* Accessed at https://work.chron.com/duties-responsibilities-school-principals-7885.html on January 6, 2022.

Doyle, M. (2022). *7 leadership styles and how to find your own.* Accessed at www.americanexpress.com/en-us/business/trends-and-insights/articles/the-7-most-common-leadership-styles-and-how-to-find-your-own on November 23, 2022.

Dunbar, F. (2016). *7 easy ways to improve school-wide communication.* Accessed at www.edutopia.org/article/7-easy-ways-to-improve-school-wide-communication-folwell-dunbar on May 13, 2022.

Dynamic Transitions. (2021). *The origins of impostor syndrome.* Accessed at www.dynamictransitionsllp.com/origins-imposter-syndrome on November 28, 2021.

Economy, P. (2016). *How the platinum rule trumps the golden rule every time.* Accessed at www.inc.com/peter-economy/how-the-platinum-rule-trumps-the-golden-rule-every-time.html on February 8, 2022.

Edmonds, R. (2022). *Educational equity: A definition.* Accessed at www.nationalequityproject.org/education-equity-definition on February 22, 2022.

The Education Trust. (2020). *Black and Latino students shut out of advanced coursework opportunities.* Accessed at https://edtrust.org/press-release/black-and-latino-students-shut-out-of-advanced-coursework-opportunities on April 8, 2022.

Education World. (2015). *School mission statements: Where is your school going?* Accessed at www.educationworld.com/a_admin/admin/admin229.shtml on February 17, 2022.

Egalite, A. J., Kisida, B., & Winters, M. A. (2015). Representation in the classroom: The effect of own-race teachers on student achievement. *Economics of Education Review*, *45*, 44–52.

Eragula, R. (2015). Confidence in leadership. *Advances in Economics and Business Management*, *2*(11), 1070–1072.

Fashiku, C. O. (2017). Effective communication: Any role in classroom teaching-learning process in Nigerian schools? *Bulgarian Journal of Science Education Policy*, *11*(1), 171–187.

Fencl, H., & Scheel, K. (2005). Engaging students: An examination of the effects of teaching strategies on self-efficacy and course in a nonmajors physics course. *Journal of College Science Teaching*, *35*(1), 20–24.

Fergus, E., & Noguera, P. (2021). The role of school leaders in advancing equity and social justice. *Educational Administration Quarterly*, *57*(1), 4–11.

Fleming, P. (2019). *What leading for equity can look like*. Accessed at www.wallace foundation.org/news-and-media/blog/pages/what-leading-for-equity-can-look-like -paul-fleming.aspx on March 23, 2022.

Fontein, D. (2022). *Your guide to transformational leadership in education*. Accessed at https://thoughtexchange.com/blog/transformational-leadership-in-education on May 28, 2023.

Francis, D. V., de Oliveira, A. C., & Dimmitt. C. (2019). Do school counselors exhibit bias in recommending students for advanced coursework? *The B.E. Journal of Economic Analysis & Policy*, *19*(4), 1–17.

Fronius, T., Darling-Hammond, S., Sutherland, H., Guckenburg, S., Hurley, N., & Petrosino, A. (2019). *Restorative justice in U.S. schools: An updated research review*. San Francisco: The WestEd Justice & Prevention Research Center.

Gabriel, J. G., & Farmer, P. C. (2009). *How to help your school thrive without breaking the bank*. Alexandria, VA: Association for Supervision and Curriculum Development.

Gale, S. F. (2019). *Leadership styles: One size does not fit all*. Accessed at www.chief learningofficer.com/2019/07/10/leadership-styles-one-size-does-not-fit-all on May 28, 2023.

Garibay, C. (2021). *Leadership styles in education: Five ways to lead in education*. Accessed at https://valiantceo.com/leadership-styles-in-education on June 10, 2022.

Gay, G. (2010). *Culturally responsive teaching: Theory, research, and practice* (Multicultural Education Series; 2nd ed.). New York: Columbia University.

Georgia Leader Institute for School Improvement for the Principal Professional Learning Community. (2014). *Shaping a vision of academic success for all students: A roadmap of key processes and effective practices.* Accessed at https://glisi.org/resources/shaping -vision-academic-success-students-roadmap-key-processes-effective-practices on January 23, 2023.

Gershenson, S., Holt, S. B., & Papageorge, N. W. (2016). Who believes in me? The effect of student-teacher demographic match on teacher expectations. *Economics of Education Review, 52,* 209–224.

Gershenson, S., & Papageorge, N. (2018). The power of teacher expectations: How racial bias hinders student attainment. *Education Next, 18*(1), 64–70.

Glaze, A. (2014). Communication: The essence of leadership. *Principal Connections, 18*(2), 7–9.

GLSEN. (2022). *Respect for all: Policy recommendations to support LGBTQ+ students.* Accessed at www.glsen.org/activity/respect-all-policy-recommendations-support -lgbtq-students on April 23, 2022.

Goleman, D. (2002). *Primal leadership: Realizing the power of emotional intelligence.* Boston: Harvard Business School Press.

Gonsalo, J. (2021). *How to improve school communication: A detailed guide.* Accessed at www.schoolvoice.com/blog/how-to-improve-school-communication on May 16, 2023.

Google Translate. (n.d.). *Translate documents and websites.* Accessed at https://support .google.com/translate/answer/2534559 on January 3, 2023.

Gregory, A., & Evans, K. R. (2020). *The starts and stumbles of restorative justice in education: Where do we go from here?* Boulder, CO: National Education Policy Center.

Gregory, A., & Weinstein, R. S. (2008). The discipline gap and African Americans: Defiance or cooperation in the high school classroom. *Journal of School Psychology, 46*(4), 455–475.

Greytak, E. A., Kosciw, J. G., Villenas, C., & Giga, N. M. (2016). *From teasing to torment: School climate revisited—A survey of U.S. secondary school students and teachers.* New York: GLSEN. Accessed at www.glsen.org/sites/default/files/2019-12/From_Teasing _to_Tormet_Revised_2016.pdf on June 18, 2023.

Grissom, J. A., Egalite, A., J., & Lindsay, C. A. (2021). *How principals affect students and schools: A systematic synthesis of two decades of research.* New York: The Wallace Foundation.

Gutierrez, L. (2014). *Cognitive science: Adult training and development.* Accessed at https:// freshapproachlearning.wordpress.com/2014/01/26/cognitive-science-adult-training -and-development on November 20, 2022.

Hallinger, P., & Heck, R. H. (2011). Exploring the principal's contribution to school effectiveness: 1980–2010. *School Effectiveness and School Improvement, 22*(4), 489–516.

Hammond, Z. (2015). *Culturally responsive teaching and the brain: Promoting authentic engagement and rigor among culturally and linguistically diverse students.* Thousand Oaks, CA: Corwin Press.

Hamre, B. K., & Pianta, R. C. (2001). Early teacher-child relationships and the trajectory of children's school outcomes through eighth grade. *Child Development, 72*(2), 625–638.

Hannigan, J., Hannigan, J. D., Mattos, M., & Buffum, A. (2021). *Behavior solutions: Teaching academic and social skills through RTI at Work.* Bloomington, IN: Solution Tree Press.

Hanson, T., Zhang, G., Cerna, R., Stern, A., & Austin, G. (2019). *Understanding the experiences of LGBTQ+ students in California.* San Francisco: WestEd.

Hanushek, E. A., & Rivkin, S. G. (2010). Generalizations about using value-added measures of teacher quality. *American Economic Review, 100*(2), 267–271.

Hasan, S. (2013). Transformational leadership in educational context: A fantasy of education scholars. Editor's choice: Selected keynote speech. *Eurasian Journal of Educational Research, 51*, 1–6.

Hattie, J. (2012). *Visible learning for teachers: Maximizing impact on learning.* New York: Routledge.

Hein, R. (2013). *How to apply transformational leadership at your company.* Accessed at www.cio.com/article/288976/careers-staffing-how-to-apply-transformational -leadership-at-your-company.html on February 8, 2022.

Hiatt, B. (2018). *Husband finds Laverton school principal Trish Antulov dead at her desk.* Accessed at www.perthnow.com.au/news/wa/husband-finds-laverton-school-principal -trish-antulov-dead-at-her-desk-ng-b88751673z on January 12, 2023.

Hill, L. (2022). *How schools can overcome the barriers of family engagement and inspire success.* Accessed at https://blog.schoolspecialty.com/how-schools-can-overcome-the -barriers-of-family-engagement-and-inspire-success on May 30, 2023.

Hill, N. (2005). *Think and grow rich: The landmark bestseller now revised and updated for the 21st century* (Revised and enlarged ed.). New York: TarcherPerigee.

Hollingworth, L., Olsen, D., Asikin-Garmager, A., & Winn, K. M. (2017). Initiating conversations and opening doors: How principals establish a positive building culture to sustain school improvement efforts. *Educational Management Administration & Leadership, 46*(6), 1014–1034.

Hopkins, G. (2017). *Principals share lessons learned about communicating with parents, others*. Accessed at www.educationworld.com/a_admin/admin/admin511.shtml on May 9, 2022.

How a Car Works. (2021). *The engine*. Accessed at www.howacarworks.com/basics/the -engine on December 21, 2021.

Howard, T. (2020). *7 culturally responsive teaching strategies and instructional practices*. Accessed at www.hmhco.com/blog/culturally-responsive-teaching-strategies -instruction-practices on May 26, 2022.

Ikemoto, G., Taliaferro, L., Fenton, B., & Davis, J. (2014). *Great principals at scale: Creating district conditions that enable all principals to be effective*. Accessed at https:// files.eric.ed.gov/fulltext/ED556346.pdf on January 12, 2022.

Illinois School Report Card. (2021–2022). *Posen Elementary School (4–5)*. Accessed at www.illinoisreportcard.com/School.aspx?source=admins&Schoolid=0701614350 22006 on January 12, 2022.

Indeed Editorial Team. (2023). *Leadership styles in education: 5 effective ways to lead*. Accessed at www.indeed.com/career-advice/career-development/leadership-styles -in-education on June 2, 2023.

Iqbal, Z. A., Abid, G., Arshad, M., Ashfaq, F., Ahsan Athar, M., & Hassan, Q. (2021). Impact of authoritative and laissez-faire leadership on thriving at work: The moderating role of conscientiousness. *European Journal of Investigation Health Psychology and Education, 11*(3), 667–685.

Jackson, K. (2018). The influence of teacher diversity on student diversity attitudes. *Education and Urban Society, 50*(6), 562–583.

Jacques, C., & Villegas, A. (2018). *Strategies for equitable family engagement*. Accessed at https://oese.ed.gov/files/2020/10/equitable_family-engag_508.pdf on May 10, 2022.

Jarvis, S. N., & Okonofua, J. A. (2020). School deferred: When bias affects school leaders. *Social Psychological and Personality Science, 11*(4), 492–498.

Joint Committee on Administrative Rules, Illinois General Assembly. (n.d.). *Administrative code*. Accessed at www.ilga.gov/commission/jcar/admincode/titles.html on January 3, 2023.

Joseph, M. X. (2021). *9 ways to promote equity in our schools*. Accessed at www.edutopia .org/article/9-ways-promote-equity-our-schools on April 23, 2022.

Kampen, A. (2019). *School mission statements: The 2021 guide (+ 6 writing tips)*. Accessed at www.prodigygame.com/main-en/blog/school-mission-statements on September 24, 2023.

Kampen, M. (2022). *8 powerful ways to promote equity in the classroom*. Accessed at www .prodigygame.com/main-en/blog/equity-in-the-classroom on September 24, 2023.

Katz-Amey, J. (2019). Interrupting inequitable discipline practices. *Multicultural Education, 27*(1), 37–42.

Kelleher, J. (2016). You're OK, I'm OK: Self-efficacy for principals. *Phi Delta Kappan, 97*(8), 70–73.

Kirk, K. (2022). Self-efficacy: Helping students believe in themselves. Accessed at https://serc.carleton.edu/NAGTWorkshops/affective/efficacy.html#references on November 20, 2022.

Kosciw, J. G., Greytak, E. A., & Diaz, E. M. (2009). Who, what, where, when, and why: Demographic and ecological factors contributing to hostile school climate for lesbian, gay, bisexual and transgender youth. *Journal of Youth and Adolescence, 38*(7), 976–988.

Kosciw, J. G., Greytak, E. A., Zongrone, A. D., Clark, C. M., & Truong, N. L. (2018). *The 2017 National School Climate Survey: The experiences of lesbian, gay, bisexual, transgender, and queer youth in our nation's schools.* New York: GLSEN. Accessed at www.glsen.org/sites/default/files/2019-10/GLSEN-2017-National-School-Climate -Survey-NSCS-Full-Report.pdf on June 18, 2023.

Kottler, J. (2018). *What you don't know about leadership but probably should.* New York: Oxford University Press.

Kraft, M. A. (2020). Interpreting effect sizes of education interventions. *Educational Researcher, 49*(4), 241–253.

Kramer, S. V., & Schuhl, S. (2023). *Acceleration for all: A how-to guide for overcoming learning gaps.* Bloomington, IN: Solution Tree Press.

Krasnoff, B. (2016). *Culturally responsive teaching: A guide to evidence-based practices for teaching all students equitably.* Accessed at www.educationnorthwest.org/sites/default /files/resources/culturally-responsive-teaching-508.pdf on September 20, 2021.

Kubic, C. (2021). *Can teachers be warm demanders during the pandemic?* Accessed at www .edutopia.org/article/can-teachers-be-warm-demanders-during-pandemic on September 7, 2021.

Ladson-Billings, G. (1995). But that's just good teaching! The case for culturally relevant pedagogy. *Theory Into Practice, 34*(3), 159–165.

Ladson-Billings, G. (2014). Culturally relevant pedagogy 2.0: a.k.a. the remix. *Harvard Educational Review, 84*(1), 74–84.

Lardieri, A. (2020). *Coronavirus pandemic causing anxiety, depression in Americans, CDC finds.* Accessed at www.usnews.com/news/health-news/articles/2020-08-13 /coronavirus-pandemic-causing-anxiety-depression-in-americans-cdc-finds on May 30, 2022.

LaRocque, M. (2013). Addressing cultural and linguistic dissonance between parents and schools. *Preventing School Failure, 57*(2), 111–117.

LEADx. (2022). *Servant leadership: Definition, examples, characteristics.* Accessed at https://leadx.org/articles/servant-leadership-definition-examples-characteristics on June 2, 2023.

Leamey, T. (2023). *Here's why drinking water is the key to good mental health.* Accessed at www.cnet.com/health/mental/heres-why-drinking-water-is-the-key-to-good-mental -health on June 18, 2023.

Lee, E., & Elliott-Lee, D. (2006). *Courage: The backbone of leadership.* San Francisco: Jossey-Bass.

Leithwood, K., Day, C. Sammons, P. Harris, A., & Hopkins, B. (2006). *Successful school leadership: What it is and how it influences pupil learning.* Accessed at www.nysed.gov /common/nysed/files/principal-project-file-55-successful-school-leadership-what-it-is -and-how-it-influences-pupil-learning.pdf on January 23, 2023.

Leithwood, K., Harris, A., & Hopkins, D. (2020). Seven strong claims about successful school leadership revisited. *School Leadership & Management, 40*(1), 5–22.

Leithwood, K., & Riehl, C. (2003). *What we know about successful school leadership.* Philadelphia: Laboratory for Student Success, Temple University. Accessed at http:// olms.cte.jhu.edu/data/ck/file/What_we_know_about_SchoolLeadership.pdf on June 27, 2023.

Les Schwab. (n.d.). *How your auto battery works.* Accessed at www.lesschwab.com/article /batteries/how-your-auto-battery-works.html on March 2, 3023.

Levin, S. (2021). *Principals matter for schools and students.* Accessed at www.niet.org /newsroom/show/blog/principals-matter-for-schools-students on January 13, 2022.

Li, L., & Liu, Y. (2020). An integrated model of principal transformational leadership and teacher leadership that is related to teacher self-efficacy and student academic performance. *Asia Pacific Journal of Education, 42*(2). Accessed at www.tandfonline .com/doi/abs/10.1080/02188791.2020.1806036 on June 18, 2023.

Ligette, R. (2022). Democratic leadership in a study of school based professional leadership culture: Policy implications. *International Journal of Leadership in Education.* https://doi.org/10.1080/13603124.2021.2009036

Long, C. (2021). *Restorative discipline makes huge impact in Texas elementary and middle schools.* Accessed at www.nea.org/advocating-for-change/new-from-nea/restorative -discipline-makes-huge-impact-texas-elementary-and on April 23, 2022.

Louis, K. S., Leithwood, K., Wahlstrom, K., & Anderson, S. (2010). *Investigating the links to improved student learning: Final report of research findings.* Accessed at https:// conservancy.umn.edu/bitstream/handle/11299/140885/Learning-from-Leadership _Final-Research-Report_July-2010.pdf on May 29, 2022.

Lozano, J. M., & Castiñeira, A. (2019). *4 types of educational leadership*. Accessed at https://dobetter.esade.edu/en/types-educational-leadership on June 10, 2022.

Lupinacci, T. M. (2019). *Key characteristics of effective leadership*. Accessed at www.bakerdonelson.com/key-characteristics-of-effective-leadership on June 1, 2022.

Lynch, M. (2015). *The eight principles of ethical leadership*. Accessed at www.theedadvocate.org/the-eight-principles-of-ethical-leadership-in-education on March 21, 2022.

Lynch, M. (2020). *Effective education leaders have self-confidence*. Accessed at www.theedadvocate.org/effective-education-leaders-have-self-confidence on December 2, 2021.

Ma, X., Yao, J., & Mu, X. (2020). Developing and implementing school vision and mission statements: A case study in a Chinese public school. *Frontiers of Education in China, 15*(1), 62–80.

Mager, D. (2017). *The 4 primary principles of communication*. Accessed at www.psychologytoday.com/us/blog/some-assembly-required/201702/the-4-primary-principles-communication on May 14, 2022.

Mahfouz, J. (2018). Principals and stress: Few coping strategies for abundant stressors. *Educational Management Administration & Leadership, 48*(3), 1–19.

Malingkas, M., Senduk, J. F., Simandjuntak, S., & Binilang, B. B. (2018). The effects of servant leader and integrity of principal performance in catholic senior high schools in North Sulawesi, Indonesia. *Journal of International Education and Leadership, 8*(1), 1–19.

Marshall, D. T., Pressley, T., Neugebauer, N. M., & Shannon, D. M. (2022). Why teachers are leaving and what we can do about it. *Phi Delta Kappan, 104*(1), 6–11. Accessed at https://kappanonline.org/why-teachers-are-leaving-what-we-can-do-marshall-pressley-neugebauer-shannon on May 31, 2023.

Masterclass. (2022). *How to be an effective leader: 8 styles of leadership*. Accessed at www.masterclass.com/articles/how-to-be-an-effective-leader on June 10, 2022.

Mattos, M. (2017). *Timebomb: The cost of dropping out* [DVD]. Bloomington, IN: Solution Tree Press.

Mautz, S. (2022). *Science says this is why you fear change (and what to do about it)*. Accessed at www.inc.com/scott-mautz/science-says-this-is-why-you-fear-change-and-what-to-do-about-it.html on May 30, 2022.

Maxwell, S., Reynolds, K. J., Lee, E., Subasic, E., & Bromehad, D. (2017). *The impact of school climate and school identification on academic achievement: Multilevel modeling with student and teacher data*. Accessed at www.frontiersin.org/articles/10.3389/fpsyg.2017.02069/full on February 21, 2022.

Mayer, G. (2018). *Subconscious mind: How to unlock its use and power.* Accessed at www.fromgnometogoliath.com/2017/06/14/subconscious-mind-power on November 30, 2021.

McCluskey, G., Lloyd, G., Kane, J., & Riddell, S. (2021). 'It's about giving them a voice and an opportunity to learn and grow': Teacher perspectives on implementing restorative approaches in schools. *Pastoral Care in Education*, *39*(2), 183–197. https://doi.org/10.1080/02643944.2020.1834348

McCormick, M. J. (2001). Self-efficacy and leadership effectiveness: Applying social cognitive theory to leadership. *Journal of Leadership Studies*, *8*(1), 22–33.

McFadden, M. (2021). *5 critical best practices for concise, engaging school communications.* Accessed at www.k12dive.com/news/5-critical-best-practices-for-concise-engaging -school-communications/607540 on May 14, 2022.

McInerney, A., & McKlindon, M. (2020). *Unlocking the door to learning: Trauma-informed classrooms and transformational schools.* Accessed at www.elc-pa.org/wp-content/uploads /2015/06/Trauma-Informed-in-Schools-Classrooms-FINAL-December2014-2.pdf on May 9, 2022.

McMorris, B. J., Beckman, K. J., Shea, G., & Eggert, R. C. (2013). *A pilot program evaluation of the Family and Restorative Conference Program, 2.* Accessed at www .legalrightscenter.org/uploads/2/5/7/3/25735760/lrc_umn_report-final.pdf on April 23, 2022.

Merriam-Webster. (n.d.a). Confidence. In *Merriam-Webster.com dictionary.* Accessed at www.merriam-webster.com/dictionary/confidence on March 20, 2023.

Merriam-Webster. (n.d.b). Discipline. In *Merriam-Webster.com dictionary.* Accessed at www.merriam-webster.com/dictionary/discipline on May 31, 2023.

Millman, D. (1984). *Way of the peaceful warrior: A book that changes lives.* Tiburon, CA: Kramer.

Monteith, A. (2018). *5 tips on communicating your vision and values.* Accessed at www .ambition.org.uk/blog/5-tips-communicating-your-vision-and-values on February 4, 2022.

Morgan. H. (2021). Restorative justice and the school-to-prison pipeline: A review of existing literature. *Education Sciences*, *11*(4), 159–169.

Morgan, I., & Amerikaner, A. (2018). *Funding gaps 2018: An analysis of school funding equity across the U.S. and within each state.* Accessed at https://edtrust.org/resource /funding-gaps-2018 on May 17, 2023.

Murez, C. (2021). *Big rise in U.S. teens identifying as gay, bisexual.* Accessed at www.us news.com/news/health-news/articles/2021-06-15/big-rise-in-us-teens-identifying-as -gay-bisexual on April 10, 2022.

Murnane, R., Willett, J., & Tyler, J. (2000). Do the cognitive skills of school dropouts matter in the labor market? *Journal of Human Resources, 35*(4), 748–754.

Murphy, J. (2009). *The power of your subconscious mind.* New York: TarcherPerigee.

National Academies of Sciences, Engineering, and Medicine. (2020). *Understanding the well-being of LGBTQI+ populations.* Washington, DC: The National Academies Press.

National Association of Secondary School Principals. (2022). *NASSP's survey of America's school leaders and high school students.* Accessed at https://survey.nassp.org/2022 /#welcome on March 20, 2023.

National Center for Education Statistics. (2015). *Public school teacher attrition and mobility in the first five years: Results from the first through fifth waves of the 2007–08 beginning teacher longitudinal study.* Accessed at https://nces.ed.gov/pubs2015/2015337.pdf on May 17, 2023.

National Center for Education Statistics. (2021a). *The condition of education 2021.* Accessed at https://nces.ed.gov/pubsearch/pubsinfo.asp?pubid=2021144 on March 3, 2023.

National Center for Education Statistics. (2021b). *Preprimary, elementary, and secondary education.* Accessed at https://nces.ed.gov/programs/coe/preprimary-elementary-and -secondary on January 18, 2022.

National Center on Safe and Supportive Learning Environments. (2016). *Quick guide on making school climate improvements.* Accessed at http://safesupportivelearning.ed.gov /SCIRP/Quick-Guide on December 21, 2022.

National Equity Project. (2022). *Creating a world that works for all of us.* Accessed at www.nationalequityproject.org on March 14, 2022.

National School Boards Association (2017). *Creating a vision for your school.* Accessed at www.nsba.org/sites/default/files/reports/Creating_a_Vision_for_Your_School.pdf on May 2, 2023.

Odiorne, G. S. (1974). *Management and the activity trap.* New York: Harper & Row.

O'Donnell, G. (2018). *Studies provide further proof that African American students benefit from having Black teachers.* Accessed at www.insightintodiversity.com/studies-provide -further-proof-that-african-american-students-benefit-from-having-black-teachers on February 24, 2022.

Olsen, L., Bhattacharya, A., & Scharf, A. (2006). *Cultural competency: What it is and why it matters.* Accessed at https://california.foundationcenter.org/reports/cultural -competency-what-it-is-and-why-it-matters on May 10, 2023.

Oplatka, I. (2017). Principal workload: Components, determinants, and coping strategies in an era of standardization and accountability. *Journal of Educational Administration, 55*(5), 552–568.

Organisation for Economic Co-operation and Development. (2007). *No more failures: Ten steps to equity in education.* Accessed at www.oecd.org/education/school/39676364.pdf on May 17, 2023.

Osher, D., & Kendziora, K. (2020). The importance of school climate. *Educational Leadership*, *77*(6), 52–57.

Owens, B. (2017). *Do you know your school's vision? Tips on making a meaningful mission statement.* Accessed at www.edweek.org/education/opinion-do-you-know-your-schools -vision-tips-on-making-a-meaningful-mission-statement/2017/11 on February 17, 2022.

Owens, K. (2015). *The five keys of safe driving.* Accessed at https://blog.steeringyourhealth .com/keys-safe-driving on May, 2, 2023.

Oyer, B. (2015). Teacher perceptions of principals' confidence, humility, and effectiveness: Implications for educational leadership. *Journal of School Leadership*, *25*(4), 684–719.

Pacheco, M., & Zeichner, K. (2021). Developing equity leadership in teacher education: Challenges and opportunities. *Journal of Teacher Education*, *72*(1), 36–49.

Parker, D. (2019). *Building bridges: Engaging students at-risk through the power of relationships.* Bloomington, IN: Solution Tree Press.

Parker, P. (2016). *White teachers are more likely to expect their Black students to fail.* Accessed at https://stateofopportunity.michiganradio.org/education/2016-04-01/white-teachers -are-more-likely-to-expect-their-black-students-to-fail on February 24, 2022.

Parker, W. D. (2020). *Pause. Breathe. Flourish. Living your best life as an educator.* Chicago: ConnectEDD.

Patrick, K., Socol, A. R., & Morgan, I. (2020). *Inequities in advanced coursework: What's driving them and what leaders can do.* Accessed at https://edtrust.org/wp-content /uploads/2014/09/Inequities-in-Advanced-Coursework-Whats-Driving-Them-and -What-Leaders-Can-Do-January-2019.pdf on December 21, 2022.

Peters, S. J., & Boser, J. A. (2021). Equity-based school improvement: A scoping review. *Journal of Educational Administration*, *59*(3), 357–376.

Picower, B. (2009). The unexamined whiteness of teaching: How white teachers maintain and enact dominant racial ideologies. *Race, Ethnicity, and Education*, *12*(2), 197–215.

Pierce, R. (2020). *Developing leaders today for education equity tomorrow.* Accessed at www .forbes.com/sites/raymondpierce/2020/12/14/developing-leaders-today-for-education -equity-tomorrow/?sh=3984850e244f on March 23, 2022.

Positive Action. (2021). *A practical guide to equity in education.* Accessed at www.positive action.net/blog/equity-in-education on September 20, 2021.

Potter, C. (2019). *Windows, mirrors, and sliding glass doors: Ensuring students see themselves and others in literature.* Accessed at https://humaneeducation.org/windows-and-mirrors-and-sliding-glass-doors-ensuring-students-see-themselves-and-others-in-literature on December 21, 2022.

Pounder, J. (2014). Quality teaching through transformational classroom leadership. *Quality Assurance in Education, 22*(3), 273–85.

PowerDMS. (2020). *Importance of clear policies and procedures in schools.* Accessed at www.powerdms.com/policy-learning-center/importance-of-clear-policies-and-procedures-in-schools on April 8, 2022.

Presence Learning. (2020). *Are you an overwhelmed school principal? How to defuse the situation.* Accessed at https://globalteletherapy.com/overwhelmed-school-principal-how-to-defuse-the-situation on October 10, 2021.

Pressley, T. (2021). Factors contributing to teacher burnout during COVID-19. *Educational Researcher, 50*(5), 325–327.

Prothero, A. (2020). *The essential traits of a positive school climate.* Accessed at www.edweek.org/leadership/the-essential-traits-of-a-positive-school-climate/2020/10 on February 21, 2022.

The Quotable Coach. (n.d.). *Sonia Sotomayor, U.S. Supreme Court Justice.* Accessed at www.thequotablecoach.com/a-surplus-of-effort-could-overcome-a-deficit-of-confidence on May 18, 2023.

Ray, B. (2017) Educational leadership coaching as professional development. *School Leadership Review, 12*(1), 29–38.

Raypole, C. (2021). *You're not a fraud. Here's how to recognize and overcome imposter syndrome.* Accessed at www.healthline.com/health/mental-health/imposter-syndrome October 10, 2021.

Reddy, K. (2021). *Why confidence is important for a leader? 18 best reasons.* Accessed at https://content.wisestep.com/why-confidence-is-important-for-a-leader-best-reasons on December 2, 2021.

Remind. (2020). *Communication between principals and teachers in successful schools.* Accessed at www.remind.com/blog/communication-between-principals-and-teachers-in-successful-schools on May 11, 2022.

Remind. (2022). *How to improve communication: Feedback between teachers, families, and students.* Accessed at www.remind.com/blog/parent-feedback-about-teachers on May 11, 2022.

Renaissance Learning. (2016). *Considerations for Using STAR™ data with educator evaluation: Illinois.* Accessed at https://renaissance.widen.net/view/pdf/w5iaxfvhup/R58187.pdf on November 10, 2022.

Restorative Practice Working Group. (2014). *Restorative practices: Fostering healthy relationships and promoting positive discipline in schools—A guide for educators.* Accessed at https://schottfoundation.org/wp-content/uploads/restorative-practices-guide_0.pdf on May 29, 2022.

Richards, R. (2020). *Increase principal capacity by expanding teacher leadership: Lessons from Denver Public Schools.* Accessed at https://eab.com/insights/blogs/district-leadership /increase-principal-capacity-distributed-leadership-model on May 28, 2023.

Riley, P. (2018*). The Australian principal occupational health, safety and wellbeing survey: 2017 data.* Accessed at https://apo.org.au/node/133796 on May 16, 2023.

Rimmer, J. (2016). *Developing principals as equity-centered instructional leaders.* Accessed at www.eecresources4justice.com/wp-content/uploads/developing-principals-equity -leaders.pdf on March 28, 2022.

Rimm-Kaufman, S., & Sandilos, L. (2015). *Improving students' relationships with teachers to provide essential supports for learning.* Accessed at www.apa.org/education-career/k12 /relationships on May 21, 2022.

Robinson, A. (2022). *The fundamentals of leadership (according to me)* [Blog post]. Accessed at www.angie-robinson.com/podcast/episode03 on May 28, 2023.

Robinson, J. (2013). *School leadership and 3 acts of integrity to practice today.* Accessed at http://the21stcenturyprincipal.blogspot.com/2013/05/school-leadership-and-3-acts -of.html on March 16, 2022.

Robinson, V. J., Lloyd, C. A., & Rowe, K. J. (2008). The impact of leadership on student outcomes: An analysis of the differential effects of leadership types. *Educational Administration Quarterly, 44*(5), 635–674.

Roegman, R., & Hatch, T. (2016). The AP lever for boosting access, success, and equity. *Phi Delta Kappan, 97*(5), 20–25.

Rosen, J. (2018). *Black students who have one Black teacher more likely to go to college.* Accessed at https://hub.jhu.edu/2018/11/12/black-students-black-teachers-college-gap on June 2, 2023.

Ross, J. A., & Berger, M-J. (2009). Equity and leadership: Research-based strategies for school leaders. *School Leadership and Management, 29*(5), 461–474.

Russell, R. (2020) *The 3 ships: Relationships, leadership, and partnerships.* Spokane, WA: RLR Leadership Consulting.

Safir, S. (2017). *The listening leader: Creating the conditions for equitable school transformation.* San Francisco: John Wiley & Sons.

Salamondra, T. (2021). Effective communication in schools. *BU Journal of Graduate Studies in Education, 13*(1), 22–26.

Schaeffer, K. (2021). *America's public school teachers are far less racially and ethnically diverse than their students.* Accessed at www.pewresearch.org/fact-tank/2021/12/10/americas -public-school-teachers-are-far-less-racially-and-ethnically-diverse-than-their-students on February 26, 2022.

Schmidt-Davis, J., & Bottoms, G. (2011). *Who's next? Let's stop gambling on school performance and plan for principal succession.* Accessed at www.sreb.org/sites/main/files /file-attachments/11v19_principal_succession_planning.pdf on February 6, 2023.

Schott Foundation for Public Education. (2014). *Restorative practices: Fostering healthy relationships and promoting positive discipline in schools.* Accessed at https://schott foundation.org/resource/restorative-practices-fostering-healthy-relationships -promoting-positive-discipline-in-schools on April 23, 2022.

Schwartz, S. (2020). *Why drinking water is important for stress reduction.* Accessed at https://ecohappinessproject.com/why-drinking-water-is-important on June 2, 2023.

Shkurina, E. (2018). *School leadership styles: Which one are you?* Accessed at https://blog .youragora.com/school-leadership-styles-which-one-are-you on June 5, 2022.

SHRM. (2012). *What is the difference between mission, vision, and values statements?* Accessed at https://shrm.pace.edu.vn/knowledge-center-/mission-vision-statements -what-is-the-difference-between-mission-vision-value-statements on February 17, 2022.

Singer, D. J. (2023). *Leading is action, not a position: Six simple rules for a better life.* Accessed at www.sixsimplerules.com/leading-is-action-not-a-position on May 16, 2023.

Singhal, M., & Gulati, S. (2020). *Five essential strategies to embrace culturally responsive teaching.* Accessed at www.facultyfocus.com/articles/equality-inclusion-and-diversity /five-essential-strategies-to-embrace-culturally-responsive-teaching on May 29, 2022.

Skiba, R. J., Arredondo, M. I., & Raush, M. K. (2014). *New and developing research on disparities in discipline (Discipline Disparities Series: New Research).* Bloomington, IN: The Equity Project at Indiana University, Center for Evaluation and Education Policy. Accessed at www.njjn.org/uploads/digital-library/OSF_Discipline-Disparities _Disparity_NewResearch_3.18.14.pdf on June 2, 2023.

Sk Md, I. (2015). *Top 10 communication skills.* Accessed at www.linkedin.com/pulse/top -10-communication-skills-irrfan-sk-md on November 23, 2022.

Slate, J. R., Jones, C. H., Wiesman, K., Alexander, J., & Saenz, T. (2008). School mission statements and school performance: A mixed research investigation. *New Horizons in Education, 56*(2), 17–27.

Sleeter, C. E. (2008). Preparing white teachers for diverse students. In M. Cochran-Smith, S. Feiman-Memser, D. J. McIntyre, & K. E. Demers (Eds.), *Handbook of research in teacher education: Enduring questions in changing contexts* (pp. 559–582). New York: Routledge.

Smith. M., Segal, J., & Robinson, L. (2022). *Burnout prevention and treatment*. Accessed at www.helpguide.org/articles/stress/burnout-prevention-and-recovery.htm on November 22, 2022.

Soika, B. (2020). *How to provide leadership for educational equity*. Accessed at https://rossier.usc.edu/news-insights/news/how-to-provide-leadership-educational-equity on March 27, 2022.

Staats, C., Bohan-Baker, M., & Meyers, C. V. (2018). *Creating a positive school climate: Strategies for school leaders*. Accessed at https://ies.ed.gov/ncee/edlabs/regions/west/pdf/REL_2018297.pdf on May 13, 2023.

Stark, P. (2014). *The critical connection between confidence and leadership*. Accessed at www.linkedin.com/pulse/20141007145901-24517615-the-critical-connection-between-confidence-and-leadership on December 1, 2021.

Steiner, E. D., & Woo, A. (2021). *Job-related stress threatens the teacher supply: Key findings from the 2021 State of the U.S. Teacher Survey*. Accessed at www.rand.org/pubs/research_reports/RRA1108-1.html on November 7, 2021.

Stobierski, T. (2019). *5 pros and cons of authoritative leadership*. Accessed at https://online.hbs.edu/blog/post/authoritative-leadership-style on June 6, 2022.

Strammer. (2021). *Leadership success: Why self-confidence is vital for leaders*. Accessed at https://strammer.com/en/why-self-confidence-is-vital-for-leaders on December 2, 2021.

Strobbe, K. (2021). *Windows, mirrors, and sliding glass doors*. Accessed at https://witschicago.org/windows-mirrors-and-sliding-glass-doors on May 22, 2022.

Synchrony Car Care. (2023). *What you should know about your car's transmission*. Accessed at www.mysynchrony.com/blog/automotive/what-you-should-know-about-your-cars-transmission.html on May 16, 2023.

Tapp, F. (2017). *Teacher burnout: Causes, symptoms, and prevention*. Accessed at www.wgu.edu/heyteach/article/teacher-burnout-causes-symptoms-and-prevention1711.html on May 17, 2023.

Tate Sullivan, E. (2022). *Principals are on the brink of breakdown*. Accessed at www.edsurge.com/news/2022-07-06-principals-are-on-the-brink-of-a-breakdown on September 28, 2022.

Tatum, B. D. (2017). *"Why are all the Black kids sitting together in the cafeteria?": And other conversations about race*. New York: Basic Books.

Tendig. (2021). *16 exercises to boost your confidence*. Accessed at https://tendig.com/16-exercises-to-boost-your-confidence on November 5, 2022.

Texas Elementary Principals and Supervisors Association. (2020). *7 ways to lead equity in schools*. Accessed at www.tepsa.org/resource/7-ways-to-lead-equity-in-schools on March 13, 2022.

Thomas, E., & Lindgren-Streicher, A. (2021). Leaders for equity: The influence of principal racial/ethnic identity on leading for equity. *Journal of School Leadership, 31*(3), 315–338.

Thompson, A., & Gomez, J. (2021). Conquering imposter syndrome. *National Association of Elementary School Principals, 100*(3). Accessed at www.naesp.org/resource /conquering-imposter-syndrome on December 21, 2022.

Thompson, J. (2019). *Advantages and disadvantages of transformational leadership*. Accessed at https://smallbusiness.chron.com/advantages-disadvantages-transformational -leadership-20979.html on June 6, 2022.

Toftdahl, S. D. (2020). *The 7 most common leadership styles (and how to find your own)*. Accessed at www.linkedin.com/pulse/7-most-common-leadership-styles-how-find -your-own-sophia on June 10, 2022.

Tucci, L. (2018). *Servant leadership*. Accessed at www.techtarget.com/searchcio/definition /Servant-Leadership on June 6, 2022.

Tunstall, E. D. (2014). *How Maya Angelou made me feel*. Accessed at https://the conversation.com/how-maya-angelou-made-me-feel-27328 on November 7, 2022.

Turner, C. S. V., & Sanders, M. G. (2021). Cultivating equity-minded leaders in higher education. *Journal of Diversity in Higher Education, 14*(2), 89–101.

Tyler, D. E. (2016). Communication behaviors of principals at high performing Title I elementary schools in Virginia: School leaders, communication, and transformative efforts. *Creighton Journal of Interdisciplinary Leadership, 2*(2), 2–16.

Understood Educators Team. (2022). *What is culturally responsive teaching?* Accessed at www.understood.org/en/articles/what-is-culturally-responsive-teaching on November 20, 2022.

United Nations Office of Drugs and Crime. (2020). *University Module Series: Integrity and ethics. Module 4: Ethical leadership*. Accessed at www.unodc.org/e4j/en/integrity-ethics /module-4/key-issues.html on March 28, 2022.

U.S. Commission on Civil Rights. (2019). *Beyond suspensions: Examining school discipline policies and connections to the school-to-prison pipeline for students of color with disabilities*. Accessed at www.usccr.gov/files/pubs/2019/07-23-Beyond-Suspensions.pdf on May 30, 2023.

Valentine, J., & Prater, M. (2011). Instructional, transformational, and managerial leadership student achievement: High school principals make a difference. *NASSP Bulletin, 95*(1), 5–30.

Veale, N. W. (2010, Spring/Summer). A comparison between collaborative and authoritative leadership styles of special education administrators. *Journal of the American Academy of Special Education Professionals*, 147–156. Accessed at https://files.eric.ed.gov/fulltext/EJ1137054.pdf on June 2, 2023.

Walker, K., & Carr-Stewart, S. (2006). Beginning principals: Experiences and images of success. *International Studies in Educational Administration*, *34*(3), 17–36.

Walker, T. (2022). *Survey: Alarming number of educators may soon leave the profession.* Accessed at www.nea.org/advocating-for-change/new-from-nea/survey-alarming-number-educators-may-soon-leave-profession on May 30, 2022.

Wallace Foundation. (2011). *The school principal as leader: Guiding schools to better teaching and learning.* Accessed at www.wallacefoundation.org/knowledge-center/school-leadership/effective-principal-leadership/Documents/The-School-Principal-as-Leader-Guiding-Schools-to-Better-Teaching-and-Learning.pdf on January 12, 2022.

We Are Teachers Staff. (2018). *What are windows, mirrors, and sliding glass doors?* Accessed at www.weareteachers.com/mirrors-and-windows on March 9, 2022.

Welborne, J. E. (2019). *Increasing equity, access, and inclusion through organizational change: A study of implementation and experiences surrounding a school district's journey towards culturally proficient educational practice.* Accessed at https://files.eric.ed.gov/fulltext/EJ1234931.pdf on June 2, 2023.

Western Governors University. (2021). *An overview of equity in education.* Accessed at www.wgu.edu/blog/overview-equity-education2107.html on September 27, 2022.

White, S. (2022). *What is transformational leadership? A model for motivating innovation.* Accessed at www.cio.com/article/228465/what-is-transformational-leadership-a-model-for-motivating-innovation.html on June 6, 2022.

Wieczorek, D., & Manard, C. (2018). Instructional leadership challenges and practices of novice principals in rural schools. *Journal of Research in Rural Education*, *34*(2), 1–21.

Wilburn, G., Cramer, B., & Walton, E. (2021). *The great divergence: Growing disparities between the nation's highest and lowest achievers in NAEP mathematics and reading between 2009 and 2019.* Accessed at https://nces.ed.gov/nationsreportcard/blog/mathematics_reading_2019.aspx on June 7, 2022.

Will, M., & Najarro, I. (2022). *What is culturally responsive teaching?* Accessed at www.edweek.org/teaching-learning/culturally-responsive-teaching-culturally-responsive-pedagogy/2022/04#definition on May 16, 2023.

Williamson, B. (2020). *Make sure you're measuring what counts.* Accessed at https://theramreview.com/15376-2 on May 26, 2023.

Wood, S. (2022). *Prison education programs: What to know.* Accessed at www.usnews.com/education/articles/prison-education-programs-what-to-know on June 2, 2023.

Wynn, S. C. (2019). *What research says about leadership styles and their implications for school climate and teacher job satisfaction.* Accessed at https://digitalcommons .cedarville.edu/education_research_projects/7 on May 31, 2023.

Xu, X. (2018). *Principal's impact on student achievement.* Accessed at https://cdn5-ss14 .sharpschool.com/UserFiles/Servers/Server_917767/File/Programs%20&%20Services /Professional%20Development/Tool%20Kit/TLE/1%20Stronge-Principal_Impact _on_Student_Achievement_9_26_18.pdf on January 13, 2022.

Yoon, E. (2020). *How can educators support LGBTQ students in K–12.* Accessed at https:// education.fsu.edu/how-can-educators-support-lgbtq-students-k-12 on June 2, 2023.

Young, V. (2021). *10 steps you can use to overcome impostor syndrome.* Accessed at https:// impostorsyndrome.com/10-steps-overcome-impostor on November 28, 2021.

Zafar, S. (2021). *Everything you should know about car transmission system.* Accessed at www.bioenergyconsult.com/car-transmission-system on May 2, 2022.

Zientek, B. (2019). *How do I know if my car frame is bent?* Accessed at www.impact autobody.com/how-do-i-know-if-my-car-frame-is-bent on June 18, 2023.

Index

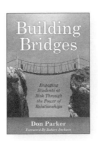

Building Bridges
Don Parker

Research shows that discipline problems are one of the greatest challenges in education. In *Building Bridges*, author Don Parker shows educators how to address this issue head-on, to build teacher-student relationships and create a welcoming learning environment that promotes engagement and achievement.

BKF846

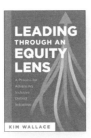

Leading Through an Equity Lens
Kim Wallace

Learn how to transform your organizational culture and improve student outcomes through advancing equity-centered initiatives. This book includes practical action steps to help school and district leaders integrate implementations that amplify opportunities and diminish systemic barriers for historically marginalized students.

BKG120

Benches in the Bathroom
Evisha Ford

Benches in the Bathroom offers K–12 leadership a wealth of field-tested, research-supported guidance to construct a school culture that values teacher contributions, operates on a framework of emotional wellness, and implements trauma-compassionate organizational strategies to ensure educator success and well-being.

BKG094

Evident Equiuty
Lauryn Mascareñaz

Make equity the norm in your school or district. *Evident Equity* provides a comprehensive method that leaders can use to integrate equitable practices into every facet of their school communities and offers real-life examples at the elementary, middle, and high school levels.

BKG032

Solution Tree | Press
a division of
Solution Tree

Visit SolutionTree.com or call 800.733.6786 to order.

Wait! Your professional development journey doesn't have to end with the last pages of this book.

We realize improving student learning doesn't happen overnight. And your school or district shouldn't be left to puzzle out all the details of this process alone.

No matter where you are on the journey, we're committed to helping you get to the next stage.

Take advantage of everything from **custom workshops** to **keynote presentations** and **interactive web and video conferencing**. We can even help you develop an action plan tailored to fit your specific needs.

Let's get the conversation started.

Call 888.763.9045 today.

SolutionTree.com